D1263797

Taleworlds and Storyrealms

The Phenomenology of Narrative

by

Katharine Galloway Young

1987 **MARTINUS NIJHOFF PUBLISHERS**
a member of the KLUWER ACADEMIC PUBLISHERS GROUP
DORDRECHT / BOSTON / LANCASTER

IV

Distributors

for the United States and Canada: Kluwer Academic Publishers, P.O. Box 358, Accord Station, Hingham, MA 02018-0358, USA
for the UK and Ireland: Kluwer Academic Publishers, MTP Press Limited, Falcon House, Queen Square, Lancaster LA1 1RN, UK
for all other countries: Kluwer Academic Publishers Group, Distribution Center, P.O. Box 322, 3300 AH Dordrecht, The Netherlands

Library of Congress Cataloging in Publication Data

```
Young, Katharine Galloway.
   Taleworlds and storyrealms.

   (Martinus Nijhoff philosophy library ; 16)
   Bibliography: p.
   Includes index.
   1. Discourse analysis, Narrative.  I. Title.
II. Title: Tale worlds and story realms.  III. Series:
Martinus Nijhoff philosophy library ; v. 16.
P302.7.Y68 1987      808.3'0141       86-23479
ISBN 90-247-3415-0
```

ISBN 90-247-3415-0 (hardback)

Copyright

© 1987 by Martinus Nijhoff Publishers, Dordrecht.

All rights reserved. No part of this publication may be reproduced, stored in a retrieval system, or transmitted in any form or by any means, mechanical, photocopying, recording, or otherwise, without the prior written permission of the publishers,
Martinus Nijhoff Publishers, P.O. Box 163, 3300 AD Dordrecht,
The Netherlands.

PRINTED IN THE NETHERLANDS

DEDICATION

To Erving Goffman,

master of these realms

TABLE OF CONTENTS

Preface   VIII

Acknowledgements   XIII

List of figures   XIV

Introduction   The Phenomenological Framework for
                 Narrative Analysis   1

Chapter One   Edgework: Frame and Boundary in the
                 Phenomenology of Narrative   19

Chapter Two   Multiple Contexting: The Story Context
                 of Stories   69

Chapter Three   Presentation of Self in Storytelling   100

Chapter Four   Joint Storytelling: The Interplay of
                 Discourse and Interaction   157

Chapter Five   Storyability and Eventfulness: Beyond
                 Referential Theories of Narrative   186

Chapter Six   Taleworlds and Real: Ontological
                 Puzzles about Narrative   211

Appendix   Transcription Devices   249

Index   257

Bibliography   261

PREFACE

> Beginning <u>is</u> the hardest moment, not because
> openers are all that scarce but because you're
> blowing into, cracking a universe.
>
> Maurice Natanson[1]

Openings are already directed toward closings. The first question in presenting a body of work is where to cut in. This is an especially difficult question since the cut-in provides a perspective on what follows. A cut is an angle of entry. Wherever I enter, from there, a realm unfolds itself. In that sense, my angle of entry is my point of view. A realm cut into has an orientation. It evidences a hierarchy of importance, relevance, accessability, value, or logic. Its content is no longer neutral and equivalent. From my perspective, the realm is not only differentiated in substance but differential in significance. There is a relation between angles and attitudes. Where I look from is tied up with how I see. The first cut opens out into a frame of reference. What count as lines of evidence in that realm materialize along with its background expectancies, its assumptions, concentrations, and confusions, its cosmology, quirks, and enchantments. Hence, once I am committed to a perspective, I am implicated in a methodology, one possessed of puzzles of a certain shape, moving toward solutions within its orthodoxy. Openings are directed toward closings. Another cut would open onto another realm.

The realm of events I cut into is a Taleworld, inhabited by characters acting in their own space and time. The Taleworld is conjured up by the Storyrealm, a realm of discourse spoken by persons who inhabit another space and time.

[1]Maurice Natanson, <u>The Journeying Self: A Study in Philosophy and Social Role</u> (Reading, Massachusetts; Menlo Park, California; London, England; Don Mills, Ontario: Addison Wesley Publishing Company, 1970) P. 115.

The Storyrealm is, in turn, an enclave in the realm of conversation, itself an aspect of the realm of the ordinary in a parish on the edge of Dartmoor, in Devonshire, England. My experience, the experience I recount here, is of multiple realities. Located in the realm of conversation, I take up a perspective on the Storyrealm. The Storyrealm has a relationship with the Taleworld, one suggested, though by no means exhausted, by the notion of representation. The Taleworld is, on occasion, mapped onto the ordinary one. And the realm of the ordinary presents, as one of its aspects, the conversation in which I find myself.

I enter a realm by turning my attention to it, as when, listening to a story, I am caught up in the relationships among characters in the Taleworld. Travel through time and space can occasion the shifts of attention which insert me into other realms. I arrive in the chill of the evening at an old stone farmhouse on the edge of the moor and find myself engaged in conversation with the inhabitants of it. I can see a realm from the inside or the outside, as it adumbrates itself around me or from a perspective I bring to bear on it from elsewhere. Now, thinking of my conversations with the natives, I am aware of their interactional strategies. Then, I was enfolded in them. Each realm provides contexts for understanding other realms as well as locations from which to perceive them, or stepping-off points from which to move into them. The old farmer who lives in the farmhouse on the edge of the moor is called Algy May and he tells stories in which he appears as a character. In the context of the occasion, I understand his storytelling as a presentation of self. I perceive the realm he conjures up from my lodgement in this one. It is another time, another place, another realm. Yet, sometimes during the storytelling, I am drawn into his Taleworld and become absorbed in it. As I listen to Algy deftly constituting that Taleworld to inhabit, my awareness of his deftness turns my attention from the Taleworld to the Storyrealm, from the realm described to the act of description, from content to performance. But his deftness is also what transports me into the Taleworld. Realms described and realms inhabited, I slip from description to habitation and out of habitation into description. In and out again, the rhythm of engagement and detachment in fieldwork.

Whether described or inhabited, realities come already differentiated. Driving across the high moor, a textured terrain of simplified forms: standing stones, tors, and grasses, I drop down toward the village into narrow winding lanes cut deep into the land, rimmed with low stone walls in the grip of the roots of enormous trees, and stop at a cluster of stone cottages. In one of them, talking with the Browns, I traverse that same region under a different ontology, as a realm that existed in Devon fifty years ago. Each realm has its own ontological presentation. I move among them, discovering their modes of being.

Descriptions reify realities; different descriptions reify different realities. Not only do their stories conjure up Taleworlds for me but also my descriptions conjure up their Taleworlds, their Storyrealms, their realms of conversation and everyday life for you. Different descriptions do not capture the same reality; a reality is reified in the description. I listen to Jack and Florence Brown tell a story together and I hear it as collaborative narration. I listen again and hear it as competitive. Which is the reality?

Descriptions approach but never arrive at realities. They are renderings of reality, at some remove from the realms they render. Transcribing the tapes of the Browns telling stories, I find myself preoccupied not with the analysis of their discourse but with the intonations of their voices. The telling, the tape, the transcription, the description, interpretation, and analysis are each another lamination away from the realm of the events. Yet each rendering can precipitate me back into another realm. The description, opaque and resistant, becomes a transparency to what it describes. Reality is not properly an attribute of any realm but a relationship between the realm I inhabit and my descriptions of it.

Descriptions, the storytellers', mine, are already angled toward understandings and understandings, in turn, inform descriptions. The mutual implication of descriptions and understandings, opened to analysis, discloses a methodology, the framework of assumptions by virtue of which I move among levels of analysis. Algy May situates a story in the realm of legend and then resituates it in the realm of the ordinary. My understanding of what has transpired in the Taleworld, the Storyrealm, and the realm of conversation is confounded by this transformation. I am myself foxed by the trick of redescription. Hence, in this inquiry I undertake to describe and redescribe, from different perspectives and in different contexts, the same realms, the Storyrealms and Taleworlds of these storytellers living on the edge of Dartmoor, to move among realms in order to arrive at a phenomenology of narrative.

The introduction moves through the writings of phenomenologists in an order of presentation designed to lead from the phenomenological perspective attached to the insertion of the body in reality to the discovery of multiple realities, in particular, the realms of narrative. Chapter One formulates the frames of Taleworlds and Storyrealms for anecdotes in ordinary conversation. Frames-of stories are also frames-for their hearers. In light of this bi-directionality, frames are not regarded as enclosures or containers of stories but as perspectives on them. The second chapter introduces the multiple contexts of stories, argues the propriety of considering a story in one context at a time, and presents an analysis of stories in the context of other stories told on the same occasion in terms of the notions of second and serial storying. Chapter three describes how a set of stories from one conversation can support a presentation of self, both as Storyrealm and as Taleworld. These three chapters are connected by their common subject matter, one evening's conversation at Algy May's farm during which thirty-three stories were told. They differ in their perspectives on that subject matter. The chapters are thus recursive, consisting of descriptions and redescriptions of the same event.

The next two chapters are also recursive; they investigate one story told by the Jack Browns from two different perspectives. Chapter Four addresses the incommensurability between treating stories as transfixes and regarding them as mutually constructed turns at talk, between, that is, the way stories hang together and the way they are articulated, punctuated, or split apart in conversation. This bears on the question of whether an anecdote can properly be considered continuous narration by a single narrator. Chapter Five investigates the assumption, pervasive in narrative analysis, that stories reflect the events they are about as words refer to things or language mirrors reality, what might be called the referential theory of narrative. The puzzle it addresses is, if the relationship between Taleworld and Storyrealm is not referential, what is it? A solution is suggested by the discovery that it is not so much that storyability originates in events as that eventfulness orginates in stories.

The sixth and final chapter permutes another story of Algy May's through two codifications. Lineal codifications foreground its sequential organization, the armature of the relation between the story and the events it is about; nonlineal codifications foreground its structural organization, the framework of the relationship between the story and the occasion on which it is told.

Movement inward from the Storyrealm toward the Taleworld draws attention to puzzles about perspective. Movement outward from the Storyrealm toward the realm of conversation draws attention to puzzles about genre. The relationship between Taleworld and Storyrealm explored in these last two chapters suggests an approach to the framing of stories as fictions or realities, truth or lies. The last chapter raises the level of analysis from inquiry into the nature of stories to inquiry into theories about the nature of stories. On the one hand, this last move encloses analysis in self-reflection, and on the other, opens it toward fresh directions of inquiry.

ACKNOWLEDGEMENTS

I would like to thank the people on Dartmoor: the ones who
told me stories, Jack and Mrs. Brown, and Algy May and his
family; the ones who kept my spirits up, Miles Fursdon, Liz and
Bill Fursdon, Peter Martin and his family, Len and Barbara
Norrish, and the Blacks, Aline herself, Hugh, young Hugh, and
the twins, Isobel and Margaret, who found me a cottage on their
farm and a place in their hearts. The inquiry was inspired in
the first instance by the teaching and writings of Maurice
Natanson, when he was at Berkeley. This phenomenology was
enchanced by the communication theory of Ray Birdwhistell and
the frame analysis of Erving Goffman, both at the University of
Pennsylvania. I am particularly grateful to my readers,
Kenneth Goldstein for his hearty support of what must have
seemed at the time eccentric propositions about fieldwork, to
Barbara Kirshenblatt-Gimblett for her fierce and illuminating
arguments about methodology and her close critical reading, and
to Brian Sutton-Smith for his engaging expatiations on
philosophy. My fourth reader, Erving Goffman, whose genius
influenced the inquiry from the beginning, died before he saw
the end. I have been lucky in my friends and colleagues,
Maxine Miska, arch-structuralist, JoAnn Bromberg, Jane Spencer
Edwards, and Phyllis Gorfain, who reformed the beginnings of
analysis, and Amy Shuman, who kept me philosophically attuned
throughout. Earlier versions of some parts of the book
appeared in the following journals: Semiotica, Western
Folklore, Cahiers de Litterature Orale, and Poetics.
Permission to use these is gratefully acknowledged. I must
thank the British Crown for permission to adapt an ordnance
survey map and the following individuals for permission to
quote at length from their work: Maurice Natanson, Barbara
Herrnstein Smith, Robert Georges, and José Limón. Quotes from
Alfred Schutz appear with permission from the University of
Chicago Press. Quotes from the lecture notes of Harvey Sacks
appear with permission from his literary executor, Emanuel
Schegloff. I would like to acknowledge the influence of the
old ones, Marcus and Ruth Young, on the shape of the
undertaking and to thank my husband, Leonard Perloff, M.D., the
boys, David and Joel, and my daughter, Ariel, for their
indulgence of my preoccupation with what Len calls realmology.
Thank you.

List of Figures

Figure 1.   Narrative Laminations.   25
Figure 2.   Beginnings and Ends.   30
Figure 3.   Openings and Closings.   32
Figure 4.   Prefaces and Codas.   37
Figure 5.   Frames that are Boundaries.   41
Figure 6.   Taleworld and Storyrealm Frames.   46
Figure 7.   Orientations.   52
Figure 8.   Evaluations.   61
Figure 9.   Distribution of Frames
                over Storytelling.   63
Figure 10.   Thematic Continuity between
                Stories.   83
Figure 11.   Stories as Contexts for Stories.   86
Figure 12.   Structural Continuity between
                Stories.   90
Figure 13.   Nested Stories.   92
Figure 14.   Nesting Structure of Seven Stories.   95
Figure 15.   Multiple Continuities among Stories.   97
Figure 16.   Laminations of Self in the
                Storytelling Occasion.   106
Figure 17.   Taleworld Map.   119-121
Figure 18.   Time Shift in the Taleworld.   126
Figure 19.   Casts of Characters.   127-130
Figure 20.   Patterns of Person, Place, and
                Time in Story Set I.   134
Figure 21.   Patterns of Person, Place, and
                Time in Story Set II.   143
Figure 22.   Genre Shift over Story System.   145
Figure 23.   The Trickster Cycle.   153
Figure 24.   Pattern of Breaks and Continuities
                at different Levels of Analysis in
                the Story System.   155
Figure 25.   The Puzzle of Natural Utterances
                and Events.   193
Figure 26.   The Relationship between the Realm of
                Discourse and the Realm of Events.   195
Figure 27.   The Realm Status of Truth and Lies;
                Fictions and Realities.   242
Figure 28.   The Transparency of the Ordinary
                in Narrative Genres.   247
Figure 29.   Transcription Conventions.   256

INTRODUCTION

THE PHENOMENOLOGICAL FRAMEWORK
FOR NARRATIVE ANALYSIS*

I find myself implicated in a universe already differentiated. My experience of the world is bound up with my understandings of it. Percepts and concepts (in a conceit of Birdwhistell's) are indiscrete. Perception is the "primordial operation which impregnates sensible being with a meaning, and which all logical mediation as well as psychological causality presupposes." (Merleau-Ponty)[1] Perception is not free of a conceptual disposition, a placement, an orientation, finally an understanding that composes a universe. Estrangement of the perceiver either from the perceived or from his perception is a trick of philosophy, "an epistemic disjunction between self and world which has always haunted the philosophic mind."

* This section presents as a unified philosophy the writings of diverse phenomenologists as if they were in amiable agreement. They are not, but it is not my part here to draw out the shades of their differences so I have presented a phenomenology as it were seamlessly. On the other hand I have wanted these remarkable philosophers to speak for themselves so my exposition is webbed between quotes, themselves pieced together like a jigsaw puzzle. To preserve continuity, the quotations have only brief parenthetical attributions for the curious in the body of the text. The exposition is directed toward a phenomenology of narrative and that orientation and its outcome are my responsibility. I should like to say at the outset how much the inquiry is indebted to the French phenomenologists Maurice Merleau-Ponty and Gabriel Marcel, to their German forebear Edmund Husserl, particularly to the American phenomenologists Alfred Schutz and Maurice Natanson, as well as to anthropologists Erving Goffman, Peter Berger and Thomas Luckman, who work in the phenomenological or ethnomethodological tradition.

1. Maurice Merleau-Ponty, Signs, tr. John McCleary (Chicago: Northwestern University Press, 1964), p. xii.

(Natanson)[2] I, my thoughts, my acts, my universe are all of
a piece. Conceptions as much as acts are relations to the
world, activities of consciousness, not events secreted inside
the skull.[3] Even my emotions are modes of participation in
the world.[4] Furthermore objects and events are implicated
with each other as with persons. My experience is of "a world,
that is...an indefinite and open multiplicity in which
relations are relations of reciprocal implication."
(Merleau-Ponty)[5] Implication and differentiation are the
paradox that roots phenomenology.

I inhabit a world of appearances, of surface phenomena.
These are neither reductive (coded clues to a more fundamental
reality) nor idealist (base manifestations of an ethereal
essence); they are real. And that reality is not
undifferentiated chaos overlaid by cognitive maps nor, by
contrast, has it a natural order apprehended by the perceiving
mind. Discriminations, disjunctions, contrasts, the texture
and grain of things, attend my insertion into the world.
Objects are appearances with a certain weight or significance.
"Let us try to unravel the complicated structural contexts that
are involved in the constitution of an external object. The
object is constituted out of appearances as we encounter them
in our stream of consciousness. Such appearances hang together
in a context of meaning." (Schutz)[6] Appearances adumbrate
themselves around me unfolding aspects whose interrelatedness
is discovered in the situation. Objects are situated
appearances. "The perspective from which and through which
that situation presents itself is the insertion of the

2. Maurice Natanson, Literature, Philosophy and the Social
    Sciences (The Hague: Martinus Nijhoff, 1962), p. 144.
3. Edmund Husserl, Ideas: General Introduction to Pure
    Phenomenology tr. W.R. Boyce Gibson (New York: MacMillan
    Co. and London: George Allen and Unwin Ltd., 1932, first
    published 1913) excerpted in ed. Morton White, The Age of
    Analysis (New York: Mentor, 1961), p. 107.
4. See Gabriel Marcel, The Mystery of Being (Chicago: Gateway
    Edition, Henry Regnery Company, 1960), Book I, Ch. VI.
5. Merleau-Ponty, Signs, p. xiii.
6. Alfred Schutz, The Phenomenology of the Social World, tr.
    George Walsh & Frederick Lehnert (Chicago: Northwestern
    University Press, 1967), p. 79.

individual in the social fabric." (Natanson)[7] Appearances are never mere, they come already meaningful, already objects. Meanings shift with percipients and occasions, generating a layered world of "multiple meaning-contexts." (Schutz)[8]

I enter the world through my perception and that entrance centers my experience.

The perceiving mind is an incarnated mind. I have tried, first of all, to re-establish the roots of the mind in its body and in its world, going against the doctrines which treat perception as a simple result of the action of things on our body as well as against those which insist on the autonomy of consciousness. These philosophies commonly forget--in favor of a pure exteriority or of a pure interiority--the insertion of the mind in corporeality, the ambiguous relation which we entertain with our body and, correlatively, with perceived things...And it is equally clear that one does not account for the facts by superimposing a pure, contemplative consciousness on a thinglike body." (Merleau-Ponty)[9]

The centrality of my body in a world which unfolds around me draws into focus the elusive relationship between the subjective and the objective. To distribute this distinction over a contrast between self and objects is to perpetrate a misunderstanding. Neither conceptualization nor objectification is prior. I enter as a material object a world rendered intelligible by virtue of my presence in it. "We grasp external space through our bodily situation. A 'corporeal or postural schema' gives us at every moment a

7. Maurice Natanson, The Journeying Self: a study in philosophy and social role (Massachusetts, California, London, Ontario: Addison-Wesely Publishing Company, 1970), p. 60.
8. Schutz, On Phenomenology and Social Relations, ed., Helmut Wagner (Chicago and London: University of Chicago Press, 1973), p. 191.
9. Maurice Merleau-Ponty, The Primacy of Perception ed. James M. Edie (Chicago: Northwestern University Press, 1964), pp. 3 and 4.

global, practical, and implicit notion of the relation between our body and things, of our hold in them. A system of possible movements, or 'motor projects,' radiates from us to our environment. Our body is not in space like things; it inhabits or haunts space." (Merleau-Ponty)[10] My lodgment so in the world has a radical contextuality: the world holds me bodily as, consciously, I hold it, "consciousness, understood as a directional force sustaining the entire range of perceptual experience." (Natanson)[11] Consciousness is always consciousness-of. It is not a mental act located in the cranium but a constitutive act, the creation of a universe. The workings of consciousness permit and imperil my apprehension of reality. I become a "self constructing for itself the shape of a world it then finds and acts in." (Natanson)[12] This paradoxical undertaking is called intentionality or the intentionality of consciousness. It is the phenomenological understanding of the problem of intention, misleadingly presented in traditional philosophy as the problem of how to get from mental events to physical acts.

On a phenomenological understanding "meaning is merely an operation of intentionality, which, however, only becomes visible to the reflective glance." (Schutz)[13] I am caught between engagement and skepticism; between my unreflective ongoing presence in the world and my speculative or detached awareness of that engagement. It is out of the interplay between these modes of attention that I come to understandings. Understanding is reflexive. Once arrived at, understandings may become fixed, typified. "A scheme of experience is a meaning-context which is a configuration of our past experiences embracing conceptually the experiencial objects to be found in the latter but not the process by which they were constituted. The constituting process itself is entirely ignored, while the objectivity constituted by it is taken for granted." (Schutz)[14] Typifications attach as well to persons. "Social life takes up and freezes into itself the

10. Merleau-Ponty, The Primacy of Perception, p. 5.
11. Natanson, The Journeying Self, p. 4.
12. Natanson, The Journeying Self, p. 23.
13. Schutz, On Phenomenology and Social Relations, p. 52.
14. Schutz, On Phenomenology and Social Relations, p. 82.

understandings we have of it." (Goffman)[15] Thus "social structure is the sum total of these typifications and of the recurrent patterns of interaction established by means of them." (Berger and Luckmann)[16] In that sense "persons are engaged in the accomplishment of social reality." (McHoul)[17]

The thrust of inquiry is to recover the reflexivity of understandings, including the mystery of other selves.[18] "Something visible to me is becoming a viewer. I am present at the metamorphosis." (Merleau-Ponty)[19] Access to the mystery lies in my reflexive awareness; "whenever I try to understand myself the whole fabric of the perceptible world comes too, and with it come the others who are caught in it." (Merleau-Ponty)[20] From my sense of intersubjectivity I come to be aware of divergent perspectives on the world. Angles of appearances are not just apparent from my point of view but from our points of view. We are implicated in a world together. This mutual implication is among its root conditions. "The world I inhabit is from the outset an intersubjective one. The language I possess was taught to me by others; the manners I have I did not invent; whatever abilities, techniques, or talents I can claim were nourished by a social inheritance; even my dreams are rooted in a world I never created and can never completely possess." (Natanson)[21] "These universal features of daily life (are) 'metaphysical constants' for human existence. Being born into a world, being born of mothers unique to us, being born into a world already inhabited as well as interpreted by others,

15. Erving Goffman, _Frame Analysis_ (New York, Evanston, San Francisco, London: Harper Colophon Books, 1974), p. 563.
16. Peter L. Berger and Thomas Luckmann, _The Social Construction of Reality_ (Garden City, New York: Anchor Books, Doubleday & Co., Inc., 1967), p. 33.
17. Alexander McHoul, "Ethnomethodology and Literature: preliminaries to a sociology of reading", _Poetics_ 7 #1 (March 1978) pp. 113-120.
18. See Marcel, _The Mystery of Being_, p. 260.
19. Merleau-Ponty, _Signs_, p. 16.
20. Merleau-Ponty, _Signs_, p. 15.
21. Natanson, _Literature, Philosophy and the Social Sciences_, p. 103.

having to grow older in this world and having to die in it are all inescapable realities." (Natanson)[22] Individuals "still must operate from the inalienable ground of their limits as human beings bound to time and space, incarnated in the world as psychophysical beings, having to live with fellow men in a shared world, and having to grow older and die." (Natanson)[23]

Metaphysical constants are the most pervasive of the "background expectancies" of everyday life, background expectencies being my assumptions about ordinary situations. "The member of the society uses background expectancies as a scheme of interpretation. With their use actual appearances are for him recognizable and intelligible as the appearances-of-familiar-events." (Garfinkel)[24] The familiarity of ordinary reality is ubiquitous in spite of

"individual perspectives and with individual adumbrations. But the order of Nature and of Society is common to all mankind. It furnishes to everyone the setting of the cycle of his individual life, of birth, aging, death, health and sickness, hopes and fears. Each of us participates in the recurrent rhythm of nature; to each of us the movements of sun and moon and stars, the change between day and night, and the cycle of the seasons are elements of his situation. Each of us is a member of the group into which he was born or which he has joined and which continues to exist if some of its members die and others enter into it. Everywhere there will be systems of kinship, age groups and sex groups, differentiations according to occupations, and an organization of power and command which leads to the categories of social status and prestige." (Schutz)[25]

22. Natanson, Literature, Philosophy and the Social Sciences, p. 94. Natanson notes in The Journeying Self, p. 198, that in his lectures Alfred Schutz used to refer to Birth, Aging, and Death as "metaphysical constants". Natanson has elaborated that usage. See Literature, Philosophy and the Social Sciences, p. 215.
23. Natanson, Journeying Self, pp. 63-64.
24. Harold Garfinkel, "Background Expectancies" in ed. Mary Douglas, Rules and Meanings (Middlexes, England: Penguin, 1977), p. 21.
25. Schutz, On Phenomenology and Social Relations, p. 246.

Such "seen but unnoticed background expectancies" are the underpinning of the commonsense world. (Garfinkel)[26] As given, that world is unremarkable, unproblematic, taken-for-granted, the primary "realm of experience" or "paramount reality" which is the universe of discourse we ordinarily inhabit. (Schutz)[27]

Such is the mundane constitution of the world from the "natural standpoint" (Husserl)[28], the "attitude of daily life." (Schutz)[29] A shift in attention transfers me to another realm, a different province of meaning, an alternate reality upon which I now "bestow the accent of reality." (Schutz)[30] "Each world whilst it is attended to is real after its fashion." (James)[31] Indeed the world turns out to be composed of "multiple realities". (Schutz)[32]

Different objects present themselves to consciousness as constituents of different spheres of reality. I recognize the fellowmen I must deal with in the course of everyday life as pertaining to a reality quite different from the disembodied figures that appear in my dreams.... Put differently, I am conscious of the world as consisting of multiple realities. As I move from one reality to another, I experience the transition as a kind of shock. This shock is to be understood as caused by the shift in attentiveness that the transition entails. Waking up from a dream illustrates this shift most simply." (Berger and Luckmann)[33]

To be sure, those experiences of shock befall me frequently amidst my daily life; they themselves pertain to its reality. They show me that the world of working in

26. Garfinkel in Douglas, Rules and Meanings, p. 22.
27. Schutz, On Phenomenology and Social Relations, pp. 243, 253, and 263.
28. Husserl, Ideas in ed. White, p. 105.
29. Alfred Schutz in Doublas, Rules and Meanings, p. 22.
30. Schutz, On Phenomenology and Social Relations, pp. 252.
31. William James in Schutz, On Phenomenology and Social Relations, p. 252.
32. Schutz, On Phenomenology and Social Relations, p. 245.
33. Berger and Luckmann, The Social Construction of Reality, p. 21.

standard time is not the sole finite province of meaning but only one of many others accessible to my intentional life.

There are as many innumerable kinds of different shock experiences as there are different finite provinces of meaning upon which I may bestow the accent of reality. Some instances are: the shock of falling asleep as the leap into the world of dreams; the inner transformation we endure if the curtain in the theater rises as the transition into the world of the stage-play; the radical change in our attitude if, before a painting, we permit our visual field to be limited by what is within the frame as the passage into the pictorial world; our quandary, relaxing into laughter, if, in listening to a joke, we are for a short time ready to accept the fictitious world of the jest as a reality in relation to which the world of our daily life takes on the character of foolishness; the child's turning toward his toy as the transition into the play-world; and so on. But also the religious experiences in all their varieties--for instance, Kierkegaard's experience of the "instant" as the leap into the religious sphere--is such a shock as well as the decision of the scientist to replace all passionate participation in the affairs of "this world" by a disinterested contemplative attitude. (Schutz)[34]

The discovery of multiple realities reveals that "all these worlds--the world of dreams, of imageries and phantasms, especially the world of art, the world of religious experience, the world of scientific contemplation, the play world of the child, and the world of the insane--are finite provinces of meaning." (Schutz)[35] Hence "realms of being are the proper objects here for study; and here the everyday is not a special domain to be placed in contrast to the others, but merely another realm." (Goffman)[36] In this sense "the imaginary is the implicit margin surrounding the horizon of the real." (Natanson)[37] However, the paramount reality, the quotidian,

---

34. Schutz, On Phenomenology and Social Relations, pp. 254-255.
35. Schutz, On Phenomenology and Social Relations, p. 255.
36. Goffman, Frame Analysis, p. 564.
37. Natanson, Literature, Philosophy and the Social Sciences, p. 112.

the realm of everyday life, remains the background to which I recur from my other provinces of meaning. "Familiar scenes of everyday activities, treated by members as the 'natural facts of life,' are mass facts of members' daily existence both as a real world and as the product of activities in a real world. They furnish the 'fix', the 'this is it' to which the waking state returns one and are the points of departure and return for every modification of the world of daily life that is achieved in play, dreaming, trance, theatre, scientific theorizing, or high ceremony." (Garfinkel)[38]

The various realms are not to be taken as contiguous with one another. In particular, the primary realm is the background for a separate reality but not its "encircling sphere.... The two worlds are present together but disconnected, apart, that is from their relation to the Ego, in virtue of which I can freely direct my glance or my acts to the one or to the other." (Husserl)[39] The realm of higher mathematics I am working out in my mind does not itself border on the physical work space I occupy. They are jointly present only to my attentiveness. This non-contiguity is true of all provinces of meaning except "enclaves," that is, "regions belonging to one province of meaning enclosed by another." (Schutz)[40] The realm of theatre for instance shares a border with the ordinary world marked by the curtain separating the stage from the house. Paintings have a physical manifestation in the material world. The medium of anecdotes, speech, is continuous with the conversations in which they occur.

A realm is defined by the metaphysical constants which inform its particular backgound expectancies. "Each province of meaning--the paramount world of real objects and events into which we can gear our actions, the world of imaginings and fantasms, such as the play world of the child, the world of dreams, the world of scientific contemplation--has its particular cognitive style. It is

---

38. Garfinkel in ed. Douglas, Rules and Meanings, p. 21.
39. Husserl, Ideas in ed. White, p. 109. Berger and Luckmann, The Social Construction of Reality, p. 25, confuse this distinction but catch the flavor of transitions between realms.
40. Schutz, On Phenomenology and Social Relations, ftnt. p. 256.

this particular style of a set of our experiences which constitutes them as a finite province of meaning...each of these finite provinces of meaning is, among other things, characterized by a specific tension of consciousness (from full awakeness in the reality of everyday life to sleep in the world of dreams, by a specific time-perspective, by a specific form of experiencing oneself, and, finally, by a specific form of sociality." (Schutz)[41]

Some realms have affinities of cognitive style and hence structural similarities. Representational art, particularly narrative, is in some measure isomorphic with the ordinary lifeworld, a microcosm of it. "'Reflect,' 'mirror,' 'represent,' are all variants for a central term of nexus between two domains held to be isomorphic in certain respects." (Natanson)[42] "Both worlds are horizonal, both presuppose a taken-for-granted set of elements, both are defined axially by metaphysical constants. What then distinguishes the fictive from the real world?" (Natanson)[43]

As a start, I submit the following characteristics of a literary microcosm which I think are essential features: first, a temporal-spatial matrix of some order is necessary for the characters and action. Second, the story presenting the action presupposes that this matrix has functional limits which set off what occurred prior to the story told as well as what might occur after the story ends. Third, the action involved is action for the characters. Their world is interpreted by them. Its meanings are disclosed originally through their action. Fourth, that there is and that there continues to be a coherent reality for the characters throughout the narrative, a reality that is intersubjective, that embraces their world. And fifth, underlying every possible element of the literary work is the horizon which defines and limits the world created. (Natanson)[44]

41. Schutz, On Phenomenology and Social Relations, pp. 252-3.
42. Natanson, Literature, Philosophy and the Social Sciences, p. 88.
43. Natanson, Literature, Philosophy and the Social Sciences, p. 96.
44. Natanson, Literature, Philosophy and the Social Sciences, p. 91.

Literary microcosms are one of "a group of otherwise most heterogeneous finite provinces of meaning, none of them reducible to the other. This group is commonly known as that of fancies or imageries and embraces among many others the realms of daydreams, of play, of fiction, of fairy-tales, of myths, of jokes. So far philosophy has not worked upon the problem of the specific constitution of each of these innumerable provinces of our imaginative life." (Schutz)[45]

Similarity or contiguity between realms "allow meaning to leak from one context to another along the formal similarities that they show. The barriers between finite provinces of meaning are always sapped either by the violent flooding through of social concerns or by the subtle economy which uses the same rule structure in each province." (Douglas)[46] The possibility of leakage points up a preoccupation of fictive realms with their own frames, that is, with the ontological conditions that make them a different order of event, their cognitive styles. Among realms that are also enclaves, the complexities of realm status are intensified by the presence of boundaries as well as frames. Boundaries reiterate the discreteness of contiguous realms. Hence the focus of fictive enclaves on edges, borders, frames, openings and closings, beginnings and ends, its points of access, thresholds of a universe.

Language has a particular faculty for realm shift: "language is capable of transcending the reality of everyday life altogether. It can refer to experiences pertaining to finite provinces of meaning, and it can span discrete spheres of reality. For instance, I can interpret 'the meaning' of a dream by integrating it linguistically within the order of everyday life. Such integration transposes the discrete reality of the dream into the reality of everyday life by making it an enclave within the latter. The dream is now meaningful in terms of the reality of everyday life rather than of its own discrete reality. Enclaves produced by such transposition belong, in a sense, to both spheres of reality. They are 'located' in one reality, but 'refer' to another." (Berger and Luckmann)[47]

45. Schutz, On Phenomenology and Social Relations, pp. 256-7..
46. Mary Douglas, ed., Rules and Meanings, p. 13 introduction.
47. Berger and Luckmann, The Social Construction of Reality, p. 40.

Stories in everyday life, unlike their literary isomorphs, are enclaves with just this sort of double orientation: stories are events themselves and they refer to events that are not themselves, to fictive realms or past worlds, Taleworlds conjured by the telling.

The casting of events into narrative is a transformation of experience, a recovery, an arrangement among others, of different realms. "Narrative may be a complementary, or alternative mode of thinking...a narrative view of life. That is to say, a view of life as a potential source of narrative." (Hymes)[48] Narrative is among the "transformations for fun, deception, experiment, rehearsal, dream, fantasy, ritual, demonstration, analysis, and charity. These lively shadows of events are geared into the ongoing world but not in a way that is true of ordinary, literal activity." (Goffman)[49] In particular, narrativity shifts my attitude to life from my engagement in it toward my reflection on it.

My life can be considered from two standpoints, that of: 1. The past. 2. That of the present, the fact that I am still living it.

1. In the past. My life appears to me as something that can, by reason of its very essence, be narrated.

But to narrate is to unfold.

It is also to summarize, i.e., to totalize schematically.

My life cannot then be reproduced by a narrative; in as much as it has been actually lived, it lies without the scope of my present concrete thought and can only be recaptured as particles irradiated by flashes of memory...

My life, in so far as already lived, is not then an inalterable deposit or finished whole. (Marcel)[50]

48. Dell Hymes with Courteney Cazden, "Narrative Thinking and Storytelling Rights: A Folklorist's Clue to a Critique of Education", Keystone 22 #1-2 (1978) pp. 21-36.
49. Goffman, Frame Analysis, p. 560.
50. Marcel, Mystery of Being, table of contents.

The sequential and summary character of narrative forwards a view of life as consequential and informed by significant incidents, these incidents being drawn toward the ordinary, the intelligible, toward their own "epistemological domestication." (Natanson)[51] Language assists this drift toward the ordinary.

The common language available to me for the objectification of my experiences is grounded in everyday life and keeps pointing back to it even as I employ it to interpret experiences in finite provinces of meaning. Typically, therefore, I "distort" the reality of the latter as soon as I begin to use the common language in interpreting them, that is I "translate" the non-everyday experiences back into the paramount reality of everyday life. This may be readily seen in terms of dreams, but is also typical of those trying to report about theoretical, aesthetic or religious worlds of meaning. (Berger and Luckmann)[52]

This capacity of language for precipitating out and transforming other realms is counterposed by its capacity for implicating and engaging them. "Language has its origins in the face-to-face situation, but can be readily detached from it.... The detachment of language lies much more basically in its capacity to communicate meanings that are not direct expressions of subjectivity "here and now".... Both of us hear what each says at virtually the same instant, which makes possible a continuous, synchronized, reciprocal access to our two subjectivities." (Berger and Luckmann)[53] The intersubjective capacity of language is located in speech. An approach to narrative as an enclave in conversation works against two traditional views of language as abstracted from speech, its insertion in the mundane world. First, structures traditionally seen as built-into language in the form of rules, syntax, or grammer, can instead be seen in speech to point

51. Natanson, Journeying Self, p. 27.
52. Berger and Luckmann, The Social Construction of Reality, p. 26.
53. Berger and Luckmann, The Social Construction of Reality, p. 37.

outward toward intelligibility, expectancy, understanding, and meaning. Interest shifts from sentences to discourse. The second view is the traditional folkloristic one of speech events and speakers as detached from the context of discourse. This underwrites a (historically crucial) view of stories as collectable but cuts away their complex realm status, their contextual implication. Such an orientation to narrative also focuses attention on stories as the exclusive production of a single individual, or, even more removed, as a fixed form independent even of its performer. The lodgement of stories in speaking situations returns attention to the mutuality of their construction, shifting interest from monologue to dialogue.

The realm of conversation has its own ontological status. Its organization is not appropriately broken down into tracings of the individual. "Our traces mix and intermingle; they make a single wake of "public durations." (Merleau-Ponty)[54] Conversation is systemic. Its points of articulation are utterance-turns. These segments roughly coincide with one person's speaking and with grammatical sentences. However, the import of an utterance is not inside it but linked to contiguous utterances. "There is mutual determinacy between any two adjacent turns at talk and from one speaker's turn to his next." (Goffman)[55] Indeed, the import of an utterance is immanent in the conversation as a whole. Utterances are themselves organized into larger units within conversation, the unit of interest here being stories. Stories take up extended turns at talk and the extended turns are accorded a different ontological status from the talk, the status of a Storyrealm. One of the differences between written and oral narrative is that written narrative closes down on the thresholds between realms, circumscribing its own horizons by separating storyteller from hearers, by withdrawing story from conversation, fixing its form, and enclosing it in a book. Oral narrative plays on, out, and through the continuities between realms, particularly between contiguous realms like the story and the conversation.

54. Merleau-Ponty, Signs, p. 19.
55. Goffman, Frame Analysis, pp. 509-510.

Stories, themselves events in conversation, direct attention to another realm of events not in the conversation, the Taleworld.[56] While opening onto the Taleworld, the story retains its own realm status as an enclave in conversation, a Storyrealm. "We have to distinguish sharply between imagining as a manifestation of our spontaneous life and the imageries imagined." (Schutz)[57] The terms "Taleworld" and "Storyrealm" discriminate these alternative ontological presentations of stories. Each realm has its own metaphysical constants. These can be elaborated, following Alfred Schutz, in terms of features of cognitive style:[58]

1) A specific tension of consciousness, from alertness to reverie or sleep;
2) a specific epoché or attitude of reflection or engagement, the suspension of belief or the suspension of doubt;
3) a prevalent form of spontaneity such as being geared into the world in order to act in it, or not;
4) a specific form of experiencing oneself, as a working self or a contemplative self;
5) a specific form of sociality such as being in communication with others in an intersubjective world;
6) a specific time-perspective, cosmic time, standard time, felt time or durée, past time.

Characters in the Taleworld are unaware of their realm as a tale. They enter into it as real, engaging, a realm to be experienced by its inhabitants as a reality. Their attitudes of interest, skepticism, detachment, partisanship follow the contours of the epoché of persons in reality (feature 2).

56. Heda Jason in "Jewish – Near Eastern Numskull Tales: an Attempt at Interpretation" Asian Folklore Studies XXXI #1 (1972) introduces the world of the tale into folklore theory. The coinage "Taleworld" is Barbara Kirshenblatt-Gimblett's and mine.
57. Schutz, On Phenomenology and Social Relations, on p. 258 has something else in mind apropos of this distinction which he plays out quite differently in terms of acting. Compare Goffman's description of innermost lamination to Taleworld and outermost lamination or rim to Storyrealm status, Frame Analysis, p. 82.
58. Following Schutz, On Phenomenology and Social Relations, p. 253, using the same numbers.

Likewise, these inhabitants have variations in the quality of their attention to their realm and their tension of consciousness may be quite different from that of storytellers and hearers: though the dreamer sleeps, the beings he dreams may be wakeful (1). The Taleworld has its own space-time horizon, experienced as such by its inhabitants and not experienced in the same way be hearers and tellers (6). It is bodily or otherwise intersubjectively inhabited by its characters who are present to each other according to the Taleworld's metaphysical conventions (5). Characters act; they are geared into the Taleworld as into a reality which demands their responses and responds to their demands (3). The inhabitants of the Taleworld, then, experience a commensurate sense of themselves as ordinary, typical, or appropriate beings in their realm: wingéd as angels, disembodied as ghosts, evil as demons (4).

The Storyrealm, unlike the Taleworld, is part of the intersubjective world of sociality and communication, an enclave in conversation, one orienting to another realm, the Taleworld. Tellers and hearers are directed to the Taleworld by the story, that direction originating in the realm of social interaction and susceptible to its strategies. Although all participants in the storytelling influence the shape of the story, tellers are understood to have more control than hearers over its angle of entry into the Taleworld and the perspective it provides on that realm (5). Insofar as they are attentive to the Storyrealm, participants in the storytelling occasion are aware of themselves as co-present with others on a social occasion. The self is a social self (4). While so engaged in the storytelling, tellers and hearers suspend skepticism, reflection, or criticism to become absorbed in the telling (2). Participants are alert to the Storyrealm as tellers or hearers, attentive to their turns, to their contributions to the story and the effects it has on them (1). Time in the Storyrealm is felt time, variable according to participants' absorption in the story. It is neither the time-span of the Taleworld nor the cosmic time or standard time of the realm of the ordinary (6). The Storyrealm is geared into the world so that I act in it, not by means of physical acts but of verbal acts. Though what transpires in the Taleworld cannot affect the real one, the stories I tell and hear can (3).

For tellers and hearers, the Taleworld is not geared into the real one:

> ... Living in one the many worlds of phantasy we have no longer to master the outer world and to overcome the resistance of its objects. We are free from the pragmatic motive which governs our natural attitude toward the world of daily life, free also from the bondage of "interobjective" space and intersubjective standard time. No longer are we confined within the limits of our actual, restorable, or attainable reach. What occurs in the outer world no longer imposes upon us issues between which we have to choose nor does it put a limit on our possible accomplishments.

> However, there are no "possible accomplishments" in the world of phantasms if we take this term as a synonym of "performable"... the imagining self does not transform the outer world. (Schutz)[59]

The design of storytelling is to set up a Storyrealm and then to move through that realm into the Taleworld. As I am drawn into the Taleworld, I become inattentive to my presence in the Storyrealm. The Storyrealm is designed to effect this inattention to itself, for instance, by taking hearers "back to the information state -- the horizon" that obtains as events begin in the Taleworld so that what follows has the character of "unforetellable unfoldings." (Goffman)[60] The paradox, then, is that to become absorbed in the Storyrealm is to move toward absorption in the Taleworld. As I move, the Storyrealm becomes invisible, I lose my sociality, my engagement with others, my sense of time as felt time, my sense of myself as a social person, to a sense of others with their own senses of time, self, and epoché, whose sociality excludes me. Tellers and hearers are not intersubjectively present to the Taleworld even if they are characters in the story and have inhabited that realm in the past.

---

59. Schutz, On Phenomenology and Social Relations, pp. 257-8.
60. Goffman, Frame Analysis, p. 508.

Inside the Taleworld, I can be anchored in the sensibility of one or several of the characters, or I can move around as an omnipresence, or I can see persons and events as if from a distance. As my perspective moves outward from the Taleworld, I become aware of my anchorage elsewhere, as teller or hearer in the Storyrealm, as conversationalist in the realm of conversation, as a participant in the realm of interaction, as a member of the social world, eventually, as an analyst in the realm of thought: I shift from absorption to abstraction. Movement among these anchorages is characteristic of my experience of stories. Too obvious attempts to draw me into the Taleworld, for instance, can have the reverse effect, making me alert to the workings of the story. Similarly, to be reminded of my bodily presence in the realm of interaction may be to lose my awareness of the Storyrealm. Complete withdrawals entail the lapse of these realms, as they are sustained only by my attention.

Relations among realms, realm-shift, and the realm status of stories are the concerns of this inquiry. Stories are considered in each of their ontological presentations separately, in relation to each other, and in relation to other realms. A constellation of realms, for which the inquiry undertakes to provide a primitive astronomy, appears, coalesces, dissolves, and vanishes.

CHAPTER ONE

EDGEWORK:
Frame and Boundary in the Phenomenology of Narrative*

Frames distinguish two ontological presentations of stories: as a realm of events transpiring in another space and time, or Taleworld; and as a realm of discourse transpiring in the here and now, or Storyrealm. Either of these realms is potentially available at any moment during a storytelling. However, for any one participant, only one will be apparent at a time. Attention shifts, whimsically or deliberately, from one realm to another. But attention is also directed from one realm to another by frames inherent in the storytelling occasion so that realm shifts systematically over the course of the telling. This chapter specifies the multiple frames of stories in ordinary conversation. These apparently ephemeral narratives turn out to be elaborately framed. Frames thus constitute and uncover the limits of narrative.

* A version of this paper was given at the 1980 American Folklore Society Meetings in Pittsburgh. It was published in Semiotica 41:1/4 (1982) under the title, "Edgework: Frame and Boundary in the Phenomenology of Narrative Communication".

Frames

Gregory Bateson describes frames as metacommunication, that is, "communication about communication",[1] or, in Ludwig Wittgenstein's phrase, the description-under-which an event is to be seen.[2] An utterence, for instance, might be seen-as a story. Frames themselves are of two sorts which Bateson distinguishes as "exchanged cues and propositions about (a) codification and (b) the relationship between the communicators."[3] That is to say, on the one hand, that frames codify stories among other kinds of events or codify kinds of stories, and on the other hand, that they invite or reveal an attitude toward the story which illuminates the relationship between its tellers and hearers. Frames of the first sort set the realm status of an event; frames of the second sort set an attitude toward the events in that realm. For narrative events, a passage of conversation can be framed in the first sense as a story and in the second sense as cruel, revealing, disingenuous, rude, clever, funny, sad, or the like.

Gerald Prince has aptly named framings of the first sort "metanarrative signs", indications of what he calls the coding of discourse as narrative.[4] Framings of the second sort are akin to what William Labov and Joshua Waletzky call "evaluative devices", about which they write: "The evaluation of a narrative is defined by us as that part of the narrative which reveals the attitude of the narrator towards the narrative by emphasizing the relative importance of some narrative units as compared to others."[5]. Labov attends only to evaluations of

1. Jurgen Ruesch and Gregory Bateson, Communication: The Social Matrix of Psychiatry (New York: W.W. Norton, 1968) p. 209.
2. Ludwig Wittgenstein, Philosophical Investigations, tr. G.E..M. Anscombe (New York: Macmillan, 1953), pp.198, 202, and elsewhere on seeing-as.
3. Ruesch and Bateson, p. 209.
4. Gerald Prince, "Narrative Guides", Chapter III in manuscript of forthcoming book, Narratology (The Hague: Mouton, 1982).
5. William Labov and Joshua Waletzky, "Narrative Analysis: Oral Versions of Personal Experience", Essays on the Verbal and Visual Arts, ed. June Helm (Seattle and London: University of Washington Press, 1967) p. 37.

the events the story is about. I am concerned with evaluations
of the telling as well as of the tale. Thus, the telling might
be comical though the events recounted in it were terrifying.
Labov's inattention to this difference confuses events with
stories by failing to distinguish, as Erving Goffman puts it,
"between the content of a current perception and the reality
status we give to what is thus enclosed or bracketted within
perception."[6]

The confusion between Taleworld and Storyrealm, between,
that is to say, the events the story is about and their
presentation in the form of a story, has been a problem in
narrative analysis. The Taleworld is a reality inhabited by
persons for whom events unfold according to its own ontological
conventions. The Storyrealm consists of tellings, writings,
performances, that is, of recountings of or alludings to events
understood to transpire in another realm. The status of one
realm bears on but does not fix the status of the other.

Frames are metacommunications of two sorts about two orders
of events: they set the realm status of or disclose an
attitude toward either Taleworlds or Storyrealms. Story frames
distinguish stories from other sorts of discoursive events like
conversations, explanations, quotations, descriptions, reports,
confessions, and so on, and from other sorts of narrative
events like plays, games, mimes, films, or dreams; and they
distinguish among genres of story, among myths, legends,
folktales, fairytales, tall tales, anecdotes, and personal
experience narratives. Story evaluations characterize stories
as good in the sense of spicy, sharp, amusing, witty, wry,
well-told, pertinent, or pointed; or not, in that they are
poorly told, pointless, malicious, maladroit, or boring.
Frames of the events that the stories are about distinguish
between real and imaginary events, among events in the ordinary
world and events in other realms such as the realms of the
dead, of dreams and dramas, of science, the supernatural, or
the extraterrestrial. Evaluations of events qualify them as
disgusting or enchanting, as romantic, adventurous, daunting,
dreadful, or dreary. This inquiry distinguishes among four
narrative frames: frames and evaluations of the story; frames
and evaluations of the events the story is about, and considers
their bearing on making stories.

6. Erving Goffman, Frame Analysis (New York, Evanston, San
    Francisco, London: Harper and Row, 1974) p. 3.

Boundaries

Information about differences, Bateson says, are stacked at the edges of events.[7] Differences between realms are at issue at the moment of transition from the realm of conversation to the Storyrealm and from the Storyrealm back to the realm of conversation. It is for this reason that frames, indications of realm status, are characteristically positioned between realms, between, that is, the event framed and the realm that event is framed for.[8] Frames, therefore, do what might be called edgework for stories.

This characteristic positioning of frames on the edges of realms gives rise to a confusion between boundaries and frames, between, that is, the literal or physical frames that lie alongside contiguous realms and the conceptual differences they reify. Boundaries locate the literal or physical borders between realms. Frames locate their conceptual limits. Events are bounded; realms are framed. Or, more precisely, events are framed as to their realm status. Boundaries occur at the same level of analysis as the events they bound: a picture frame is a material object among material objects; a story boundary is a verbal event among words. Setting a boundary implies a frame by separating, setting off, and tying together the events within the boundary. Defining a frame likewise implies a boundary by relating events to be conceived of in one realm. However, though all boundaries are frames, not all frames are boundaries.

Frames communicate about the ontological status of other events, but they have a different ontological status from the events they communicate about. Unlike boundaries, they do not

7. Gregory Bateson, Unpublished Lecture at the University of Pennsylvania (Philadelphia: 1973).
8. Maurice Natanson, Literature, Philosophy and the Social Sciences (The Hague: Martinus Nijhoff, 1962) p. 81: "The act of framing, of literally surrounding a canvas with sides of wood or metal, is the astonishing sorcery of the art apprentice. To frame a picture is to separate a part of experience from its context... To create, then, is to separate, to exclude, to deny a whole by attending a fraction of that whole."

count as part of the events they frame. As Bateson points out, "... the analogy of the picture frame is excessively concrete. The psychological concept which we are trying to define is neither physical nor logical. Rather, the actual physical frame is, we believe, added by human beings to physical pictures because human beings operate more easily in a universe in which some of their psychological characteristics are externalized."[9]. Boundaries, then, are differences themselves, drawn along the edges of realms of events whose differences they thereby come to represent. Boundaries serve as cues, or, more closely, concrete metaphors, for conceptual frames.

Boundaries are positional: they enclose, or, in the case of narrative, open and close, an alternate realm of experience. Frames, by contrast, are transfixual: they are pervasive qualifications of the events they span and inform. Framing transforms into a story a possible first hearing of that event as conversation. The frame imputes an ontological status to events wherever they are located, rendering them constituents of a realm. By its nature, then, a frame can lie within the same realm as the event it frames, in some other realm, or, most commonly, along the border between. So story frames are either disclosures in the course of storytelling, remarks in the course of conversation, or transitional structures.

The distribution of frames inside, outside, or alongside the realm of events they frame reflects their bi-directionality: frames are directed from one realm and toward another, for instance, from the realm of conversation toward the Storyrealm. The instructions they bear on how to see that other realm of events implies a realm to see the events from. Frames are frames-for tellers and hearers as well as frames-of events. As Goffman points out, "assumptions that cut an activity off from the external surround also mark the ways in which this activity is inevitably bound to the surrounding world."[10]. Frames do not just enclose one realm, they specify a relationship between two. Hence, this inquiry extends attention from how stories are framed to what stories are framed for.

9. Gregory Bateson, <u>Steps to an Ecology of Mind</u> (New York: Ballantine Books, 1972) p. 188.
10. Goffman, p. 249.

Edgework

In virtue of their frames, stories can be identified as a different order of event from the conversations in which they are enclaves, a Storyrealm. The Storyrealm, that region of narrative discourse within the realm of conversation, then directs attention to a third realm, the realm of the events the story is about, or Taleworld. Events in the Taleworld are framed by the story, itself framed by the conversation. A single event can, in this way, be multiply framed so that, as Erving Goffman suggests,

> it becomes convenient to think of each transformation as adding a layer or lamination to the activity. One can address two features of the activity. One is the innermost layering, wherin dramatic activity can be at play to engross the participant. The other is the outermost lamination, the rim of the frame, as it were, which tells us just what sort of status in the real world the activity has, whatever the complexity of the inner laminations.[11]

This chapter analyzes relations among three realms: the Taleworld, the Storyrealm, and the realm of conversation. These realms are conceived to open out onto one another in such a way that the innermost or deepest realm is the Taleworld, a realm of unfolding events and enacting characters. The next lamination or level is the Storyrealm, the recounting of events and acts in narrative discourse. And the outermost or presented realm is the occasion of this recounting, the realm of conversation. Frames, on this analysis, orient one realm to another. (Figure 1 shows these narrative laminations.)

11. Goffman, p. 82.

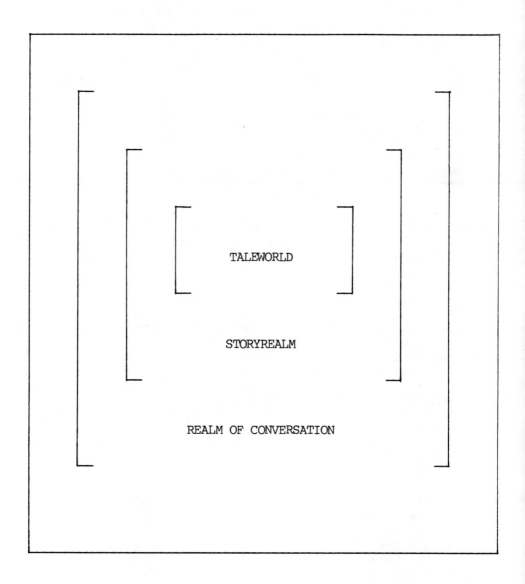

Figure 1: Narrative Laminations.

Framing characteristics are exemplified in the stories told
in the course of an evening's conversation at Algy May's farm,
Rowbrook, on Saturday the 29th of March, 1975. This is the
first of many such conversations with Algy, tape-recorded
during a year's fieldwork on Dartmoor. On this occasion,
stories are exchanged among five participants: Algy May, the
primary storyteller (abbreviated A in the transcription); his
wife, Jean (J); his niece, Marian (M); and his two visitors,
Miles Fursdon, a local farmer (MF); and myself (K). Algy is a
sturdy sprightly sixty-seven year old countryman with bright
blue eyes and bright white hair. His wife, Jean, spare and
skittish, with a long folded face, is a painter who used to
breed thoroughbred horses and greyhounds. Marian, stocky,
ruddy-faced, dark-haired, does the farmwork with Algy and helps
Jean with her breeding. Miles, tall, lean, and swarthy, is a
young farmer from nearby and an old friend of the Mays. I
appear as a folklorist and a foreigner, to follow the Devon
practice of so describing anyone from outside of the shire.

We talk in the dark, stone-flagged kitchen of their
nineteenth century farmhouse in the company of three dogs, a
huge cat, and a baby lamb being warmed and fed by the fire. In
the background is the murmur of the television. They know I am
interested in stories and after half an hour's conversation
Algy mentions a story connected with the main house on Rowbrook
Farm, just over the hill from Algy's farmhouse. Do I know it?
At this point I get permission to start tape-recording and
continue from this, the first story told on this occasion and
the first I have ever heard Algy tell, to the last story told
as Miles and I were leaving an hour and a half later. These
are the stories and their tellers.

1	Three Brothers	Algy
2	Snailly House	Algy
3	Dolly's Cott	Algy
4	Jan Coo and the Piskies	Algy
5	Hangman's Pit	Algy
6	The Devil at Tavistock Inn	Algy
7	The School Inspector	Algy
8	Foxy's Cremation	Algy
9	Foxy's Surplice, the Bentley, and the Deerstalker	Marian, Algy
10	Foxy and the Cartwheel	Marian
11	Foxy and the Flywheel	Miles
12	Algy and the Flywheel	Algy
13	Bill Hamlyn and the Cable Spool	Algy

14	The Plough and the Hare	Algy
15	Michael and the Hay	Algy
16	Michael and the Master of Hounds	Algy
17	Not 'Xactly and the Cigarette	Algy
18	Not 'Xactly and the Waterbuckets	Jean
19	Polly and the Runaway Cart	Algy
20	The Witchcraft-Exorcism Trial	Algy
21	Herman French's Aerial Photographs	Miles
22	Richard and the Dock Seed	Miles
23-26	Ferreting	Algy
27	Sheepshearing	Algy
28-30	Dog-training	Algy, Miles, Marian
31	The Dog Breaks his Neck	Algy
32	The Tom Sawyer Readings	Katharine
33	Going Jiggoty	Algy

Beginnings and Ends

William Labov claims it is characteristic of what he calls
personal experience narratives that the sequential organization
of narrative clauses in the Storyrealm matches the temporal
organization of events in the Taleworld.[12] However, it is
crucial to remember that sequence is merely a convention for
time: "... time does not belong to discourse proper, but to
the referent," writes Roland Barthes.[13] In the Taleworld,
one event happens after another. In the Storyrealm, one event
follows on from another. Construing consecutive events as
causally related gives stories their consequentiality. "The
sense of closure," writes Barbara Herrnstein Smith, "is a
function of the perception of structure."[14] Consider the
first story about three brothers by the name of French who once
lived in the main house on Rowbrook Farm.*

```
Opening        A:  The point was
                   .....
Beginning          there were
                   three
                   teenage
                   Frenchs
                   sleeping in one bed over here
                   in the cottage- in the old house.
                   Thunderstorm
End                Father French comes down
                   finds the center one
                   struck
                   by lighting.
Closing            Three boys in one bed center one killed.
Closing            Tchew.
```

(Story 1)

*See appendix for transcription devices.

12. Labov and Waletzky, p. 13, ".... narrative will be
    considered as one verbal technique for recapitulating
    experience, in particular, a technique of constructing
    narrative units which match the temporal sequence of that
    experience.:"
13. Roland Barthes, "An Introduction to the Structural
    Analysis of Narrative", New Literary History Volume VI
    (1974-75), pp. 237-272, p. 252.
14. Barbara Herrnstein Smith, Poetic Closure (Chicago and
    London: University of Chicago Press, 1968) p. 4.

In order to arrive at its end, the story of the three brothers opens up and spins out earlier events in such a way that they orient to the death of the middle brother. The story then moves from the beginning toward that end as its completion. The appearance of consequentiality in narrative is produced by counting the last event taken from the Taleworld an end, and then constructing the story backwards to include whatever is necessary to account for it, thus arriving at the beginning. Beginnings do not so much imply ends as ends entail beginnings. Paul Ricoeur writes: "By reading the end in the beginning and the beginning in the end, we learn also to read time itself backward, as the recapitulating of the initial conditions of a course of action in its terminal consequences."[15] Succeeding events are presented as consequent on preceding events. Thus, the points where the sequence of events starts and finishes in the Taleworld become the beginning and end of the story. (Figure 2 locates beginnings and ends on the edges of the Taleworld.)

15. Paul Ricoeur, "Narrative Time", Critical Inquiry VII, 1 (Autumn 1980) p. 180. See also p. 174: "Following a story, correlatively, is understanding the successive actions, thoughts, and feelings in question insofar as they present a certain directedness. By this I mean that we are pushed ahead by this development and that we reply to its impetus with expectations concerning the outcome and completion of the entire process. In this sense, the story's conclusion is the pole of attraction of the entire development. But a narrative conclusion can be neither deduced nor predicted. There is no story if our attention is not moved along by a thousand contingencies. This is why a story has to be followed to its conclusion. So rather than being predictable, a conclusion must be acceptable. Looking back from the conclusion to the episodes leading up to it, we have to be able to say that this ending required these sorts of events and this chain of actions. But this backward look is made possible by the teleological movement directed by our expectations when we follow the story."

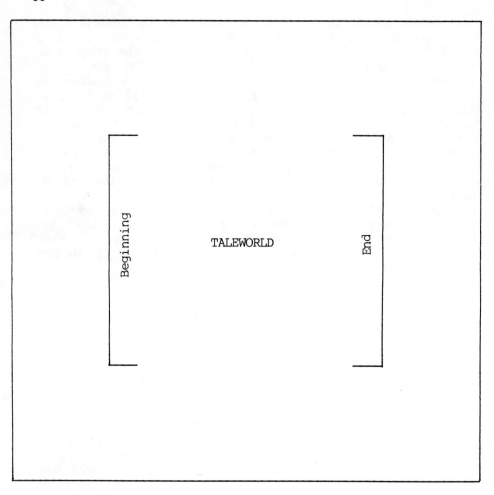

Figure 2: Beginnings and Ends.

Taleworlds do not have beginnings and ends. They are realms experienced by their inhabitants not as beginning and ending, but as ongoing. The story cuts out a portion of the Taleworld to recount, but the Taleworld extends beyond the boundaries set in it by the story. Other events are understood to have happened before and after, as well as at the same time as, those being recounted. Beginnings and ends are introduced into the Taleworld by the Storyrealm, thus rendering consequential what is merely consecutive. These boundaries set up by the story in the Taleworld frame events in that world for the Storyrealm. They constitute, that is, instructions that the events within the boundary are to be taken in relation to one another. Framing events as stories invests them with the sense of an ending. Beginnings and ends are frames-of the Taleworld and frames-for the Storyrealm.

Openings and Closings

The stories, unlike their Taleworlds, are enclaves in another realm, the realm of conversation. Story enclaves are a different order of discourse from the conversation that encloses them, namely, a representation of events not present to the occasion. They are also a different order of event from other events likewise enclosed in conversation. They are set off from the enclosing conversation by openings and closings, which mark the entries and exits between the Storyrealm and the realm of conversation. Openings and closings can also distinguish a narrative event from other enclaves in conversation. A distinction must be made between beginnings and ends, on the one hand, and openings and closings, on the other. Beginnings and ends are the points where the events stories are about start and finish; openings and closings are the points where the stories start and finish. Beginnings and ends create boundaries in the Taleworld. Openings and closings constitute the boundaries of the Storyrealm. (Figure 3 locates openings and closings on the edges of stories.)

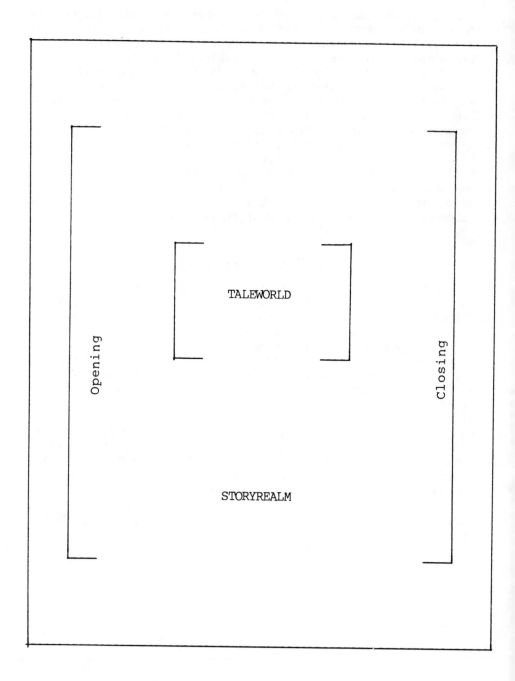

Figure 3: Openings and Closings.

Characteristically, openings and closings neatly bracket beginnings and ends, as in "Three Brothers", where the opening frame, directed to the Storyrealm, is tucked in next to the beginning of the Taleworld.

Opening   The point was

               .....
Beginning   there were
               three
               teenage
               Frenchs

The closing phrases, there are two, closely follow the end.

End   Father French comes down
               finds the center one
               struck
               by lighting.
Closing   Three boys in one bed center one killed.
Closing   Tchew.

                                                    (Story 1)

Occasionally, though, the beginning of the Taleworld is used to open the Storyrealm and the end closes both realms. For instance, after Algy finishes his frames of the ferreting stories, he opens the next story about Marian shearing a sheep by moving straight into the Taleworld to describe the film crew's intentions.

Evaluation A: I swear it's perfectly true.
Coda   We got a fiver for that.   (Story 26)
                (He he)
Beginning/   Then the other thing they wanted to film Marian
Opening   shearing a sheep   (Story 27)

The end of the story of Foxy and the flywheel is followed by an evaluation of the events in the Taleworld. There is no separate frame to close the Storyrealm.

End/Closing [[MF: [and he was knocked flat.   ]
Evaluation   A: [Cor he was lucky wasn't he.]   (Story 11)

A result of this condensation of opening and beginning as well as end and closing frames is that the story is more slightly differeniated from the conversation in which it occurs. For instance, the activities of the Canadian film crew are carried over into the story of the sheepshearing. The result of layering openings along beginnings and closings along ends is a density of frames at the edges of the story, these serving to set it off further from conversation.

When openings and closings are formulaic, like "Once upon a time", and "The end", not only do they mark a discontinuity in the order of discourse, but also, by convention, they specify the realm status of the enclave as fairytale-like. The openings and closings of conversational anecdotes are not usually formulaic in this traditional sense and, although they do mark discontinuities in speaking, they do not necessarily specify the realm status of the event they bound. In the story of the three brothers, the opening phrase, "The point was", alerts hearers that a story is about to commence, in much the same way that the formulaic opening "Once upon a time", does. The phrase is technically a re-start, indicating that the storyteller is picking up where he left off doing preparatory work for the story before I interrupted to ask if I could record. The closing phrase, "Three boys in one bed center one killed", draws attention to and reiterates the end of the story. The formulaic closing, "The end", similarly positioned just after the end of a story, likewise draws attention to what has already happened, though without repeating it. "The end" is not itself the closing event in the Taleworld, though it refers to that, but the closing utterance in the Storyrealm. The phrase which follows this closing, "Tchew", appears to be a form of what Goffman has entitled "expression speech", that is, utterances which convey by rhythm and intonation the feeling of a prior remark without replicating its content.[16] It is the sort of utterance adults often use with infants and animals. Here, the sound, "Tchew", catches the quality of lightening striking, thus reiterating the end of the story in another key. Repetition appears to create a closural effect both by creating a sense of saturation with the pattern repeated, and by laying an evaluative emphasis on the element to be taken as the end of the story.[17] The effect is produced by doubling back over and thus reversing the flow of discourse.

Besides doing closure on the Storyrealm, closings direct attention inward or backward to the Taleworld and forward or outward to the realm of conversation. They can signal on the

16. Goffman, p. 527.
17. Smith, p. 42. Consider also the structuralist view that redundancy draws out pattern, Bateson, _Steps_, p. 130.

one hand that hearers have missed the ending in the Taleworld
and they can signal on the other hand for hearers to resume the
transition property of utterance completions, suspended for
storytelling.[18] These   Storyrealm   closings   have   been
deceptively classified by Labov as codas, though they do not
fulfill his own criterion that codas follow on from events in
the Taleworld.[19] Storyrealm closings orient hearers to the
Taleworld and to the realm of conversation while providing a
transition between the two. During the course of Algy's story
about Marian shearing the sheep, Miles interpolates the brief
supportive utterances characteristic of hearers, but no remark
to indicate awareness of its end, though this is marked by Algy
and Marian's laughter. So Algy follows the laughter with a
Storyrealm closing to which Miles responds appropriately both
by his appreciative utterance and also by the fact of taking up
his own turn.

	A:	But at the end of the shearing
		this- the camera was stopped for a second
		then this huge fleece that I'd got from the
		wool merchants- (he he he)
		huge thing-
		Marian throws it out you know as you do after
		shearing
		but unfortunately the-
End		the old sheep had a green mark on it and this had
		bright red.
	[[M:	[(Hm hm hm)
		(He he he)]
Closing	A:	That's the only thing about that.
	MF:	Tsh.

(Story 27)

18. Emmanuel Schegloff and Harvey Sacks, "Opening up Closings"
     in Ethnomethodology, ed. Roy Turner (Middlesex, England:
     Penguin, 1974) p. 256: "Having initially formulated the
     closing problem for conversation in terms of the
     suspension of the transition property of utterance
     completions, a technique was described to come to terms
     with that problem --- the terminal exchange."
19. Labov, "The Transformation of Experience in Narrative
     Syntax" in Language in the Inner City (Philadelphia:
     University of Pennsylvania Press, 1972) pp. 365-366.

If beginnings and ends frame the Taleworld for the
Storyrealm, openings and closings frame the Storyrealm for the
realm of conversation. Both pairs of frames bound the story.
This lodgement of beginnings and ends, as well as openings and
closings, in the boundaries of the story enhances its
discreteness from surrounding discourse.

Prefaces and Codas

Frames in the form of prefaces and codas located in the
conversation also lie along the edges of the story enclave,
already neatly bounded by beginnings and ends, and by openings
and closings. Openings and closings lie just inside the
Storyrealm. Prefaces and codas, on the other hand, lie just
outside the story in the realm of conversation, thus layering a
third frame onto the boundaries of the story. Openings and
closings frame the Storyrealm they bound, but they also appear
as boundaries of the story. Prefaces and codas likewise bound
the story and also bound off the realm of conversation,
creating the enclosure for a story enclave. While codas only
frame the Taleworld, prefaces can frame either the Taleworld or
the Storyrealm. All three pairs of frames, whether of the
Taleworld or the Storyrealm, are also boundaries of the realm
of conversation. (Figure 4 locates prefaces and codas on the
edges of conversation.)

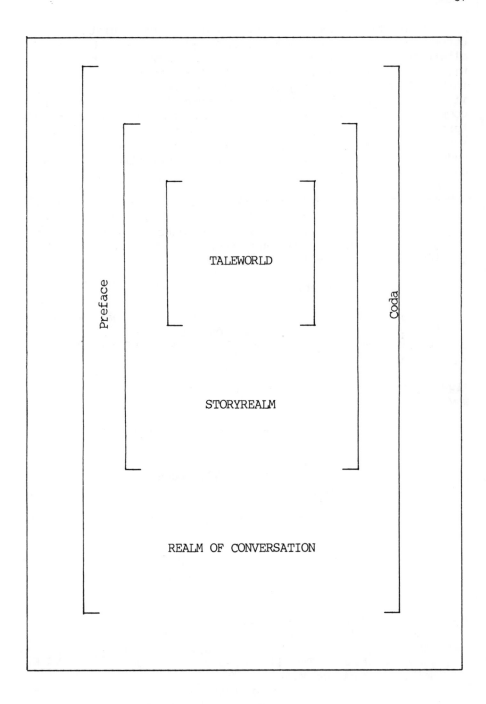

Figure 4: Prefaces and Codas.

Conversation consists of what sociolinguists call utterance turns, arrangements for participants to speak alternately. At the completion of a turn, other participants will feel expected or entitled to take their own turn at talk. Sentence ends signal utterance completions.[20] Thus, if a speech event is going to take more than one sentence to complete, speakers must get permission to take an extended turn, or risk being interrupted on completion of the first sentence.[21] Because of the sequential relationship between ends and beginnings, even the briefest story takes more than one sentence utterance to tell.[22]

> The consequence of that (Sacks says) is that one produces for what turn out to be stories what I'll call a "story preface" which is an utterance that asks for the right to produce extended talk and says that the talk will be interesting, as well as other things.

> At the completion of that "interest arouser" if you like, one stops and it's the business of others to indicate that it's okay and maybe also that they're interested, or it's not okay, or they're not interested. If one looks at stories one finds that prefaces of this sort are present.

Algy May prefaces his story of Snailly House in the following way:

```
            A:  But you don't know probably any of the old
                    stories
                about
                Dolly's Cott Snailly House.
                Do you.
            K:  About what?
Preface      [[ A: [Never heard anything ] about Snailly House.
               K: [Snailly House?        ]
            A:  Yes.
                It's a-
                it's in the forest now but there used to be a
                    house up there
```

20. Schegloff and Sacks, p. 236.
21. Sacks, "On the Analyzability of Stories by Children" in John Gumperz and Dell Hymes, eds., Directions in Socioligistics: The Ethnography of Speaking (New York: Holt, Rinehart and Winston, 1972) pp. 325-345, pp. 344-345.
22. Harvey Sacks, Unpublished Lecture Notes (University of California, Irvine: 9 April, 1970) Lecture II, p. 10.

```
Response        K:  No I didn't know that.
Beginning       A:  Two old women lived in it
                    .....                    (Story 2)
```

Conversation moves from the preface to the beginning of the story, "Two old women lived in it", as soon as the storyteller receives an appropriate acceptance of his preface, namely, "No I didn't know that". Prefacing can be done neatly in three utterance turns: preface, response, opening; and would have been so done here if I had not been puzzled by the referents, "Dolly's Cott", which turns to be short for Dolly's Cottage, and "Snailly House", which is another cottage named after its association with snails. The preface, "But you don't know probably any of the old stories/ about/Dolly's Cott Snailly House./Do you", would neatly have been followed by "No I don't", thus arriving at the opening on the third turn. The work of prefacing can be accomplished in two utterance turns if a second speaker requests a story, that request serving as both preface and response. Thus Algy's wife, Jean, asks him to tell the story of Michael the carthorse:

```
Preface/        J:  Tell them about um mm Harold
Response            Bluett darling in Cornwall
                    and uh
             [[ A: [and Michael ]the  horse.
                    Yes.        ]
                J:  Um
                    (They'd like to know.)
Opening         A:  This is true.
Beginning           There was a great big carthorse in Cornwall
                    got out on the common.
                    .....                    (Story 15)
```

Prefaces can be addressed to either the Taleworld or the Storyrealm, arousing interest in the events or the story. Contrast the preface to "Foxy's Cremation" with the preface to "Foxy's Surplice, the Bentley, and the Deerstalker." The preface to "Foxy's Cremation" focuses on a character in the Taleworld, Foxy.

```
Preface to
Events          A:  But in more recent times Miles will remember
                        Foxy
Response        MF: Yeah.
                A:  Do you?
Response        MF: Yeah.
```

```
A:    Well he- you know took seventeen tries to get
         a-
      to be a
      parson
      .....                                    (Story 8)
```

The preface to "Foxy's Surplice, the Bentley, and the Deerstalker" directs attention instead to the quality of the story.

```
Story
Preface   M:    Now I think the best- one of the best stories
                   about Foxy is that
                he used to do the service at Princetown and
                   he used to=
Response  A:    Umhm.                              (Story 9)
```

The use of what sociolinguists call laminator verbs like "think", "tell", "know", "hear", "say", "dream", and so on, can orient the preface to the Storyrealm though the verbs within the lamination are directed to the Taleworld.[23] Appropriate responses can be exceedingly slight, serving merely to return the floor to the storyteller in the awareness that he is embarking on an extended turn at talk.

Since prefaces arrange to suspend the transition property of sentence completions during storytelling, a difficulty can arise about when the story ends so that turntaking can be resumed. Apparently, ends do not always so clearly complete beginnings that closure is evident from the Taleworld. That can be remedied or reinforced by closings in the Storyrealm which draw attention to the completion of the events in the Taleworld. Despite, or in the absence of, such framing devices, hearers sometimes overlook or fail to display appreciation of the end of a story by taking up their turn. In such an instance, storytellers can alert hearers that the story has ended with what Labov calls a coda. "Codas close off the sequence of complicating actions and indicate that none of the events that followed were important to the narrative."[24] A nice parity is evident between prefaces and codas; one opens up a realm the other closes down, both working from the conversational side. These conversational frames thus parallel the edgework of openings and closings on stories, and of beginnings and ends on events. (Figure 5 shows these sets of frames as boundaries.)

23. Goffman, P. 505.
24. Labov, p. 365-366.

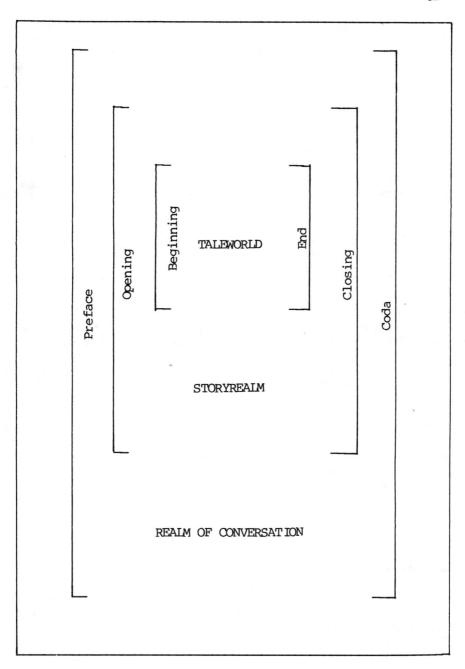

Figure 5: Frames that are Boundaries.

An elegant alternative to dependence on such closing frames is to build into the preface information about how to monitor a story for its end. According to Sacks:[25]

> It turns out that among the jobs of the story preface is that of giving information about what it will take for the story to be over; again, there's an obvious rationality to putting information about what it will take for it to be over, right at the beginning so that people can watch from there on in to see when it will be over.

Thus the preface to "Bill Hamlyn and the Cable Spool" instructs hearers to monitor the story for its similarity to the story before:

```
Preface       A:    But then you see Hamlyn
                    the
                    contractor
                    told us a very similar story
                    .....                               (Story 13)
```

Prefaces can take the form of what Labov calls "abstracts", consisting "of one or two clauses summarizing the whole story."[26] Abstracts can also be used as openings for stories where they do not elicit responses but only offer instructions about how to monitor the story for its end. Abstracts are not to be understood as part of the story or a replica in miniature, but as another metacommunication or frame about how to listen to it.[27] Algy's abstract to the story of Marian shearing sheep acts as its opening and indicates how to watch for what will be its end, namely, the sheepshearing.

```
Abstract      A:    Then the other thing they wanted to do was to
                        film Marian
                    shearing a sheep.
                    This is in October so I said O likely.
              MF:   Tsa.
              A:    Anyhow.
Beginning           Went down to Buckfastleigh and got
                    two very big Scottish fleeces
                    .....                               (Story 27)
```

25. Sacks, (9 April 1970) Lecture II, pp. 13–14.
26. Labov, p. 363.
27. Compare Labov, p. 364, and Labov and David Fanshel, Therapeutic Discourse (New York, San Francisco, London: Academic Press, 1977) p. 106.

Prefaces to invite stories from other participants quite characteristically take the form of abstracts, as in Algy's preface to Marian's story of Foxy and cartwheel, thus indicating at once which story is being elicited and providing its response.

```
Preface/
Abstract/
Response      A:   Tell them about- Marian tell them about the
                        um-
                  putting the mm-
                  pushing the cartwheel down Meltor cause that
                        was
              [[ M:       [really Foxy ]
                          [Yes.
              [[ A:   [started that again      ]
Opening       [[ M:   [when- when he was um]
                  vicar at Leusden he thought he'd- he'd
                  .....                            (Story 10)
```

Codas consist of frames following the close of the story which are designed to link the story back onto conversation. They relate the Taleworld to the realm of conversation by interposing events sequential but not consequential to the story between its completion and the resumption of conversation. As Labov describes this, "all codas are separated from the resolution by temporal juncture."[28] Thus, he argues: "Codas have the property of bridging the gap between the moment of time at the end of the narrative proper and the present. They bring the narrator and the listener back to the point at which they entered the narrative."[29] Such codas take the form of residues of the events recounted in the story, as in Marian and Algy's codas to the story of Foxy and the cartwheel.

```
Coda          M:   You can still see the old- old um
Coda          [[ A:   [You can down the ] wood now yeah.
              [[ M:   [remnants down-
                  down in the wood.             (Story 10)
```

28. Labov and Waletzky, p. 40.
29. Labov, p. 366.

The continuing presence of these artefacts ties the present setting to the past realm of events. Their persistence in everyday life, of which conversation is an aspect, appears to authenticate the story, to attest to its relevance. Codas can also be spun out into conversation, as they are after the story, "Foxy and the Flywheel", where generator flywheels are taken up as a topic and become a theme of the following story, "Algy and the Flywheel", even though that topic shift entails discontinuing the topic of Foxy, the vicar, which has connected all four of the preceding stories in conversation.

```
                   .....
          MF:   And she went down there and
                found him lying on the floor
           J:   She knew.
          MF:   and the flywheel had come off the
                generator
        [[J:   [O how awful.]
        [[M:   [Dreadful.    ]
          MF:   and rolled- went right over him I think it did
                     and-and smashed a chair against the wall
End                 [and he was knocked flat.        ]
        [[A:        [Cor he was lucky wasn't he.]
          MF:   Yeah.
Coda          And mother had to pick him up and get him-
                stir him to life again.
        [[J:   [Good heavens.]
        [[M:   [(            ]
        [[A:                    [God he's]lucky to be[alive    ]
        [[J:                                          [Yes yes.]
        [[MF:  Yeah.
Coda          We got the generator at home now.
           K:   O.
          A:    He was certainly[lucky to be alive.      ]
        [[MF:                    [The one that did it uh]
           K:   Uh.
Coda      MF:   got it down in the river.
           A:   Well
Preface         it's funny you should say that because uh
                   .....                    (Stories 11 and 12)
```

Codas mark closure in the Taleworld as closings mark closure in
the Storyrealm. However, the relationships between each of
these realms and the realm of conversation for which they do
closure are quite different. The Taleworld is not present to
the storytelling occasion whereas the Storyrealm is an enclave
in conversation. For this reason, while codas construct
continuities between disparate realms, closings discriminate
contiguous realms. The boundaries of stories provide junctures
for the insertion of information about ontological differences
in the form of frames. Frames that are also boundaries lie
between the realms they are frames-for and the realms they are
frames-of. So positioned, frames point in two directions:
toward the events they frame, and toward the realm they frame
those events for. (Figure 6 shows the relation between the
realms these frames are located in and realms to which they
direct attention.)

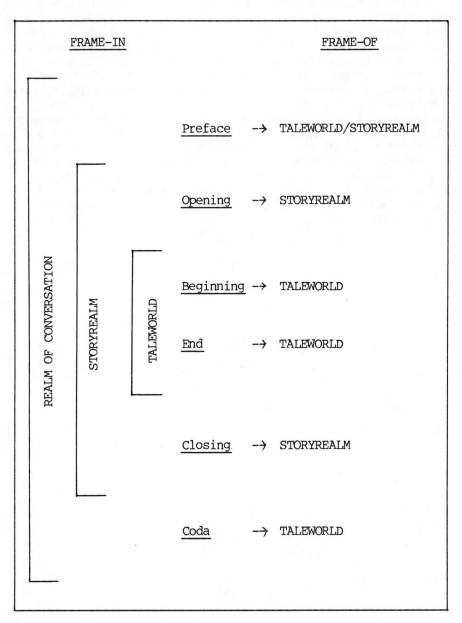

Figure 6: Taleworld and Storyrealm Frames.

Orientations

Frames that are boundaries must be contrasted with frames
that are not or not necessarily boundaries. Such frames bear
on events in a realm but do not mark the edges of that realm of
events. Orientations, for instance, provide information deemed
necessary in order to understand what is transpiring in the
Taleworld. For instance, Algy tells a story about a narrow
escape which he begins with a geographical orientation.

```
Beginning/         A:  Jean and I were going up a narrow lane
Orientation            in Cornwall
                       and we saw a very white-faced chap
                       looking at us.
                       Cor thank God you're well.
                       I said what's the matter.
                       He says the bloody flywheel's come off.
                       And he's pointing to the top of the hill
                   MF: ((Chuckles))
End                A:  And apparently it had come down so fast it
                          had
                       jumped over this
                       low lane
                   MF: Tcha.
                   A:  Yeah.
                       missed us
                   MF: Tss.
                   A:  and gone into the-
                       well miles away ((chuckles)).      (Story 12)
```

To assure that hearers understand the story, Algy precedes it
with another orientation that describes the flywheels on
threshing engines.

```
Preface/
Orientation     A:  But Miles
                    years ago
                    there used to be threshing engines
Ticket  MF:         Yeah.
Orientation     A:  Steam engines.
                MF: Yeah.
Orientation     A:  Bloody good flywheels on them
                    (              )
Beginning           and we were going up-
                    Jean and I were going up a narrow lane
                    .....                         (Story 12)
```

Placed as these are around the beginning of the story,
orientations provide background for the sequence of events. In
this position, as Labov suggests, they "serve to orient the
listener in respect to person, place, time, and behavioral
situation. We will therefore refer to this structural feature
as an orientation section: formally, the group of free clauses
which precede the first narrative clause."[30] However,
orienting remarks explanations, or clarifications can also be
inserted into or after the story, directed to those particular
aspects of it they are designed to elucidate. After this
story, it occurs to Algy that his hearers may not all realize
that Cornish lanes are cut so deeply into the land by ancient
usage that a projectile skimming along at ground level could
cross the lane and miss the people in it, so he adds another
orientation later on in the conversation, one which expands on
the orientation to Cornwall inside the story. This orientation
does not lie along a boundary of the story.

```
Orientation    A: These
                  real old sunken
                  Cornish lanes you know way down it was.
                  And of course it just bounced   over
        [[MF:                                   [Right ]
                      over the top.                      (Story 12)
```

Orientations can thus transfix a narrow span of events within
the sequence. In such a case, Sacks notices, "What we have is
a sense of context being employed by the teller, which involves
fitting into the story, in carefully located places,
information that will permit the appreciation of what was
transpiring which is not information which involves events in
the story sequence at that point."[31]

Orientations disclose the Taleworld as a realm of events
not given to hearers in the way events in everyday life are
given, one for which some metaphysical constants or background
expectancies are therefore made explicit.[32] The geographical

30. Labov and Waletzky, p. 32.
31. Sacks, (1970) Lecture VII, p. 10.
32. Maurice Natanson notes that Alfred Schutz used to refer to
    birth, death, and aging as "metaphysical constants," The
    Journying Self (Massachusetts: Addison Wesley Pub. Co.,
    1970) p. 198. Harold Garfinkel, "Background
    Expectancies," Rules and Meanings ed. Mary Douglas
    (Middlesex, England: Penguin, 1977) p. 21.

location of two cottages strung out along the East Dart River, Dolly's Cott and Snailly House, serve as orientations for two stories about them strung together in conversation:

Preface	A:	But you don't know probably any of the old stories about Dolly's Cott Snailly House Do you.
Preface	[[K: A:	[About what? [Never heard anything]about Snailly House.
	K:	Snailly House?
	A:	Yes. It's a-
Orientation		it's in the forest now but there used to be a house up there
Ticket	K:	No I didn't know that.
Beginning	A:	Two old women lived in it
	MF:	Where's this?
	A:	Snailly House.
	K:	Where.
Orientation	A:	At East Dart.

(Story 2)

. . . . .

Orientation	A:	Then further down the East Dart you get Dolly's Cot.
Orientation		And Dolly was um a girl that worked at Prince Hall and uh- no sorry Torre Royal and the-
Orientation		it's the Torre Royal outside Princetown
Orientation		and the Prince Regent used to come down
Beginning		and a chap that was courting Dolly

. . . . .

(Story 3)

This passage introduces situational and social orientations as well as the spatial orientation mentioned. Orientations can also be temporal, historical, philosophical, and so on. The orientation to the next story locates the events in the geographical space the conversationalists are inhabiting, Rowbrook Farm, but two hundred years earlier:

	A:	And Jan Cou.
Orientation		The one for here- Rowbrook.
Orientation		He was a boy about seventeen hundred and

> something
> looked after the cattle- only a youngster
> ....

(Story 4)

Attention to ontological differences qualifies orientations as frames even when they do not provide information about how to regard the Taleworld as a whole. Harvey Sacks argues that the strategic use of such information keeps hearers attentive to how to interpret what is being told.[33] Algy orients to the story of Marian shearing the sheep in this way.

Abstract	A:	Then the other thing they wanted to do was to film Marian shearing a sheep.
Orientation		This is in October so I said O likely.
	MF:	Tsa.
	A:	Anyhow.
Beginning		Went down to Buckfastleigh and got two very big Scottish fleeces
		.....

(Story 27)

Sheep's wool thickens over the winter and moults over the summer, so shearing is usually done in the spring when the wool is thickest. An October fleece is a fairly motley proposition. Miles, himself a farmer, is therefore alerted by the orientation to monitor Algy's story for a solution to the problem of shearing a sheep in October.

Orientations can be offered by other participants who so display just the kind of attention to the story orientations by the teller are intended to evoke. Thus, orientations can not only insert information for understanding the story but also insert it at just the point where its teller or other participants figure the information will be needed. Its nicety of placement then indicates when it is to be used.[34] Orientations can be understood to introduce hearers into the realm codas then draw them out of, codas and orientations consisting of aspects or fragments of the Taleworld set out in discourse beforehand and afterwards. Orientations afford an angle of entry into the Taleworld, an angle that can disclose a perspective on that realm. In setting up the background against

33. Sacks, (1970) Lecture VII, p. 11.
34. Sacks, (1970) Lecture VII, p. 10.

which events unfold they set up the angle from which hearers apprehend those events. They point from the context of the story to the context of the events, from hearers to hearings, and tie them together.[35] Orientations are frames—of the Taleworld and frames—for the realm of conversation, in the Storyrealm, thus neatly interrelating three realms of experience. (Figure 7 shows the interrelation of these three realms.)

35. Jane Spencer Edwards describes the way orientations relate Taleworlds to the social realms of storytellers and hearers in "Orientation to the Contexts of Oral Narrative," presented at the American Folklore Society Meetings (Los Angeles: October, 1979).

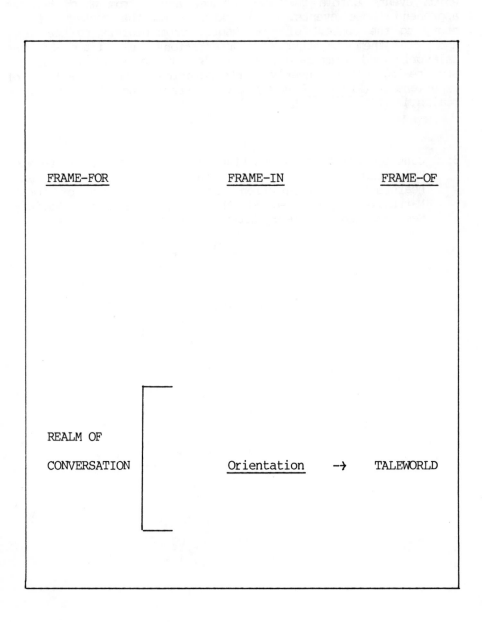

Figure 7: Orientations.

Evalulations

The frames examined so far bear on the realm status of events and stories, on whether a piece of discourse is a story, what sort of story it is, and what sort of realm the events it recounts come from. These frames determine orders of event, in contrast to evaluations, which disclose perspectives on, attitudes toward, or feelings about events of that order. Labov describes evaluation as, "the means used by the narrator to indicate the point of the narrative, its raison d'etre: why it was told and what the narrator was getting at."[36] He writes as if all these means were roughly equivalent. In fact, a nice distinction between the point of the story and the point of telling the story is involved. The first pertains to the events in the story and the second to the relationship between the story and the occasion on which it is told.

Evaluations of events argue that the Taleworld is reportable in its own right. Labov claims: "To identify the evaluative portion of a narrative, it is necessary to know why this narrative --- or any narrative --- is felt to be tellable; in other words, why the events of the narrative are reportable."[37] For Labov, whatever warrants their telling is inherent in the events. That quality is presented or enhanced by evaluations. The evaluations give differential weight to some events over others, especially to last events, so that events do not just succeed one another, they come to a point. In that way, the point comes to have a bearing on the end. However, points are not ends, they are recognitions of the relation of ends to beginnings as cogent. If the end can be seen as the final element in the narrative sequence, then the point bears on the relationship among narrative elements or between these elements and non-narrative aspects of the story. For instance, the evaluation after "Foxy's Cremation", "he'd only just got his bloody ticket", meaning had just recently qualified as a vicar, links the orientation before the story to its end. That Foxy had some difficulty becoming a vicar makes his vagaries especially culpable: one might expect the freshly invested to take exceptional care, as, according to succeeding evaluations, the Bishop did.

36. Labov, p. 366.
37. Labov, p. 370.

	A: But in more recent times Miles will remember Foxy.
	MF: Yeah.
	A: Do you?
	MF: Yeah.
Orientation	A: Well he you know took seventeen tries to get a- to be a parson.
	MF: Did he?
	A: Yeah and he got in on the eighteenth try.
	MF: Hmhmn.
Beginning	A: And one of his first jobs was to- to- (ha) them in um t- O what do you call it-
	MF: ((Chuckles)) /
	A: cremation he had to chuck the ashes about you see and he went in to- into
Evaluation	Huccaby Church and the bloody wind blew
End	chucked them up and they went out over the wall you see.

[[All: ((Laughter))
   A: Out over the moor.]

End

(Ha)

[[MF: Well that- that-
        ((Chuckles))]

Evaluation   A: he'd only just got his bloody ticket.

All: ((Chuckle))

[[K: Why did it
   A: The Bishop was hopping mad.

Evaluation

Evaluation   He said how dare you Foxy.   (Story 8)

The relationships between Foxy's recent qualification, his first job, and its outcome are forms of intention, in this case of intention foiled or flawed, or what is more commonly described in literary theory as motivation.

The point appears to be lodged in the arrangement of events, whether it was inserted there by nature or teller. But it is evident that this story could be extracted from its evaluative nest and told on another occasion with a different point, one about sacred ground or botched jobs or cremations, say, rather than eccentric vicars. Clearly, though the point is introduced into the story, a narrative sequence without one would fail in some sense to be a story. The question is, does the story make the point or the point make the story. Events, it turns out, are not just tellable, but tellable on occasions. It is their relevence to this occasion which is the point of the telling. Point is what connects stories to occasions. The point of the telling can, though it need not, invest itself in the point of the story. To miss the point of the story, then, is either not to see how the events in it connect together or not to see how they are relevant to the occasion of their telling.

Taleworld evaluations can not only evaluate events in the Taleworld but also specify the ontological status of those events for the occasion on which they are told. They can frame the events, that is, as real or fictitious. In this set of stories, evaluations of events as true is one of the warrants for telling them. The truth of the tale enhances the authoritativeness of the teller. In this vein, Algy accompanies several of his stories with truth evaluations. They are positioned before and after, as well as during the story:

This is absolutely true.   (During Story 2)

That is true and you won't beat that anywhere.
Tis absolutely gospel.   (After Story 5)

That's supposed to be true.   (After Story 14)

This is true.   (Before Story 15)

No it's absolutely true.   (After Story 15)
Absolutely true.

I swear it's perfectly true.   (After Story 23-6)

Truth evaluations identify the Taleworld as one of those realms we call realities: the events in that realm are understood to have or have had an instantiation in space and time. Such realities are quite diverse and can include the realms of the past, present, and future; of the supernatural or the scientific; of dreams, play, and work, the realm of the dead and the realm of the gods. Evaluations of Taleworlds as fictive identify them as imaginary realms, fairyland or hell, the supernatural or the extraterrestrial. Clearly, understandings about which realms are fictitious depend on differences in individual or cultural cosmologies. Legends, for instance, depict extraordinary events located in the geography of the ordinary. Whether that realm is seen as continuous or discontinuous with the world of everyday life depends on the skepticism or belief of teller and hearer. The displacement of extraordinary events to distant times or exotic places enhances their credibility. Thus, Algy's orientation to the legend of Jan Cou and the piskies (the proper Devon pronunciation of pixies) locates it in a realm that existed in "seventeen hundred and something", permitting hearers to perceive as unremarkable otherwise extraordinary events. He goes on to discriminate the story of the Devil at Tavistock Inn from the story that follows it with the evaluation:

A: This is nothing to do with
     fiction at all this is true.

                                              (Story 7)

This suggests that the story of the Devil, along with the stories about the piskies, the prince, and the gypsies, which also preceded it, can be regarded as fictions. The frame thus operates backward as well as forward.[38] Evaluations offered in the course of the storytelling are not, in spite of Labov, necessarily uttered by the storyteller. Jean and Marian interpose evaluations in the course of Miles' telling of "Foxy and the Flywheel", as if to offer the teller ongoing encouragement on this, his first story on this occasion.

```
                        .....
           MF:   and mother thought
            A:   (He he)
           MF:   she'd better go and find out what was wrong.
                 And she went down there and
                 found him lying on the floor
            J:   She knew.
           MF:   and the flywheel had come off the
                 generator
Evaluation   [[ J:   O how awful.
Evaluation      M:   Dreadful.
           MF:   and rolled- went right over him I think it
                 did and-
                     and smashed a chair against the wall
End        [[   and he was knocked flat.
Evaluation    A:   Cor he was lucky wasn't he.        (Story 11)
```

38. See Goffman, pp. 543, 544, and 545, on prospective and
     retrospective framing.

The suspension of these evaluations in the narrative sequence between complication and resolution serves, just as Labov suggests, to emphasize the climax. "The evaluation of a narrative is defined by us as that part of the narrative which reveals the attitude of the narrator toward the narrative by emphasizing the relative importance of some units as compared to others."[39] This emphasis can be as aptly provided by hearers as tellers and located outside as well as inside the story, like Algy's evaluation, "Cor he was lucky wasn't he." Hearers appear to be as attentive to the structure of stories as tellers and to contribute to their construction.[40]

The evaluations observed so far are part of the Storyrealm, comments by tellers and hearers on events transpiring in the Taleworld. Evaluations are also located in the Taleworld in the form of remarks or other indications by characters in that realm of an attitude toward the events. These "embedded evaluations", to use Labov's term, are quoted by tellers or hearers to disclose that attitude.[41] Embedded evaluations characteristically transpire in the course of the events they evaluate. Here, though, Algy appends an observer's comment about the vicar's driving to give emphasis to his account of "Foxy's Surplice, the Bentley, and the Deerstalker". Both observer and his observation are located inside the Taleworld. The first comments on the events and the second on their storyability.

```
     .....
A:   Somebody stopped me once
     who was that.
     Foxy absolutely tearing down Dartmeet Hill.
K:   (Ha)
A:   Deer- deerstalker.
     Bentley with a bloody great leather strap over its
          bonnet and everything (he).
K:   (he he)
```

39. Labov and Waletzky, p. 37.
40. See Charles Goodwin, "The Interactive Construction of the Sentence Within the Turn at Talk in Natural Conversation", presented at the American Anthropological Society Meetings (San Francisco, 1975) on the mutual construction of turns at talk.
41. Labov, p. 372.

```
        A:   Brooom.
       All:   ((Laughter))
         A:   Who on earth's that.
Taleworld      O I said our local vicar my God he said what
Evaluation     extraordinary people you got on.  (He he)
       All:   ((Chuckles))
         A:   ((Chuckles))
Storyrealm     Um he said that's an extraordinary story.
Evaluation                                        (Story 9)
```

As is evident from this transcription, laughing often counts as taking a turn, not, as some linguists have supposed, as a way of punctuating discourse. As a turn, the utterance has the weight of evaluation. What is being evaluated can be inferred only by proximity since laughter, unlike talk, does not carry linguistic directions to its referent.

Evaluations need not work, as Labov supposes, by drawing attention to one event among others. They can instead transfix and evaluate the sequence of events or the story itself. Transfixual evaluations bear on a realm of events rather than on events in the realm. Such evaluations by different persons can be layered together:

```
Evaluation     K: That's extra=
Evaluation     A: Well that's true                     (Story 2)

Evaluation     K: Isn't that extraordinary.
Evaluation     A: Well that's true you'll see- you'll find it
                     tis really.                        (Story 7)
Evaluation     K: Heaven's sake.....
               A: Do you remember that.
               J: Yes.
Evaluation     A: Yeah then well that's true.           (Story 12)
```

Presenting events as extraordinary but true at once deflects incredulity and accepts appreciation, while modestly redirecting astonishment to the Taleworld.

Labov elucidates evaluations exclusively in terms of how they frame the events stories are about. They are discovered here to frame stories as well as events. Storyrealm evaluations lodge value in the story. Hearers attention is warranted by the quality of the story, not the events. In this vein, Algy follows his story of the three brothers with the evaluation:

Fantastic story isn't
to strike one in a bed of three.   (Story 1)

Evaluations of both realms can be done for a single story at different times by the same person:

Storyrealm	
Evaluation	A: Now I like the story of when his old man was about seventy driving a tractor
Taleworld	...
Evaluation	A: That's supposed to be true.
	...
Storyrealm	A: You like that one don't you.
Evaluation	MF: Hm.
Storyrealm	
Evaluation	A: It's lovely too (Story 14)

Or evaluations can be done by different persons at the same time.

Storyrealm	A: Well
Evaluation	his best story I didn't tell you.
Storyrealm	MF: O good.
Evaluation	K: Um.
	A: No
Taleworld	
Evaluation	This is really true .... (Story 33)

Both kinds of interlayering, frames of the same realm by different persons and frames of different realms by the same person, are designed to strategically manage attention to the Taleworld and the Storyrealm on the storytelling occasion.

Harvey Sacks describes evaluations as instructions for hearing-as.[42] Such instructions can be designed to preclude interactional awkwardness by disclosing the attitude of teller or hearer to the story being told. For instance, Jean May follows her husband's story about an idiot boy with the evaluation:

J: It was awfully embarrassing cause he always
          used to stare at you.
      And the horses as well.   (Story 17)

42. Sacks, (28 May 1970) Lecture VII, p. 2, and (4 June 1970) Lecture VIII, p. 4.

This suggests that the rest of us hear the story as an account of embarrassement rather than, for instance, as mocking an idiot. Evaluations also provide information on how a story has been heard. Jean follows Algy's account of her own misadventures in a runaway cart with the evaluation, "Poor pony.", suggesting an interpretation of the episode on her part as unfortunate rather than courageous, and so modestly circumventing compliments on her adventurousness. Evaluations are thus used in the management of relationships among persons on storytelling occasions.

Evaluations are of two sorts: evaluations of the Taleworld and evaluations of the Storyrealm. Evaluations of the Taleworld focus on the events the story is about, rendering the story a transparency to another realm. Evaluations of the Storyrealm focus on the telling, constituting the story a realm in its own right. Evaluations of the Taleworld can be located inside that realm, in the Storyrealm, or in the realm of conversation. Evaluations of the Storyrealm are located in the Storyrealm or the realm of conversation. (Figure 8 shows the extension of evaluations from the outermost realm of conversation to the innermost Taleworld.) Though they can modulate the internal dramatic structure of the story, evaluations have more general uses which can be characterized as the management of attitudes, interest, and attention on storytelling occasions.

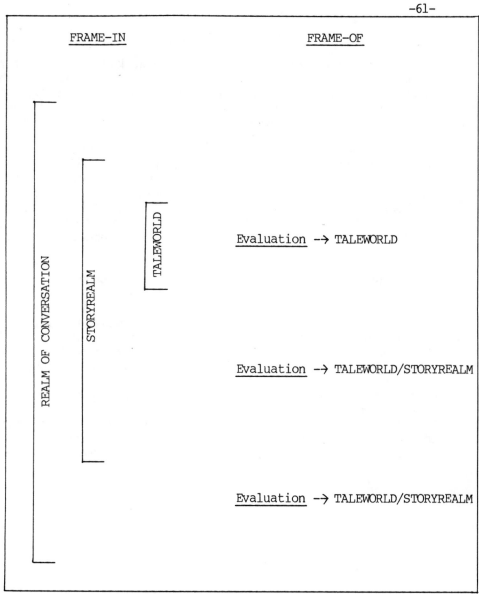

Figure 8: Evaluations.

Narrative Laminations

The clustering of frames along the boundaries of the story accomplishes a kind of edgework for storytelling. The clustered frames give a neat parity to the literal and ontological limits of the Storyrealm. The edgework undertaken on the storytelling occasion also lends an appearance of circumscription to the events in the Taleworld. The Storyrealm invests boundaries in the Taleworld so that events there take on some of its discretion. In reality, story boundaries are not neatly fitted down over the Taleworld. Events in that realm have their own boundaries. However, access to the Taleworld is only through the story. So apprehensions of the realm status of events in the Taleworld are not contingent on experience of that realm but on its framework on the storytelling occasion.

Attention to the Storyrealm implies an awareness of the occasion as performance, in the sense that it involves an undertaking by story tellers and hearers to tell and hear stories. Attention to the Taleworld draws awareness away from the performer and the performance toward the events recounted by them. This renders the occasion conversational. During actual storytellings, attention to the Taleworld or Storyrealm shifts over the course of a single telling, and over the course of the storytelling occasion as a whole. Roughly speaking, the fixed frames move hearers from the Storyrealm into the Taleworld and out again; moveable frames create a shifting emphasis on one or the other of those narrative realms. (Figure 9 shows the shift from Storyrealm to Taleworld and back again.)

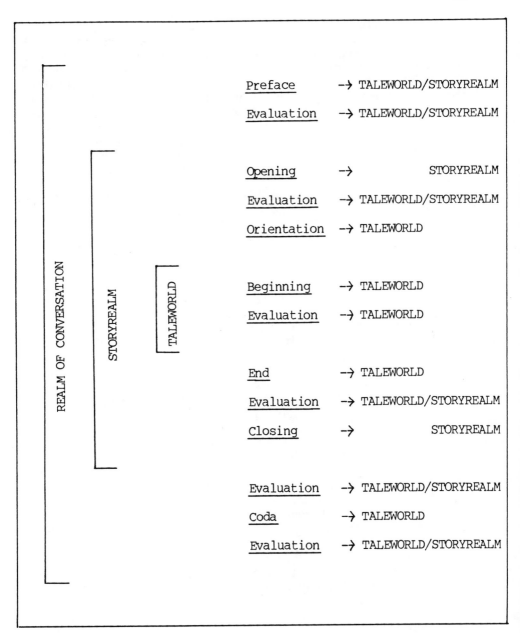

Figure 9: Distribution of Frames over Storytelling.

Algy May's story, "The Plough and the Hare", is neatly bracketed by Storyrealm evaluations. Attention inside the brackets is turned to the Taleworld. The story opens with an evaluation which directs attention to its status as a story: "I like the story of". This modulates directly into orientations to the Taleworld in which events transpire. Attention to the Taleworld is sustained by the coda and evaluation that follow. Frames in subsequent conversation redirect attention to the Storyrealm, reiterating evaluations of it. These are succeeded by evaluations and frames of the Taleworld which result in the content of that realm, hares, being taken up as a topic of conversation.

The Plough and the Hare

Storyrealm
Evaluation/
Storyrealm
Opening   A: Now I like the story of when his old man was
              about seventy
Taleworld   driving a tractor
Orientation   MF: ((Clears throat))
Taleworld   A: ploughing
Beginning   with Bill
         [[J: [(   )]
         A: three furrow plough.
           You know up and down the bloody field
           and a hare got up.
           And the old man
           forgot about his furrow and he
      [[All:[((Laughter))]
           A: took it out
Taleworld   [[[and gave chase.]
End   Hm.
       All: ((Laughter))
Taleworld   [[A: Had a lovely furrow
Coda   [[[right   ]
        [[[following this   ]
        [[[hare all across the field.]
        [[All:[((Laughter))   ]
       MF: (He he he he)
        K: (He he he)
Taleworld
Evaluation   A: That's supposed to be true.
         .....
Storyrealm   A: You like that one don't you.
Evaluation   MF: Hm.

Storyrealm		
Evaluation	A:	It's lovely too.
Taleworld		Lovely straight furrows up and down (he he
Orientation		he).
		You know they'd been doing it for all day.
Taleworld		Buuullwoom.
Abstract	All:	((Laugh))
	A:	Away he went in top.
Taleworld	J:	There's something magic about the hare
Coda		perhaps that's why- perhaps it cast a spell
		on him.
		..... (Story 14)

Not all kinds of frames turn up in each story and only four kinds are essential; a preface, the beginning and end, and some sort of evaluation. These essential frames can all be directed to the Taleworld, but not all to the Storyrealm. Attention to the Storyrealm takes special direction. "Foxy's Cremation", for instance, never draws attention to itself as a story:

Foxy's Cremation

Taleworld		
Preface	A:	But in more recent times Miles will
		remember Foxy.
Response	MF:	Yeah.
	A:	Do you?
Response	MF:	Yeah.
Taleworld	A:	Well he- you know took seventeen tries to
Orientation		get a-
		to be a
		parson
	MF:	Did he?
	A:	Yeah and he
		got in on the eighteenth try.
	MF:	Hmhmm.
Taleworld	A:	And one of his first jobs was to-to-
Beginning		to- (ha) them in um- t- O what do you call
		it-
	MF:	((Chuckles))
		/
	A:	cremation
		he had to
		chuck the ashes about you see and he went
		in to-
Taleworld		into
Evaluation		Huccaby Church and the bloody wind blew

```
Taleworld              chucked them up and they went out over the
End                          wall you see.
                  [[ All: [((Laughter))              ]
                     A:  [Out over the moor.]
                     (Ha)
                           [Well that- that-]
Taleworld       [[ MF: [((Chuckles))    ]
Orientation/       A:  he'd only just got his bloody ticket.
Evaluation       All:  ((Chuckles))
                     K: [Why did it ]
Taleworld       [[ A:  [The Bishop]was hopping mad.
Coda/                  He said how dare you Foxy.          (Story 8)
Evaluation
```

A frame that can be directed to either realm is of particular interest in determining realm shift. Prefaces, for instance, can be directed to either the Taleworld or the Storyrealm, thus focusing attention at the outset on one or the other. Evaluations, turning up over the course of storytelling, can closely control attention to both realms. The preface to "Three Brothers", about practicing a story more than once, is directed toward the Storyrealm, and the story's opening sustains that direction. Frames then move into the Taleworld until the closing, "Tchew", which draws away from the events to comment on them, and is in that respect evaluative. Codas and evaluations by tellers and hearers, clustered together after the story, juggle attention between realms, on the one hand earthing the events in surrounding geography and contemporary society, and on the other, charging the story with preternatural intimation.

Three Brothers

```
Storyrealm
Preface        A: Because you want to
                  go through these things more than once
                  before you start.
               K: You don't
                     [What a silly idea.        ]
                  [[ J: [Want some more sherry]dear.
                  Have some more sherry.
               MF: Not for me thank you.
Storyrealm        /
Opening        [[ A:[The point was]
                  J:[Would you?   ]
```

Taleworld Beginning	A: there were three teenage Frenchs
Taleworld Orientation	sleeping in one bed over here in the cottage- in the old house. Thunderstorm? Father French comes down finds the center one
Taleworld End	struck by lightening.
Taleworld Abstract	Three boys in one bed center one killed Tchew.
Storyrealm Closing	.....
Taleworld Coda	One of the survivors was Herman French's Father
	K: Excuse me.
	A: Yeah?
Taleworld Coda	the other one's his uncle.
	M: Old Fred- Fred wasn't it.
	A: Fred
Taleworld Orientation	yeah. M: Used to be up at Ollsbrim.
Taleworld Coda	[[A: [Fred was the M: [Or just at the end of the]war
	A: other survivor. Hm.
Storyrealm Evaluation	K: That's OK. ((Refuses sherry))
Taleworld	[[A: [Fantastic story wasn't it.] M: [He was always a bit-
Evaluation Storyrealm Evaluation	[[[He was always a bit funny actually wasn't he. K: [It was extraordinary.
Taleworld Evaluation	A: Course he was funny. Damn funny.
Taleworld Evaluation	K: That's very strange.

.....

Storyrealm Evaluation	A: Fantastic story isn't it
Taleworld Abstract	to strike one in a bed of three.

(Story 1)

The unusual number of Storyrealm frames in "Three Brothers"
appears to be due to the use of that story to initiate

storytelling on this ocassion. Part of its business is to establish the Storyrealm. Once this is accomplished, interest turns to the Taleworld, as evidenced by the framing in a later story, "Foxy's Cremation". Storyrealm frames are noticeable again in the last story told on this ocassion. The framework of this storytelling thus replicates the framework of a single story, moving from Storyrealm into Taleworld and out again. The choice of frames can strategically manage attention to the Taleworld or the Storyrealm. These alternative ontological possibilities then inform the storytelling occasion.

Stories are enclaves in conversation, events in one realm bounded by another.[43] The boundaries between these realms constitute natural junctures for presenting information about their differences in the form of frames. Positioning frames between realms reiterates their dual orientation: frames are oriented to the realm of events they frame and to the realm they frame those events for. The frames-of a story, for instance, can be frames-for conversation. Frames are never of and for the same realm. They can be located in the realm they frame, as beginnings and ends are located in the Taleworld or openings and closings in the Storyrealm, and evaluations in each. They can be located in the realm they are frames-for, as prefaces and codas, along with some evaluations, are located in the realm of conversation. Or they can be located in a third realm, as orientations to the Taleworld and for the realm of conversation are located in the Storyrealm. Frames do not enclose, or open and close, one realm; they specify a relationship between two.

The Taleworld, the Storyrealm, the realm of conversation, indeed any realm, can engage perceivers as an ongoing reality. Framing has the capacity to detach it from that engagement, to render it subject to reflections, attitudes, evaluations, to draw perceivers back and lodge them in another realm, a realm from which they have a particular perspective on their experience. That perspective is called here a frame. In that sense, frames separate as well a connect realms. To become aware of such perspectives on stories is to undertake the frame analysis of narrative.[44]

43. Schutz, footnote, p. 256.
44. I am indebted to Erving Goffman not just for the phrase "frame analysis" but for the ontological concerns it implies.

CHAPTER TWO
MULTIPLE CONTEXTING:
The Story Context of Stories*

The manner of the search is plain to me and might be
called the method of double or multiple comparison.

Gregory Bateson[1]

Stories are implicated in as well as distinct from the occasions
on which they are told. Their implication is a matter of context
and their distinctness is a matter of frame. Contexts are the
continuities between stories and some aspects of their surround, and
of other relevant events. Frames mark the discontinuities between
stories and these other present or pertinent contexts. Contrasting
puzzles about stories thus present themselves to narrative
analysis: one, distinguishing stories from contexts; and the other,
connecting stories with contexts. Stories can be seen as contextual
events that are situated and occasioned or they can be seen as
discrete objects that can be detached and resituated. Seeing
stories as events and seeing stories as objects are not
incommensurable. In the koan of a philosopher, Stanley Eveling, an
event is a quick object and an object is a slow event.[2] Stories
move along the continuum from events to objects as possibilities of
presentation.

* A version of this paper was given on the panel "On Context" at the
1979 American Folklore Society Meetings in Los Angeles. The opening
section on the notion of context was given in the forum, "The
Significance of the Text/Context Debate for the Future of Folklore
Research", at the 1980 American Folklore Society Meetings in
Pittsburgh and subsequently published in Western Folklore
44:2 (1985) 115-122.

1. Gregory Bateson, Mind and Nature (New York: E.P. Dutton,
   1979), p. 87.
2. Stanley Eveling, Unpublished Lectures in Philosophy
   (University of Edinburgh, Scotland: 1967).

In an ongoing argument, skeptical contextualists have challenged the primacy of texts and skeptical formalists the propriety of context. The argument has been canonized in folklore as the text/context controversy, and so instantiated in its traditions of analysis that folklorists now fall into one or the other orthodoxy.[3] My own skepticism about context is not its impropriety but its imprecision. The intent of this chapter is to move beyond questions of propriety to an account of the multiplicity, differentiation, and constitutiveness of contexts.

I The Notion of Context

To begin, it is crucial to distinguish context from surround. Not all of what surrounds an event contextualizes it. Context is a matter of relevance, not proximity. A surround is whatever is contiguous whether it bears on the event or not; a context is whatever bears on the event whether it is contiguous or not. Not only is not all of the surround context but also not all of the contexts are in the surround. Erving Goffman suggests that "context can be defined as immediately available events which are compatible with one frame understanding and incompatible with others."[4] Thus frames exclude some of what is in the surround as context. But, I propose they also include as contexts some of what is not in the surround. Hence, contexts must be regarded as multiple.

The performance theory of folklore is flawed by a fine confusion between context and surround: context has been taken indiscriminately to be everything in the surround. This results in the fallacy of inventory, that is, the attempt to exhaust surround in the name of context. For instance, Kenneth Goldstein's catalogue of contexts in his Guide for Fieldworkers in Folklore includes physical setting, interaction among participants, performance, time and duration, sentiments

3. See the interchange between Steven Jones and Dan Ben-Amos in Western Folklore 38 (January 1979), pp. 42-55.
4   Erving Goffman, Frame Analysis (New York, Evanston, San Francisco, London: Harper Colophon, 1974), p.441.

expressed, miscellaneous observation, and the observer.[5] (To be fair, Goldstein also includes a list of contexts which are not in the surround, including personal history of informants, aesthetics of informants, knowledge, feelings, and meanings, the transmission of folklore materials, descriptions of folklore situations collectors is unable to observe, and informants' repertories). The implication of exhaustiveness in such lists is deceptive for two reasons. On the one hand, the number of possible contexts for an event is limitless and, on the other, the number of relevant contexts for understanding that event is limited. The immediate surround as a context for a spoken story is both inexhaustible and incomplete. However, as Barbara Herrnstein Smith notes: "It is usually not necessary and of course it is usually not possible to ascertain all the conditions that make up the context of an utterance."[6] What is necessary is that in invoking a context, its bearing on the event is specified. Contextual analysis properly addresses relations between contexts and events not collections of contexts.

Events, that is, are context-specific in two senses. One, contexts are contexts-of events. Each context brings a different perspective to bear on the event and the event presents itself in a different perspective to each context. The number of contexts potentially bearing on any one event is infinite but not all are brought to bear at once. They shift with shifts in the mode of attention of perceivers as well as from one perceiver to another. That is to say, two, contexts are also contexts-for perceivers. Participants in storytellings, like analysts of them, are perforce selective about contexts, the difference being that analysts, unlike participants, are obliged not to keep their criteria for selection hidden. Contexts can perfectly properly be suited to perceivers' purposes, including the purposes of analysis. Different analyses draw on different contexts.

5. Kenneth Goldstein, A Guide for Field Workers in Folklore Hatboro, Pennsylvania: Folklore Associates, 1964), pp. 91 - 93.
6. Barbara Herrnstein Smith, On the Margins of Discourse (Chicago and London: University of Chicago Press, 1978), p. 94.

The initial choice of perspective on the story orients analysts to other events as contexts. As Henry Glassie writes: "The object is composed and it is related; the whole is the object's system, the system being arbitrarily but precisely delimited by the choice of the object."[7] Some contexts for a story come to be understood as part of the story from other perspectives, for instance, as Barbara Kirshenblatt-Gimblett notes, tellings of tellings.[8] Fixing on the context as itself an event directs attention to other events as contexts. Stories can be contexts for other events, including other stories. The same event seen in a different context is, in a sense, a different event.[9] Events and contexts are mutually implicated, as Gregory Bateson expresses it, in a relation "in which two or more information sources come together to give information of a sort different from what was in either source separately.[10] Stories, for instance, are not the same to teller and hearer, from the perspective of what they recount and what they accomplish, as discourse and interaction. Hence, contexts are not just multiple, they are constitutive.

Contexts condition the form, content, or occurence of an event. As Smith puts it, "every event can be conceived of as the center of a causal nexus, that is, a set of causes and consequences, corrollaries and entailments, both gross and subtle, that obtain at every level of potential organization;

7. Henry Glassie, "Structure and Function, Folklore and the Artifact," Semiotica 7:4 (1973), pp. 313 - 351, p. 315.
8. Barbara Kirshenblatt-Gimblett, Personal Communication, 1983.
9. It would be just as inaccurate to say that an event in two different contexts is two different events, or two simultaneous events, as to say that an event in two different contexts is the same event. A closer understanding might be arrived at through Ray Birdwhistell's characterization of alternate presentations of an event as "transforms" of each other. Unpublished Lectures on Interpersonal Communication Codes (Philadelphia: University of Pennsylvania, 1976).
10. Bateson, p. 21.

and that total set can be conceived of as the total meaning of the event."[11] Utterances, she argues, are events of this kind. So utterances are not merely situated, they are occasioned, occasioned not in the sense that they are set pieces triggered by accidents of circumstance, but in the sense that they are linguistic structures engaged in an ongoing way with their contexts. Smith elaborates her notion of context:[12]

> .... the historical "context" of an utterance does not merely surround it but occasions it, brings it into existence. The context of an utterance, then, is best thought of not simply as its gross external or physical setting, but rather as the total set of conditions that has in fact determined its occurence and form. That total set of conditions, what makes us say something at a particular time and also shapes the linguistic structure of our utterance -- the specific words we choose, our syntax, our intonation, and so on -- is likely to be manifold and complex no matter how simple the utterance. Moreover, the total set of conditions that determines what we say and how we speak is by no means confined to the objects and events "spoken about," or what linguistic theorists of various persuasions refer to as "referents," "designations," "denotations," or "significations."

Contexts, then, are multiple, constitutive, and finely differentiated. Once the notion of context is separated from surround, pertinent contexts are seen to be remote from the events they bear on as well as present to them.

Among the remote contexts for stories, I would argue, are the events the story is about, whether these events come from imaginary realms or those we call realities. Stories evoke for us a Taleworld not present to the storytelling occasion, which is understood to bear on how we understand the story. If that realm is a reality, for instance, we may have knowledge of it from other sources. In semiotic theory it is argued on the contrary that the relationship between stories and the events they are about is referential: the Taleworld is supposed to provide the story its content. Other contexts, on this view,

11. Smith, p. 94.
12. Smith, p. 16.

merely offer glosses on what is taken to be the root sense-reference or story-event relationship. The flaw in this view is most clearly exposed if we see that the events the story is about, like other contexts, are conjured up by hearers as well as tellers, each after his or her own fashion, on the storytelling occasion. Contextual analysis confounds the assumption that the relationship between events and stories is fundamental and relationships between the story and its other contexts superficial. In fact, as will become clear in the contextual analysis undertaken here, some of the content of the story comes not from the events it is about but from the occasion on which it is told, in this instance, from other stories in the conversation.

Stories can be informed by the experience of past tellings as well as by the experience of past events. In both instances, storytellers assess the relevance of their past experiences for the present occasion. Until recently, folklorists of a formalist cast were more concerned with retellings of past tales than with recountings of past events, where retellings are understood by them to be portable texts inserted into variable contexts. They are more accurately described as tales seen in the context of other tellings, a context known, quite properly, as the context of tradition. It is not that formalists do not look at stories in contexts but that the contexts they see them in are remote rather than present.

Their preoccupation with past tellings has focused formalists on what they think of as the fixity of texts. Steven Jones claims that "while the social context of a folklore item may change, the folklore itself remains the same. In other words, a particular item of folklore (for example, a proverb, joke, or story) can appear in many different situations."[13] The illusion of fixity is enhanced if, as Jones proposes, the story is pruned to the text. But the text is not the story, it is only one cutting of the story-in-context system, a cutting that has no claim to primacy for analysis. What it does have a claim to is recoverability.

13. Steven Swann Jones, "Slouching towards Ethnography," Western Folklore 38, p. 45.

As Smith notes: "Although we may, for certain purposes, describe an utterance exclusively in terms of its linguistic form ....., a natural utterance can never be adequately specified or described as an event except in relation to the context in which it occured. In other words, a verbal event, like any other event, is individuated as much by its context as by its form."[14] Texts are not stories. Stories make their appearance as incidents in a social world from which texts are an abstraction: they capture, and inevitably transform, that aspect of the storytelling event that happens to be transcribable. So retellings are not constant events transported intact among shifting contexts. On the contrary, they display contextual influences in changes formalists grapple with as versions and variants, which have the peculiar virtue of lodging contextual considerations inside texts. Alan Dundes' notion of "texture" might be understood as what orients text to context.[15]

If formalists err in granting primacy to texts over contexts, performance theorists err in granting primacy to present over remote contexts. This, coupled with their failure either to distinguish context from surround, or to distinguish among present contexts, has precluded precision in the analysis of the story in any one context. Contexts do not constellate conveniently around stories. They are brought to bear on stories by tellers and hearers. Among present contexts, it is possible to distinguish between importations and encounters, that is, between contexts participants carry with them and those they come across on the occasion. Mood, personal history, cognitive style, past experiences and associations, for example, are internal contexts imported by tellers and hearers into situations, whereas relationships among participants, interactional strategies, postures, gestures, and spatial arrangements can be seen as external contexts encountered there. Edward T. Hall describes the etiology of this distinction.[16]

14. Smith, p. 18.
15. Alan Dundes, "Texture, Text and Context," Southern Folklore Quarterly 28 (1974): 251 - 265.
16. Edward T. Hall, Beyond Culture (Garden City, New York: Anchor, 1977), p. 95.

Contexting probably involves at least two entirely
different but interrelated processes --- one inside the
organism and the other outside. The first takes place in
the brain and is a function of either past experience
(programmed, internalized contexting) or the structure of
the nervous system (innate contexting), or both. External
contexting comprises the situation and/or setting in which
an event occurs (situational or environmental contexting).

These contexts are related in that external contexts come
into the awareness of persons on occasions and so become
internal while those they apprehend as internal color their
participation in the external situation. They are
distinguished by their boundary conditions: external contexts
must be distinguished from the stories that are implicated in
them whereas internal contexts must be brought to bear on
stories. Henry Glassie investigates the relationship between
what he calls particular, that is, external, and abstract, or
internal, contexts.[17]

Social scientists call two different conceptualizations
"context". Often no distinction is made between them. The
particularistic context is the observable environment of an
expression of culture ... For observable interpersonal
relations, the particularistic context consists of a hugely
complicated communicative interchange. For an old house,
the particularistic context would consist of the land
concentrically ringing its walls... The particularistic
context surrounds the object in the real world... The
abstracted context is a structure of potential source and
consequence. It relates the object being composed in the
designing mind to the maker's view of himself and to human,
natural, and supernatural forces that exist beyond him.
When the object is placed in its abstracted context, a
prediction is made about the object's effect within the
maker's design field... The structure of the abstracted
context is internal, in mind, but it binds the object to

17. Glassie, Folk Housing in Middle Virginia (Knoxville:
University of Tennessee Press, 1979), pp. 114 - 116.
Glassie's book is itself a model of multiple contexting.
Each chapter angles in on architecture from a differen
perspective, using different theoretical frameworks ar
writing in different styles.

such external variables as the materials available in nature or the expectations of the maker's group.

These three sets of contexts are not perfectly fitted together. Each captures and discriminates a slightly different field so that kinds of context, imported and encountered, internal and external, abstract and particular, appear not just multiple but finely differentiated.

Among present contexts of any kind, another distinction might be made, between proximity and immediacy, that is, between contexts continguous in space and those previous, concurrent, or subsequent in time. The physical setting for storytelling. can be seen as a spatial context whereas other stories and surrounding conversation are temporal. Remote contexts can also be distinguished as spatial or temporal: the geographical setting is spatially remote while previous tellings of the same story are temporally remote. It is tempting to suppose spatial contexts, at least, dispose themselves around events with a neat concentricity but of course, like other contexts, these cut across and overlap each other. For instance, the visual field of a storytelling might be differentiated from its aural one so that some participants are hearing the story but not seeing the storyteller, some are seeing the storyteller but not hearing the story, some are doing both, and some neither.

Stories are not equally pervious to all of their contexts. Anecdotes in conversation, for instance, are characteristically interlaced with non-narrative talk, at the least with appreciative murmurs. Whether these are artefacts of turntaking or evidence of attention to storytelling, such interpositions appear to breach the boundaries of the story. Folktales, by contrast, are characteristically protected from such breaches by their framing as performance.

The intelligibility of events depends on contextual information. What Edward T. Hall calls high-context events require hearers already to command certain understandings in order to grasp what is being conveyed. These events are highly context-dependent. Low-context events, on the other hand, make themselves so explicit that they retain intelligibility detached from their contexts of presentation. They are relatively context-free.[18] The contrast is akin to Basel

18. Hall, chapters six, seven, and eight, pp. 85 - 128.

Bernstein's distinction between restricted and elaborated codes.[19] The intelligibility of conversational anecdotes diminishes outside of the context of conversation while folktales are relatively intelligible separate from performance situations. Contextual information, available in the surround of high-context events, can be seen as packed into low-context events. Literary narratives embody the sort of directional cues and background information that are implicit in the storytelling situation. Insofar as contexts can be lodged inside stories, to just that extent are stories detachable from those contexts. The same story is context-dependent in some respects and context-free in others. There is a congruence between high-context events and their perviousness to context, on the one hand, and between low-context events and their boundedness, on the other. Interest in folklore has been shifting from low to high contexts and from bounded to previous events, as analysts gain mastery over their discovery, codification, and analysis.

Each context draws out different aspects of the story: aspects of the story in turn draw in other contexts. Stories are not held constant through shifting contexts, nor are contexts fixed constellations around the story. The two are interdependent: stories are shifting and contexts multiple. For that reason, the investigation of context is properly the investigation of a single story-in-context system. Thus, this chapter focuses on the bearing of stories on other stories told on the same occasion as a system of stories in the context of stories.

19. Basel Bernstein, "Social Class, Language and Socialization" in Language and Social Context, ed., Pier Paolo Giglioli (Middlesex, England: Penguis, 1972), pp. 157 - 178.

II The Story-in-Context System

One puzzle about stories is the way they cluster in conversation. Study of such story clusters discloses that each story is in some respects constituted by the story before and constitutes the story after. This constitution of stories by stories is here considered a question of context.[20] Stories in conversation have two patterns of distribution, a dispersed pattern of what Barbara Kirshenblatt-Gimblett calls "story-subordinated conversation" and a pattern of clustered stories in what she calls "story-dominated conversation'.[21] Single stories are immediately contextualized by the conversations in which they occur. Study of story clusters discloses, on the contrary, that each story is in some respects constituted by the story before and constitutes the one after. Stories so interconnected form what can be seen as a nesting structure.

20. David Evans, "Riddling and the Structure of Context", Journal of American Folklore 89 (1976), p. 170, entertains a similar conception of riddle sessions. He writes, "clearly then, if one is going to study the structure of context for riddles, he must study the riddle session as a whole. The riddles must be analyzed not only in respect to the social and behavioral context in which they are told but also in respect to all the other riddles that are told at the session. The total number of riddles told and the order in which they are told constitute part of the context of any single riddle." Evans himself holds a different view of the comparison between riddles and stories, namely that riddle sequences can be compared with single stories, not storytelling sessions. "For if riddling can be a part of storytelling sessions, then it is possible that consecutive series of riddles could fulfill roles similar to those of individual narratives in such sessions." Evans, p. 186.
21. Barbara Kirshenblatt-Gimblett, "The Concept and Variaties of Narrative Performance in Each European Jewish Culture" in Explorations in the Ethnography of Speaking, ed., Richard Bauman and Joel Sherzer (New York: Cambridge University Press, 1974), pp. 291 and 293.

The nesting structure investigated here consists of a closely worked set of seven stories from the conversation with Algy May analyzed in Chapter One. The passage of conversation is story-dominated: continuity runs from story to story, conversation merely does linkage work. It consists of both runs of stories told by one storyteller, called here serial stories, and stories by a second storyteller following on stories by a first, called by Harvey Sacks second stories. The analysis of story clusters comes of noticing, in Sacks" words: "First, that stories come in clumps, and second, clumped stories have an apparent similarity between them."[22] These seven stories are part, I will argue the heart, of a longer story-dominated passage of twenty stories, itself the first of two such passages in the course of the evening's conversation.

I will focus on the eighth story in a series of loosely associated stories Algy has been telling on this occasion. This story follows on from another which was set in the same place, Huccaby Church. It is about an eccentric English vicar called Foxy. Intervening conversation is subordinated to the two stories, serving to link them together:

Story Eight

FOXY'S CREMATION*

A: But in more recent times Miles will remember Foxy.
MF: Yeah
A: Do you?
MF: Yeah.
A: Well he- you know- took seventeen tries to get a-
    to be a
    parson.
MF: Did he?
A: Yeah and he
    got in on the eighteenth try.
MF: Hmhmm.
A: And one of his first jobs was to-

*See appendix for transcription conventions.

22. Harvey Sacks, "Storytelling in Conversation" (University of California, Irvine: April 30, 1970), Lecture Five, p. 1.

```
        to (ha) them in um t- O what do you call it
   MF:  ((Chuckles))
        /
    A:  cremation
        he had to
        chuck the ashes about you see and he went in to
        into
        Huccaby Church and the bloody wind blew
        chucked 'em up and they went out over the wall you see.
   [[ All:  ((Laughter))
    A:   [Out over the moor.]
        (Ha)
   [[      [Well that- that-]
      MF:  [((Chuckles))  ]
    A:  he'd only just got his bloody ticket.
   All:  ((Chuckle))
   [[ K:  [Why did it]
    A:   [The Bishop]was hopping mad.
        He said how dare you Foxy.
```

The next story in the cluster of seven is initiated by
Algy's niece, Marian, and jointly constructed by the two of
them, making it another serial story for Algy and a second
story for Marian. Continuities between first stories and what
Goffman calls "following-on stories" are apparent; the way
these continuities are constituted is less so.[23] First
stories appear to dictate the thematic possibilities of
following-on stories. In reality, something like the reverse
is the case. Next stories select out of a first story's
possibilities those that thereby come to count as thematic.
Possibilities in "Foxy's Cremation" include clerical vagaries,
vicars, English eccentricity, Huccaby Church, consecrated
ground, cremation, sacrilege, death, chance, the moors, botched
jobs, first jobs, wind, angry bishops, Foxy, and so on.[24]
The following-on story, "Foxy's Surplice, the Bentley and the
Deerstalker", is again about Foxy, the eccentric vicar, his
further infringement of orthodox procedure, and the wind as
agency: instead of ashes falling on unconsecrated ground,
Foxy's surplice blows away over the moor. (The detail about
wearing a deerstalker was interpolated later.)

23. "Following-on stories" is a usage suggested by Erving
    Goffman, arrived at in consort with William Labov,
    Personal Communication (University of Pennsylvania: 1977).

Story Nine

FOXY'S SURPLICE, THE BENTLEY, AND THE DEERSTALKER

M: Now I think the best—one of the best stories about
     Foxy is
  that he used to do the service at Princetown
     and he used to
A: Umhm.
M: hurry out to Huccaby
A: Yeah.
M: to do the service there.
  And he- he'd sort of rushed out of Princetown Church
     and
  took off his surplice and put it on the roof of his
     car and
  forgot it was there.=
A: Forgot it.=
M: Forgot about it so it blew off on the way (hehe)
     across- coming across ⌈Princetown plain.⌉ ((Coughs))
[[J: ⌊(   )⌋
M: In his Bentley or whatever it was he was- you know-
     coming.

    A first story, then, presents an array of possibilities out of which second or serial stories fix on a few. Sacks points out that, "the question of whether there is topic similarity can't procede (sic) by listing the set of topics that the first story had and then seeing does the second have one of those? but topic similarity is something that the second can, with the use of similarity, exhibit, though you wouldn't have thought from the first that the second would be a coherent topic with the first. That is to say, the relationship "topic similarity" is one in which the second is crucial. Given the second you can see they're topically similar."[25] The appearance of thematic continuity is reconstituted backwards, the constitution of the pair of stories not being what is intended by the first but what is foregrounded by the second. (Figure 10 shows the relationship beween themes in these first two stories).

24. These ephemera of conversation are of course untitled by their tellers and hearers though ways of briefly calling to mind a particular story can have the aspect of a title. The ways of referring to stories here I have invented.
25. Sacks, (April 30, 1970) Lecture Five, p. 13.

Story Nine

Story Eight

FOXY'S CREMATION

FOXY'S SURPLICE, THE
BENTLEY, AND THE
DEERSTALKER

Huccaby Church   .

Consecrated ground   .

Cremation   .

Clerical vagaries   Clerical vagaries

Vicars   Vicars

English eccentricity   English Eccentricity

Foxy   Foxy

Moors   Moors

Wind   Wind

Botched jobs   Botched Jobs

First jobs   .

Trying for jobs   .

Angry bishops   .

Funerals   .

Ashes   .

.   .

.   .

.   .

Figure 10: Thematic Continuity between Stories

The third story in this cluster is told by Marian, a serial to her own previous story and a second to her uncle's. It is again about Foxy, making it third in what turns out to be a run of four stories featuring the same character. While he was vicar at Leusdon Church, Foxy decided to revive the local midsummer's eve custom of rolling a cartwheel off the top of Mel Tor into the river below to bring good luck. Unfortunately, since the time of the original custom, trees had grown up along the sides of the tor, so the cartwheel was smashed to bits before it ever got to the river. The fourth story is by Miles Fursdon. It is his first story on this occasion and the first pure second story. Miles' mother was playing the organ in Leusdon Church when the lights went out, so Foxy, who was vicar there, went into the cellar to start up the electric generator:

Story Eleven

FOXY AND THE FLYWHEEL

MF: I can remember mother saying once when she was
playing the organ in the Church
J: Yes.
MF: that- I think it must have been-
I suppose it was Leusdon
and they just had to-
A: Yeah?
MF: they had an electric pump fitted on the organ I
think or whether-
whether it was the lights he-
he went down to start the generator anyway
J: Umhm.
MF: and he
went away and then-
didn't take very long to start it up
[[A: (He he he)]
MF: and no lights came on and they
waited and waited (he) in the Church for the
lights to come on
[[A: (Ha)]
MF: and nothing happened.
A: No of course not.
MF: And mother thought
A: (Hehe)
MF: she'd better go down and find out what was wrong.

```
             And she went down there and
             found him lying on the floor
      J:     She knew.
      MF:    and the flywheel had come off the
             generator
   [[  J:   ⌈O how awful.⌉
       M:   ⌊Dreadful.    ⌋
      MF:    And rolled- went right over him I think it did
                  and- and smashed a chair against the wall
   [[        ⌈and he was knocked flat.      ⌉
       A:   ⌊Cor he was lucky wasn't he⌋
      MF:    And mother had to pick him up and get him-
             stir him to life again.
```

Prior stories are contexts for subsequent stories which in turn contextualize them. The third story, "Foxy and the Cartwheel" continues to take place out on the moor and involves the further characterization of behavior on the fringes of ritual orthodoxy. Concentration of the second and third stories on willfully wayward acts conveys the impression that these have been intended as thematic from the outset. But the fourth story is not about an act of Foxy's at all, instead it is an object that is wayward and Foxy is its victim. In light of this, it is possible to see the previous story as likewise about a wayward object, the cartwheel, and, more tenuously, to see the surplice and the ashes of the first two stories as wayward, instead of so seeing the vicar who mishandles them. Mishaps now appear as the theme for all four stories. Wayward objects can be seen to shift from the unpredictable but harmless to the dangerous over the course of the four stories, and the objects have been specified, twice in a row, as wheels. The character of Foxy is held constant through all four stories but the scene of the fourth is inside a church instead of outside on the moor. (The juxtaposition of church and moor in the first story is unlikely to have influenced this choice since contextual relationships do not usually jump four stories.[26]) Adjacent stories are mutually constitutive. Each points up or plays out elements of the other. Elements come thereby to thread through and tie together two or more stories. Tying elements can be built up into sets, more or less densely layered depending on how closely the stories are related. (The variously sequenced and overlapped sets of elements are represented in Figure 11 by brackets nested one inside the other. Their density indicates the intimacy of the relation between stories as contexts for each other.)

26. See Harvey Sacks and Emmanual Shegloff, "Opening up Closings" in Ethnomethodology, ed., Roy Turner (Middlesex, England: Penguin, 1974), p. 238, on adjacency pairs.

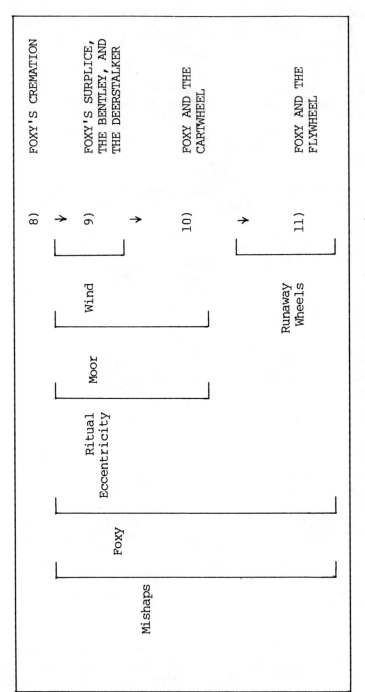

Figure 11: Stories as Contexts for Stories.

Second stories are both a recognition of something in first stories and an elaboration of something out of them. As Sacks notes: "It obviously would take some sort of work on the part of the second teller to achieve a similar second story. That work would obviously involve such sorts of things as some sort of attention to the first story, some sort of analysis of the first story, some sort of use of the analysis of the first story in building a second."[27] The distinction between serial and second stories is evidenced in the sorts of attention they show first stories: serial stories show attention to content; second stories show attention to form.[28]

Serial stories, that is, series of stories by the same storyteller, pick up elements from first stories and play them out in different arrangements. The wheel, for instance, falls down a hill in "Foxy and the Cartwheel" and flies off a machine in "Foxy and the Flywheel". Continuities between serial stories can appear perfunctory since any element can serve to spin off a story. Second stories, that is, following-on stories by a different storyteller, pick out relations between elements, that is, actions, or what Vladimir Propp calls functions, and work them into the story.[29] The function taken from "Foxy and the Cartwheel" by the second story, "Foxy and the Flywheel", could be specified as "wheels get out of control". Content can be quite different in second stories provided form is constant. The elements being related are substitutable, it is the relation that is fixed. Serial stories spin out the possibilities of elements in an unfolding set of stories whereas seconds elaborate its structure.

27. Sacks, (April 30, 1970), Lecture Five, p. 5.
28. Barbara Kirshenblatt-Gimblett argues that inversions of these patterns can occur when, for instance, second story tellers, who are closely related to first story tellers, take up an alignment with them and produce next stories which are, in effect, serial stories, or when serial story tellers, to make a didactic point, effectively second their own stories. Personal Communication, New York, 1983.
29. Vladimir Propp, Morphology of the Folktale (Austin and London: University of Texas Press, 1968), p. 21: "Function is understood as an act of a character, defined from the point of view of its significance for the course of the action."

The attention next stories show first stories is evidenced by the continuities between them, and this attention is part of the warrant for telling them.[30] But second story tellers are not asserting a community of experience with first story tellers, though a superficial reading can suggest this, they are asserting an affinity of understanding. Second stories are specifically designed, according to Sacks, to display understanding of firsts. "I want to suggest that part of the common business of storytelling occasions involves story recipients positioning an appreciation of the story on its completion. So that it's an altogether common feature of storytelling occasions that, on some story's recognized completion, recipients will offer understandings of the story."[31] One of the understandings so offered is the second story. This extends, Sacks continues, "from an obvious base, things like questions and answers, the relevance of positioning of utterances for determining the kinds of jobs they do."[32] Attention to form, I suggest, is precisely what accomplishes this display of understanding.

By the fourth story, "Foxy and the Flywheel", the operation of these mixed second and serial stories on first stories have pared down both elements and functions so that the possibilities for subsequent stories are severely restricted. At this juncture of the conversation, for the first time since storytelling began, Algy May has lost the floor as storyteller, and he has lost it for two turns in a row. Given the tight constraints on the constitution of stories now being unfolded, he has two alternatives for recovering the floor. One is to permit Miles' story to do closure on storytelling and pursue conversation in another vein which could open out again into stories later. Closure is, in fact, characteristic of second stories because the way seconds close down on the open possibilities of firsts severely restricts subsequent seconds to those few explicit functions. The elaborate redundancy of

30. Erving Goffman, <u>Frame Analysis</u> (New York, Evanston, San Francisco, London: Harper Colophon, 1974), p. 510, in which Goffman suggests that telling a story provides other participants with an occasion to match it with one from their own repetoire.
31. Sacks, "Storytelling in Conversation", SS132 Lecture One (University of California, Irvine: 8 October 1971), p. 7.
32. Sacks, (11 October 1971), Lecture Two, p. 6.

seconds seems to work something like the final couplets of
Shakespearean plays, at once summing up and exhausting their
formal resemblances and thereby closing the sequence. Algy's
alternative is to come up with a second story that fits the
constraints now set up. And so he does:

Story Twelve

ALGY AND THE FLYWHEEL

```
A:   But Miles
     years ago
     there used to be threshing engines
MF:  Yeah.=
A:   bloody good flywheels on them
     (                )
     and we were going up-
     Jean and I were going up a narrow lane
     in Cornwall
     and we saw a very white-faced chap
     looking at us.
     Cor thank God you're well.
     I said what's the matter.
     He says the bloody flywheel's come off.
     And he's pointing to the top of the hill.
MF:  ((Chuckles))
A:   And apparently it had come down so fast it had
     jumped over this
     low lane
MF:  Tcha.
A:   yeah
     missed us
MF:  Tss.
A:   and gone into the-
     well miles away.
```

In this second story one element, the flywheel, has been
carried over from the previus story, "Foxy and the Flywheel";
two elements have been transformed, Algy is substituted for
Foxy and the threshing-engine for the generator; and the
function has stayed the same, "flywheels flung dangerously and
unpredictably at people's heads cause narrow escapes."
Continuity is structural as well as thematic. (Figure 12 shows
the structural continuity between the two stories.)

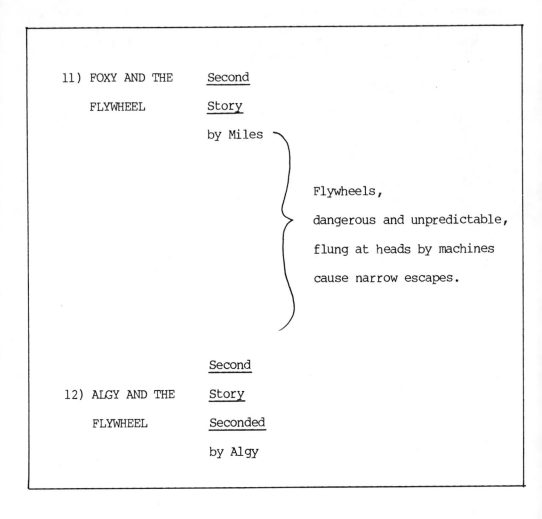

11) FOXY AND THE   Second
    FLYWHEEL   Story
                       by Miles

                                Flywheels,
                                dangerous and unpredictable,
                                flung at heads by machines
                                cause narrow escapes.

                       Second
12) ALGY AND THE   Story
    FLYWHEEL   Seconded
                       by Algy

Figure 12: Structural Continuity between Stories.

This second story of Algy's is a much more difficult
accomplishment than ordinary second storying, it seconds a
second. The trick now, for Algy, is to retain the floor as
storyteller. As I have suggested, the conventions for serial
storying, that is, following one's own story with another
oneself, are looser than for second storying, and they work in
divergent directions: if second stories close down on the
functions of firsts, serial stories pick up elements of firsts
and open out toward other functions. Continuity between serial
stories is merely topical, pivoting on common elements in
different relations. So, to show precedence at this juncture
over possible seconds by other storytellers, Algy offers a
serial story that retains both the element, "wheels", and the
function, "getting out of control": a huge spool of telephone
cabling fell off Bill Hamlyn's truck and bounded down Bilberry
Hill. In shifting the element from a little flywheel to a big
spool and the function from flying off a machine to falling
down a hill, the story of Bill Hamlyn and the cable spool comes
to resemble the story three back of Foxy and the cartwheel.
The matched outer stories bracket the matched inner stories in
quite a neat fashion. (Figure 13 shows the double bracketing.)

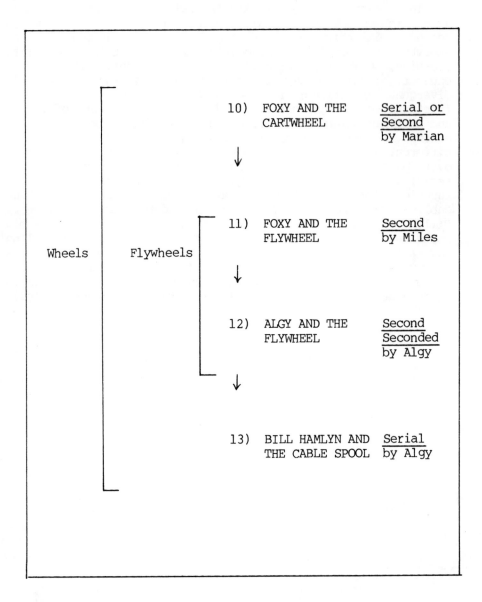

Figure 13: Nested Stories.

By virtue of the contextual constraints constructed by the sequence of second stories, Algy's serial story, "Bill Hamlyn and the Cable Spool", unlike the earlier following-on stories, either second or serial, has come to be constrained by the story before. The backwards reconstitution of first stories by following-on stories has come round to the frontwards constitution of following-on stories by first stories. In this instance, both the thematic and structural continuities created in the previous stories constrain this one. Algy continues with the seventh and last story of the cluster analyzed here, relating it to the previous story by tying Bill Hamlyn to his father, and to the cluster of stories by describing another wayward object:

Story Fourteen

THE PLOUGH AND THE HARE

MF: That's typical of Bill I can believe anything
        about him.
A: Um.
    Now I like the story of when his old man was about
        seventy
    driving a tractor
MF: ((Clears throat))
A: ploughing
        with Bill
[[J: [(   )]
A: Three furrow plough.
    You know up and down the bloody field
    and a hare got up.
    And the old man
    forgot all about his furrow and he
[[All: [((Laughter))]
[[A: [took it out
        and gave chase.]
    Hm.
All: ((Laughter))
A: Had a lovely furrow
    right-
    following this
    hare all across the field.
All: ((Laughter))
A: That's supposed to be true.

The flywheel element that ties the fourth and fifth stories can be seen as a particular kind of wheel, which is the element that links these stories to the two that bracket them. The wheel in all four stories is a wayward object of the kind characteristic of the cluster of seven stories. The stories about wayward objects are themselves part of a larger set of what might be called perversity tales, that is, tales about a world out of control, of which they are a particular kind. From the pivotal second story seconded, thematic continuity opens outward in both directions, moving from the particular to the general, so that the outer elements entail the inner. (Figure 14 discloses the nesting structure.)

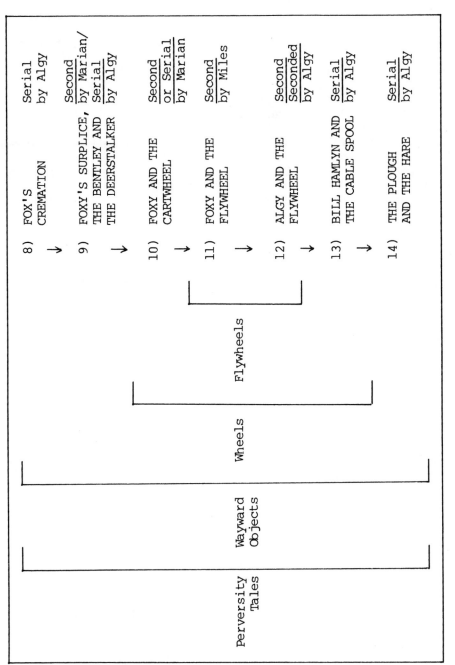

Figure 14: Nesting Structure of Seven Stories.

Thematic continuity between serial stories gives the cluster its circumscribed content; structural continuity between second stories gives the cluster its characteristic form. Serial stories extend the boundaries of the Taleworld, elaborating and exploring its content. Second stories tie together the Storyrealm, relating the structures of adjacent stories, regardless of content. Thus, serial stories point toward the Taleworld, transparencies to the events the story is about. Second stories point toward the Storyrealm, shaping the relationship between stories, and, by extension, between storytellers. Not all particular thematic elements are tidely entailed by more general thematic elements in the way that the element "flywheels" is entailed by "wheels", itself entailed by "wayward objects" which is in turn entailed by the reversals of circumstance characteristic of perversity tales. Commonly, sets of thematic elements form a pattern of overlapping relationships. (These are represented in Figure 15 by layered brackets. Structural continuities are expressed as shared functions.)

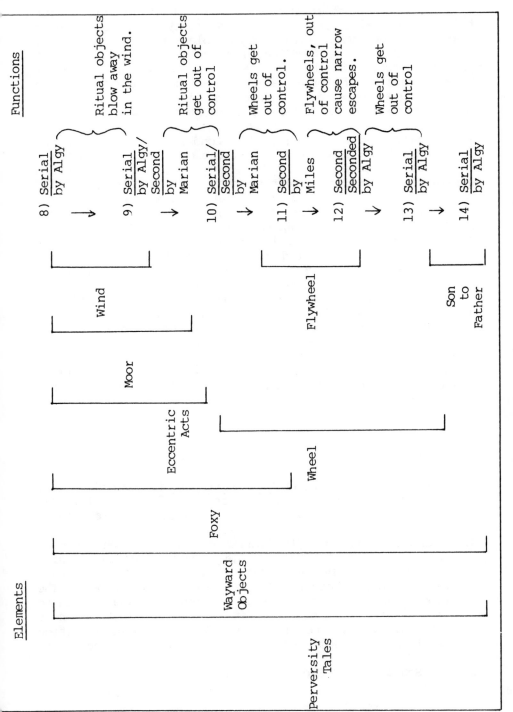

Figure 15: Multiple Continuities among Stories

A function is not located in a story, but foregrounded out of it by a second as its context. The function of story two as it entails story one, "ritual object blows away in the wind", is different from the function of story two as it is entailed by story three, "ritual object gets out of control". One of the difficulties of formal analysis is the fixity with which functions are rendered. A function that is apprehended as content in a story is, in fact, contingent on context.

The study of story singles, seconds, serials, sets, and systems discloses some of the intricacies of the organization of stories in conversation. The interplay between seconds and serials can be used to explicate relationships between stories and conversation as well as relationships among stories. Clustered stories in the same conversation can be taken together as a system in which stories relate to each other, spanning intervening talk.[33] Single stories or the story system can also be related to the context of conversation. Stories on the edge of a cluster follow on from or lead in to conversation.[34] In shifting from the Storyrealm to the realm of conversation, serials take the form of topical continuity and seconds take the form of displayed understandings. Stories constitute and invite seconds and serials from conversation as well as from other stories, thus playing out the overall sequential implicativeness of the storytelling occasion.[35] Conversation is among the multiple contexts for stories, contexts that are likewise constitutive after their fashion.

33. John McDowell, Children's Riddling (Bloomingdale and London: Indiana University Press, 1979), p. 111 and Chapter 7 on clusters of riddles relating to each other, not to talk.
34. Evans, p. 181, comes to similar conclusions about what he calls sections of riddles. "The structure of the session consists of twelve sequential sections of riddles. Each section is united by one or more common themes. The riddle at the end of each section is usually linked thematically to the riddle at the beginning of the next section, or else the riddle at the beginning of a section is linked to some aspect of the immediate behavioral context."
35. See Schegloff and Sacks, pp. 233 - 264.

If other stories clearly constitute the occasion for telling a story, this analysis demonstrates how they constitute its form and content as well.

It may be remarked that for a contextualist the analysis I do here is peculiarly formalist in character. Sacks' notion of second storying and its mate, my notion of serial storying, are described in terms of formal resemblances between stories. This can be regarded as an attempt to see as contextual what is usually seen as formal and so, by implication, to show the formality of contextual relationships. The fact is that contextualism, unlike formalism, is not a theory. It is a way of locating a laboratory for analysis in which the analysis can be of any theoretical persuasion whatever, including what is often taken as its antithesis, formalism. Formal analysis turns out to be equally bound to contexts, not to a present context but to any of a number of remote contexts. Stories, that is to say, are never context-free. The contexts for stories include the events the story is about as well as the occasion on which it is told; they include other stories told on the same occasion, the same story told on other occasions, and tellings and hearings of the same story on the same occasion; they include gestures, postures, orientations and relationships; distributions in space, time, and circumstance; analytical schemas and interactional strategies; the constancies of human communication and the ephemera of turns of mind. The story context of stories is only one of their multiple contexts.

CHAPTER THREE

PRESENTATION OF SELF IN STORYTELLING*

"......the self constructing for itself the shape of the world it then finds and acts in."

Maurice Natanson[1]

Stories are enclaves in conversation, framed as a different order of discourse from the discourse that encloses them, namely, as narrative discourse within ordinary conversation. The enclaves so framed share their realm status as stories. For that reason, stories relate to each other, spanning intervening conversation. Hence, all the stories in one conversation can be taken together as a system.[2] As a consequence of the systemic character of storytelling in

---

*A brief version of this chapter was given at the 1976 American Folklore Society Meetings in Philadelphia and later appeared as an article in the Journal of Western Folklore (January 1978) under the title, "Indirection in Storytelling". I am indebted to Phyllis Glazier for the critical eye and metaphysical wit she brought to an early reading of it.

1. Maurice Natanson, The Journeying Self: A Study in Philosophy and Social Role (Reading, Menlo Park, London, Ontario: Addison-Wesley Publishing Company, 1970), p. 23.
2. David Evans argues analogously that there can be a structure to a complete riddling session. "The riddles must be analyzed not only in respect to the social and behavioral context in which they are told but also in respect to all the other riddles that are told at the session. The total number of riddles told and the order in which they are told constitute part of the context of any single riddle." "Riddling and the Structure of Context", Journal of American Folklore 89 (1976), p. 170.

conversation, stories are not appropriately treated as tracings of an individual. They are aspects of a mutually constructed universe of discourse, a universe in which individuals make appearances, presentations of self.[3] This chapter is concerned with the presentations of Algy May in the universe mutually constructed over the course of the evening's conversation at Rowbrook. Thirty-three stories were told during that conversation, twenty by Algy May himself, and the remaining thirteen by the other four participants on the occasion, Jean, Marian, Miles, and myself.

The stories are clustered in two subsets in the conversation, a set of twenty stories told during the first half hour of storytelling and a set of eleven more told near the end of the occasion.[4] Two other stories scattered through the intervening half hour are subordinated to the conversation and have no bearing on the story system. Clustered stories, as Barbara Kirshenblatt-Gimblett observes, dominate conversation.[5] Not only do these clustered stories share the same ontological status, but also they are formally and thematically related. Serial stories, runs of stories by the same teller, carry across from one to the next certain thematic elements and thus have the property of expanding a universe or Taleworld. Second stories, stories by a second teller parasitic on stories by a first, replicate certain formal relations between elements and so have the property of structuring the narrative discourse or Storyrealm.[6] Stories that so entail seconds and serials are called first stories. Relationships among first, second, and serial stories create

3. This turn of phrase and the interactional design behind it come from Erving Goffman, The Presentation of Self in Everyday Life (New York: 1959).
4. David Evans describes twelve sequential sections of riddles told on one occasion, each section linked by one or more common themes. The end riddle of one section is linked to the first riddle of the next or the first riddle is linked to the behavioral context.
5. Barbara Kirshenblatt-Gimblett, "The Concept and Varieties of Narrative Performance in East European Jewish Culture", in Explorations in the Ethnography of Speaking, ed., Richard Bauman and Joel Sherzer (New York: Cambridge University Press, 1974), pp. 291 and 293.
6. Harvey Sacks, Unpublished Lectures on Storytelling in Conversation (University of California, Irvine, 1970), lectures five and six.

what Sacks calls "observable similarities across clumps" of stories.[7] On this occasion, the first and last stories of both sets, some of the second stories, and all of the serial stories are told by one storyteller, Algy May. Other conversationalists only do second storying, that is, the registration and replication of a pattern introduced by the preceding story. Because of the interdependency of the stories and Algy May's dominance as storyteller, the story system sustains his presentations of self even when he is neither telling the story nor in the tale.

Storytelling is about both messages and relationships.[8] The story consists at the message level of acts and events by characters inside the Taleworld, the realm evoked or invoked by the story. But the message is itself an act or event delivered for and with other persons as part of the Storyrealm, in a way that bears on the relationships among participants in that realm. On this occasion, presentations of self are undertaken by one person in the form of two presentational routines, one in each realm, these presentations having an elegant relationship to each other.

Story Set I: Presentation of Self as Storyteller

The first presentation is a legitimation routine, that is, an interactional undertaking designed to provide evidence that the person is what he purports to be, here, that Algy May is a

7. Sacks, Lecture Five, p. 4.
8. See Robert Georges, "Toward on Understanding of Storytelling Events", Journal of American Folklore 82 (1969), p. 322: "Once the storyteller begins to receive and decode the responses of the story listener and to interpret and respond to them as feedback, the storyteller and the story listener begin to shape the message jointly (stage 60). As the interactions of the storyteller and story listener intensify through their joint participation in the shaping of the message, the message increases in prominence, relatively speaking, and begins to create its own tensions, which reach a peak as the message itself generates maximum interaction between the storyteller and the story listener (stage 7)."

storyteller.[9] The undertaking involves a shift from participant to what Erving Goffman calls the "specialized and functionally differentiated role of raconteur and storyteller".[10] Such a role can be slight and transient, briefly assumed to tell a story and lightly discarded afterwards, especially if the story is one of those ephemera of conversation, personal anecdotes. But Algy is not just telling stories, many stories and good ones, he is pointing out that he is telling stories and how good they are. And the stories he tells are not, at the outset, personal anecdotes. Metanarrative and evaluative frames of the stories draw attention, respectively, to the realm status of the discourse as narrative and to the quality of the narrative discourse. Algy's first story is framed by metanarratives like these which are also evaluations:

> A: Fantastic story wasn't it.
> ......
> A: Fantastic story isn't it
> to strike one is a bed of three

The second frame not only establishes the discourse as narrative but also remarks on the surprising storyability of events in the Taleworld.

These frames draw attention to the Storyrealm, directing hearers to attend to storytelling as performance. Frames can be directed to either the Storyrealm or the Taleworld and the emphasis shifts over the course of the first group of twenty stories from the first to the second. Not only do both Storyrealm and Taleworld frames speak to the ontology and aesthetics of stories but also they separate and set off stories from conversation, thus serving as boundaries as well as frames. Such boundaries make it clear, Goffman argues, that

9. See Roger Abrahams, "Negotiating Respect", Journal of American Folklore 88 (1975), p. 59. Abrahams writes in a similar vein about "presentational routines", "presentational strategies", and "repetoire of self-presentational routines".
10. Erving Goffman, Frame Analysis (New York: Harper and Row, 1974), p. 538.

the storyteller "means to stand in a relation of reduced
responsibility for what he is saying".[11] The Taleworld, that
is, sustains a life of its own, one only lightly invested in
the occasion by the story. Discourse in the Storyrealm,
therefore, is not so firmly attached to the occasion as
unframed remarks are supposed to be.

Meanwhile, inside the Taleworld, the groundwork is being
laid for another presentation of self, one laminated in that
realm as a character so that, Goffman writes, "what the
individual presents is not himself but a story containing a
protagonist who may happen also to be himself".[12] This
second presentation of self is protected and enhanced by its
lamination in a story. It circumvents what Goffman refers to
as the modesty rule by framing as storytelling what might
otherwise appear to be self-description.[13] And the teller's
ability to guide and shape the self he is presenting is
enhanced by his control of the story in which he presents
himself.

Algy May's presentation of self is accomplished in two
moves: 1) the presentation of self as storyteller and 2) the
presentation of character as self. The presentations are
distributed over the occasion so that the first move, the
legitimation routine, is established during Story Set I and the
second move, the self-description, comes into play during the
stories in Set II. Algy uses the role he has established as
storyteller in Set I to describe a character in Set II who is
himself. However, the groundwork for that second self is

11. Goffman, p. 512.
12. Goffman, p. 541. See also Goffman, p. 278, where he
     alludes to "the power of dramatic scriptings to insulate
     performers from their parts." Roland Barthes goes
     further, isolating the grammatical "I" from the person
     articulating it: "indeed, the psychological person
     (belonging to the referential order) has nothing to do
     with the linguistic person, which is never defined by
     natural dispositions, intentions, or personality traits,
     but only by its (coded) point of insertion in the
     discourse." Barthes, "An Introduction to the Structural
     Analysis of Narrative", New Literary History VI (1974-5),
     p. 263.
13. Goffman, p. 531.

laid from the first story on and the first self continues to support the second to the end. Thus, the first constituted self is used to constitute a second self indirectly: the storyteller sustains the realm in which the character is lodged. (Figure 16 shows laminations of self in storytelling.)

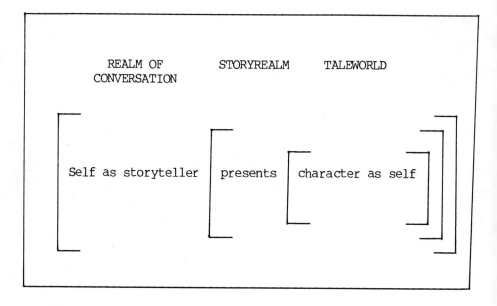

Figure 16: Laminations of Self in the Storytelling Occasion.

Multiple selves apear to be variously layered or laminated in conversation.[14] The presenting self who appears in the flesh to initiate conversation might be taken as the root self. Over the course of the conversation some elaboration occurs, this self is fleshed out somewhat, disclosing more of who it is, revealing attributes imported into the occasion from other occasions, each of these disclosures producing trifling shifts or changes on the presenting self. Such presentational possibilities can be concentrated or focused in personal anecdotes, these being designed to knit up the separations between persons by spinning out what has befallen them in each other's absence. They can be straightforward representations of what tellers were up to when hearers were not present. But they are used more cunningly to produce a controlled impression and thereby elicit appreciation of the sort of person the teller is. Thus, anecdotes that connect or reconnect persons can also be used to do the interactional work of presenting a self. The presenting self exudes a second storytelling self who elaborates a third past self, creating an ongoing self who develops over the conversational occasion, each of these subsequent selves being at some remove from the first one. The storytelling self is only slightly removed from the presenting self, partaking of its body and animacy, the self as character is more removed, partaking of that body and animacy only at some other temporal juncture. But some of its attributes leak into the storytelling occasion and inform the onging self appearing there. These transformations of self are available in brief with any anecdote. Here, they are spun out over a whole storytelling occasion, an arrangement that enriches and complicates the interactional project of presenting a self.

The first story told on this occasion nicely establishes Algy May's provenance as a storyteller in two respects. He tells a story, and he tells hearers he is telling a story and how good the story is. And he begins describing a Taleworld to which he has special access or entitlement. That description is lodged in orientations and codas to the story, orientations preceding or accompanying the narrative proper and codas following after it. Both serve to connect the Taleworld to the storytelling occasion. The story is about three brothers by the name of French who lived at Rowbrook House toward the end of the nineteenth century. It is presented with spatial, temporal, and personal frames:

14. See Goffman, pp. 516-530.

Three Brothers*

	A:	The point was
	J:	Would you
	A:	there were
		three
		teenage
		Frenchs
Spatial		sleeping in one bed over here
Orientation		in the cottage- in the old house.
		Thunderstorm
		Father French comes down
		finds the center one
		struck
		by lightening.
		Three boys in one bed center one killed
		Tchew.
Personal		One of the survivors was Herman French's
Coda		father
	K:	Excuse me.
	A:	Yeah?
Personal		the other one's his uncle.
Coda	M:	Old Fred.
Personal		Fred wasn't it.
Coda	A:	Fred
Spatial		yeah.
Coda	M:	Used to be up at Oldsbroom.
	A:	Fred was the
Temporal	M:	Or just at the end of the war
Coda		

*See Appendix for transcription devices.

Personal Coda	A:	other survivor.
		Hm.
	K:	That's OK. ((Refuses sherry from Jean.))

```
       A: ┌Fantastic story wasn't it.┐
   [[  M: └He was always a bit-     ┘
```

```
           ┌He was always a bit ┐funny actually wasn't he.
   [[  K:  └It was extraordinary.┘
```

A: Course he was funny.
     Damn funny.

K: That's very strange.

      ....

A: Fantastic story isn't it
     to strike one in a bed of three.

```
      MF: ┌O well          ┐
   [[ A:  └I mean┘three in a bed
```

     teenage boys.

MF: Yeah.

Personal
Coda

A: And Herman French brought down photographs the
                other day
     of the two
     his father
     and the other two
     that would have been un-
     well they were- aren't alive now.
     I think Herman French's father would have been
         a hundred
       and something now.
        /

Temporal
Orientation

All this happened about eighteen seventy-
six.

Person, Place, and Time

The initial orientation locates the story in the old house
on Algy's own farm, not the farmhouse we are in but the original
house just over the hill, a location that entitles him to tell
it. Stories attached to a person's property come to be his own
stories. Anchored here in space, the story opens out toward
other people and past times, their relevance to the storytelling
occasion being contingent on the story's spatial location.
These characters from 1876 turn out to be ancestors of present
inhabitants of the parish, a genealogy traced in the
conversation to connect them with those present. The geography
of the story is extended in the codas from the two houses on
Rowbrook Farm to Ollsbrim Cottage just down the road.

Evidently, alternate realities lodged, as this one is in the realm of everyday life must display some relevance to that environing world. So stories use continuers, links, bridges from the Taleworld to the ordinary one. Local storytellers can map their stories onto the geographical surround or fit their characters into a social or genealogical system. Conversationalists who do not share such a closely inhabited world preserve relevance by connecting the two realms through their own persons or the present time. An intricately connected social order in a precisely delineated geographical setting is characteristic of storytelling in traditional communities. By the same token, personal anecdotes are the characteristic genre of non-traditional populations whose continuers are themselves. In these stories, the threads that connect the Taleworld and the conversational occasion are drawn down through time, tied to present persons, and spun out through social and geographical space.

The next two stories are alluded to by the storyteller as "Snailly House", a story about two old women who lived on snails, and "Dolly's Cott", short for Dolly's Cottage, about a local beauty and the Prince Regent, these brief references taking on the quality of titles for conversational anecdotes. (Even these forms of reference are rare, the other titles used here having been concocted up by the author.) Notably, both titles refer to houses, houses with specific geographical locations mapped out by the storyteller along the East Dart River, part of the eastern boundary of the parish. So the first three stories are set in three houses, Rowbrook House, Snailly House, presently visible as a ruin along the river, and, further downstream, Dolly's Cott, to each of which the hearers are oriented from the farmhouse on Rowbrook Farm, where the conversation takes place. The fourth story, about Jan Coo and the piskies (the Dartmoor pronunciation of pixies) is set in the very old house on Rowbrook Farm where we are talking.

It is not the houses which are significant, however, but the building up of a familiar geography over the series of stories, the mapping being designed to test as well as to substantiate hearers' orientations to this small parish on the edge of the moor: Snailly House in the forest along the East Dart River, Ponsworthy and Poundsgate, the two nearest hamlets, Dartmoor itself, Dolly's Cott, further down the East Dart, the Torre Royal Inn at Princetown, site of the famous Dartmoor Prison, Brimpt's Cottage and Badger's Holt, other cottages along the river, the farmhouse at Rowbrook, Langamarsh Pit,

part of a curious rock formation on the farm, Brent, a nearby
town, Hexworthy, the village just out on the moor beyond Algy's
farm, Hangman's Pit, folkname of a local canyon, and Stoat,
another nearby town.

Snailly House,
Dolly's Cott, and
Jan Coo and the Piskies

(Stories 2, 3, and 4)

Temporal   A: But you don't know probably any of the old
Orientation   stories
                    about
                    Dolly's Cott Snailly House.
                    Do you.
      [[K: [About what?]
          A: [Never heard]anything about Snailly house.
          K: Snailly House?
          A: Yes.
             It's a-
Spatial   it's in the forest now but there used to be
Orientation   a house up there.
          K: No I didn't know that.
          A: Two old women lived in it
Spatial   MF: Where's this?
Orientation   A: Snailly House.
Spatial   K: Where.
Orientation   A: At East Dart.
             /
Spatial   A: It's in the forest now.
Orientation   But in actual fact it's-
Spatial   it's above Dolly's Cott
Orientation   J: (   )
Spatial   A: (It's there now.)
Coda   J: (   )
          A: Snailly House?
          J: Really.
          A: Two old women
          J: Yes.
          A: lived there.

One died.
And they went to take here away to bury her
and the people went up there to see her
looked around and they couldn't see-
they'd never seen these two old women
come anywhere when- it's at the East Dart
now you've

Spatial
Orientation

got to walk either to
Ponsworthy
or

J,M: ((Side conversation.))

Spatial   A: mm Poundsgate haven't you.
Orientation
Well there was nothing.
No one had ever seen them come shopping
and all they could find in the house-
this is absolutely true-
was a tin bath
full of snails.
And that's what they lived on.
And they took the old-
they took the old lady away
and buried her.
And the other one
remained.
Without any visible means of support except
this tin bath of snails.
No food.
And she lived for several years.
And eventually died
and then they took her away.
But that's all the food-
no one had ever seen them- these two old
ladies go further than
just round the

Spatial
Orientation
Orientation
Coda and
Orientation

Snailly House.
Up the East Dart
in the wood.
There now.
In the forest it is.
And they lived on snails.

```
                     /
                  Snails they gathered too.
                  Not escargots as such
                  ((chuckles)) you know from France.
                  They lived on Dartmoor ((chuckle)) snails.
                  (He he)
                  Twas the only food they had hm.
              K:  That's extraor- ((chuckles))
              A:  Well that's true.
              K:  Hm.
              A:  Nevermind that.
              K:  Hm.
Spatial       A:  Then further down the
Orientation       East Dart you get Dolly's Cott.
                  And Dolly
                  was um
Spatial           a girl that worked at Prince Hall
Orientation       and uh-
                  no sorry
Spatial           Torre Royal
Orientation       and the-
Spatial           it's the Torre Royal outside Princetown
Orientation       and the Prince Regent used to come down
                  and a chap that was courting Dolly
                  thought well the Prince Regent's still
                        pretty keen on my-
                  my girl you see
                  so I'll take her away
                  and built this house
Spatial           which you can see below Brimpt's now-
Orientation             haven't you ever seen it?
Spatial           There's not much of it left
Codas             there's a chimney and
                  mm a wall or two.
Spatial           Do you know that? Up the East Dart?
Orientation   MF: How far away from Brimpt's is it then.
              J:  Well
```

Spatial   A: It's down
Orientation   to the river.

Spatial   J: Just above the river
Orientation   Yes.

Spatial   A: Not very far up above
Orientation   old Badger's

            [[J: [It's]in a lovely position.
                A: [Holt.]

Spatial   MF: So- so it isn't there- it's between
Orientation   [there and]
Spatial   [[M: [It's about]
Orientation   quarter mile up above.

             A: He put her-
                he took her there you see and said right
                come on
                my woman

          [[M: [Not well hello Dolly]
                J: [You'll live here.]

             M: goodbye Dolly.
             K: Yeah.
          MF: Hm.
                (He he)

             A: And actually Crossing says there was no
                    need for all that
                he was
                rather jumping the gun (ha.)
                Cause the Prince Regent wasn't all that
                    keen hm.
                But he built there the house he says
                called Dolly's Cott.
                You don't know anything do you.

          [[K: He's always teasing[me
                A: [Really]when you come
                to look round
                there's (all sorts of) stories in-
             K: Hm.

Spatial   A: And Jan Coo.
Orientation   The one for here- Rowbrook
Temporal   He was a boy about seventeen hundred and
Orientation   something
                looked after the cattle- only a youngster
                and um

Spatial Orientation	he used to come up with the other labourers
	from the river or above the river
Spatial Orientation	and come up to Rowbrook- the old house which
	I think must've been
Spatial Orientation	not that one
	another one down here
	because the workmen would-
	he used to come up at- in the evening
	and
	he said O they're calling my name- Jan Coo
	Jan Coo.
	And the other workmen said don't be stupid
M:	They were the piskies.
A:	Yes only the pixies or piskies.
	Nope I can hear it- well this went on all
	the autumn
	and in the spring one
	evening
	he came up with the other workmen and-
	calling me I can't stop and he rushed down
	and um
Spatial Orientation	crossed the river
	and the other workmen came up here
	opened the kitchen door and
	got lanterns and
	said O Jan Coo's gone
	we'll have to go and look for him they went
	down of course they never found him.
Spatial Orientation	Cause he crossed the stepping stones which
	are down there
Spatial Coda	You can see them now
	and he's sitting
	at the pixie's throne-
	the female pixie he
	heard her calling all this time you see and
	he
	thought ah I can't stop any longer I must
	go and see her.
	There he is.

```
Spatial
Orientation    [[ M: [In the Langamarsh Pit.
               A: [Only two hundred years ago.  ]

               [[ K: [Or two hundred and fifty.
                     [C-]
               A: Um?
Spatial        K: Can I go up there and see him then.
Orientation    M: Langamarsh Pit.
Spatial        A: Langamarsh Pit's down there now.
Coda           K: O must go and look at it.
               A: That's Jan Coo.
```

The geography of the Taleworld is laid over the parish, spun out across the moor, and caught at the edges on surrounding towns. Subsequent stories, even those by other storytellers, are inserted into the contours of this unfolding region. At the outset they recur to Rowbrook Farm as their central point of reference. Later they range increasingly further afield, till the twelfth story, "Algy and the Flywheel", is set altogether outside of Devon in the next shire to the southwest, Cornwall. This is the first of six Cornish stories, the other five following all in a row three stories later. These Cornish stories break away from the familiar geography of the Taleworld to create a second geographical region, one whose topography must be specified for hearers who might not know, for instance, that old Cornish lanes are sunk so deeply into the ground from ancient usage that the heads of persons in the lane might not appear above the bank:

                    Algy and the Flywheel
                         (Story 12)

```
               A: But Miles
Temporal          Years ago
Orientation       there used to be threshing engines
              MF: Yeah=
               A: Steam engines.
              MF: Yeah.
               A: Bloody good flywheels on them
                  (                              )
Personal          Jean and I were going up a narrow lane
Orientation
```

```
Spatial
Orientation                  in Cornwall
                             and we saw a very white-faced chap
                             looking at us.
                             Cor thank God you're well.
                             I said what's the matter.
                             He says the bloody flywheel's come off.
Spatial                      and he's pointing to the top of the hill.
Orientation        MF       ((Chuckles))
                   A:        And apparently it had come down so fast it
                                 had
                             jumped over this
Spatial                      low lane
Orientation        MF:      Tcha.
                   A:        Yeah.
                             Missed us
                   MF:       Tss.
                   A:        and gone into the-
                             well miles away ((chuckles)).
                   K:        Heaven's sake.
                   J:        Yes.
                   A:        Do you remember that.
                   J:        Yes.
                   A:        Yeah then well that's true.
                   J:        I'm=
                   A:        Gaw he said
                             you all right? (he he)
                             Bang (he he)
                             misses us.
                   MF:       ((Chuckle))
                   A:        We never saw it even
                 J,MF        ((Chuckle))
                   A:        It'd come down
                             missed us.
                   MF:       Um.
                             Cor.
              [[   A:        Those were those great big flywheels
                   J:                                       Was
                                  that when we had the jeeps that
              [[   A:             with the great=
                             Yeah.
                             Coming up in the lane now I remember it
                                 very well
                   MF:       Cor ((chuckles))
                   A:        These
                             real old sunken
```

Spatial
Orientation   Cornish lanes you know- way down it was.
                     And of course it just bounced ⌈over ⌉
          MF: ⌊Right⌋over
                the top.

    If the mapping procedure for Devon works from the inside
out, starting with Algy's farm and spiralling out into the
parish, over the moor, and on to the towns, it works for the
Cornish stories from the outside in. They start in the Cornish
lanes, draw toward a cluster of adjoining farms in the next two
stories, move in the following two stories to the village of
Trelow, and come, in the last of the Cornish stories, in to
Algy and Jean's farm there. The drift from familiar to
unfamiliar geographies culminates in the setting of the
twentieth and last story of Set I, an account from the
newspaper of a witchcraft and exorcism trial in Leeds, a city
in the north of England with which neither storyteller nor
hearers is familiar. (Figure 17 maps out places mentioned in
or in connection with the stories in Sets I and II.)

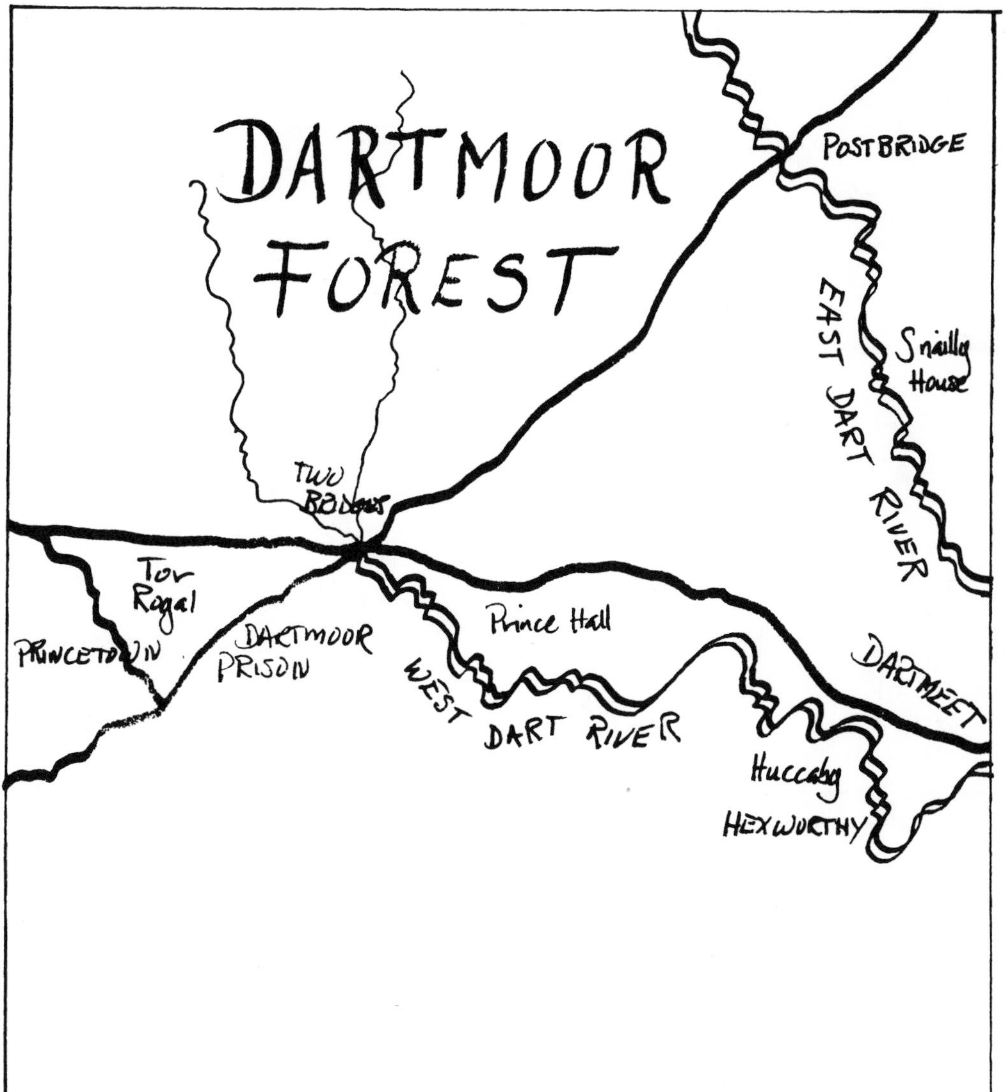

Figure 17: Map of the Taleworld
(Based upon the Ordnance Survey map with the permission of the controller of Her Majesty's stationery Office, Crown copyright reserved.)

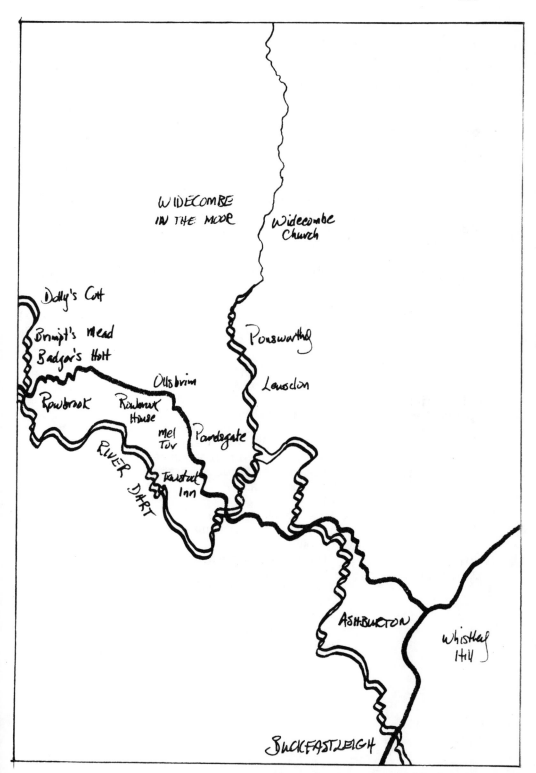

WIDECOMBE
IN THE MOOR

Widecombe
Church

Dolly's Cott

Brimpt's Mead

Badger's Holt

Ollsbrim

Ponsworthy

Leusdon

Rowbrook

Rowbrook
House

Mel
Tor

Pandsgate

RIVER DART

Tavistal
Inn

ASHBURTON

Whistley
Hill

BUCKFASTLEIGH

The first seven stories transpire in the past, that is, without the lifespan of the storyteller, Algy May, but except for two, within the possible lifespans of his immediate forebears. The exceptions are both stories about supernaturals, the piskies and the Devil himself, inserted into the distant past, which has the effect of shielding them from incredulity. Hearers appear to be willing to credit or at least countenance extraordinary events if they occur in distant times or exotic places. Thus, the story, "Three Brothers", takes place in 1876, "Snailly House" and "Dolly's Cott" about 1900, "Jan Coo and the Piskies" in 1700, "Hangman's Pit" about 1850, "The Devil at Tavistock Inn" in 1638, and "The Inspector at Huccaby Church" again about 1900. Suitable characters are situated in the period thus evoked. These characters are all old inhabitants of the parish and two of them, the Frenchs in the first story and Perriman's grandfather in the fifth, are also direct ancestors of present inhabitants. Residence and genealogy link and separate the Taleworld and the world of everyday life.

Hangman's Pit
(Story 5)

	A: Then there's the chap
Spatial	who came from Brent.
Orientation	Um he went to Brent Fair
Spatial	from Hexworthy.
Orientation	Nice horse- everything- he got drunk in the pub you see.
	And he sold his nice horse
	or swapped it for a horrible old thing.
	All bones and
	old.
	Rode it back
	in the early morning he
	K: Go on.
Spatial	A: stopped at Hangman's Pit which is across
Orientation	the river.
	He suddenly realized
	Cor I've been done.
	K,MF: ((Chuckle.))
	A: This is nothing like the one I used to bring back with my wife ((chuckles)).

Or I set out on.
Nothing like as good as my
previous horse.
So he thought n- O bugger I can't face her
    any longer you see and he hung
    himself.

[[[Yeah-
   K: [O (ho ho).]

<table>
<tr><td>Spatial
Orientation</td><td>A: Yeah but that's not the end of the story.
Hangman's Pit there's a Hawthorne tree
   where he hung himself.
The best part of the story is the fact that
somebody walking by next morning saw him
   hanging
with a new halter
which this
gypsy chap had given on this horse you see.
And this fellow walking by thought
Cor not going to leave it
that's a waste of a good halter and he cut
   the halter off.
And um ((chuckles))</td></tr>
</table>

   K: ((Chuckles))
   A: Yeah and
  MF: ((Chuckles))
   A: took the halter away and left the chap
     there.
That is true and you won't beat that
    anywhere.
  /
Tis absolutely gospel (   ).
  MF: ((Clears throat and chuckles))
   A: (Ha)
He said I'm not wasting a new halter like
    that.
   K: ((Chuckles))
   A: (Ha)

Personal   And that's Perriman's grandfather did that
and Spatial   over at Stoat.
Coda

    Time and person shift in the eighth story. Time shifts to
the recent past, within the lifespan and even the lifestage of
the storyteller. Characters shift to associates, or what
Alfred Schutz has called consociates, that is, persons present

to the storyteller in everyday life.[15] Place, by contrast, is held constant: both the seventh and eighth stories are in Huccaby Church, locality thus sustaining continuity despite changes in persons and time:

Foxy's Cremation
(Story 8)

Temporal
Orientation

A: But in more recent times Miles will remember Foxy.

MF: Yeah.

A: Do you?

MF: Yeah.

A: Well he- you know took seventeen tries to
    get a-
to be a
parson.

MF: Did he?

A: Yeah and he
got in on the eighteenth try.

MF: Hmhmm.

A: And one of his first jobs was to-to
to (ha) them in um t- O what do you call it

MF: ((Chuckles))
/

A: cremation
he had to
chuck the ashes about you see and he went in to
into
Huccaby Church and the bloody wind blew chucked them up and they went out over the
    wall you see.

[[All: [((Laughter))
   A: [Out over the moor.]
(Ha)

[[[Well that- that-
  MF: [((Chuckles))   ]

A: he'd only just got his bloody ticket.

M,MF: ((Chuckle))

[[K: [Why did it
    A: [The Bishop]was hopping mad.
He said how dare you Foxy.

15. Alfred Schutz, <u>On Phenomenology and Social Relations</u> (Chicago and London: University of Chicago Press, 1970), pp. 218-235.

Time stays constant from the eighth through the nineteenth stories but in the twelfth story person shifts with place: Algy appears as a character in his own story, set in Cornwall, and reappears in the other five Cornish stories, numbers fifteen through nineteen. These six anecdotes maintain relevance to the storytelling occasion through continuity of person rather than continuity of place. As the stories shift toward the present and the self, their spatial lodgement loosens. (Figures 18 and 19 consist of a Time Chart and a Cast of Characters for the stories.)

Story	Time
1	1876
2	
3	Circa 1900
4	1700 or 1750
5	Circa 1800
6	1638
7	Circa 1900
8	
9	
10	Circa 1950
11	
12	Circa 1940
13	Circa 1950
14	
15	
16	
17	Circa 1940
18	
19	
20	Now
23	
24	
25	
26	
27	the Present
28	
29	
30	
31	
32	Circa 1950
33	

Figure 18: Time Shift in the Taleworld

Figure 19:   Casts of Characters

Story 1:   Three Brothers

    three teenage brothers:
    one brother, Herman French's father
    the second brother, Fred
    the third brother
    Father French, their father, old inhabitant
    Herman French, son and nephew, present inhabitant

Story 2:   Snailly House

    two old women, old inhabitants of the parish
    local people

Story 3:   Dolly's Cott

    Dolly, a barmaid
    her beau, old inhabitants of the parish
    the Prince Regent of Great Britain

Story 4:   Jan Coo and the Piskies

    Jan Coo, shepherd, old inhabitant
    his fellow workmen at Rowbrook Farm
    the piskies and their queen

Story 5:   Hangman's Pit

    a chap from Hexworthy, old inhabitant
    his wife
    a gypsy
    the grandfather of Perriman, present inhabitant

Story 6:   The Devil at Tavistock Inn

    the Devil
    a man at the Inn
    the landlady, Mrs. Foley, present inhabitant
    her forebear, old inhabitant

Story 7:   The School Inspector

    the inspector
    the teacher at Huccaby, old inhabitant
    the school children

Story 8:   Foxy's Cremation

        Foxy, vicar of the parish, consociate
        the Bishop

Story 9:   Foxy's Surplice, the Bentley, and the Deerstalker

        Foxy, the vicar, consociate
        an onlooker

Story 10:   Foxy and the Cartwheel

        Foxy, the vicar, consociate
        the local people

Story 11:   Foxy and the Flywheel

        Foxy, the vicar, consociate
        Miles' mother, present inhabitant
        the congregation

Story 12:   Algy and the Flywheel

        Algy May, the storyteller himself
        Jean May, his wife
        a local farmer, inhabitant of Cornwall

Story 13:   Bill Hamlyn and the Cable Spool

        Bill Hamlyn, present inhabitant

Story 14:   The Plough and the Hare

        Bill Hamlyn's father, present inhabitant
        Bill Hamlyn
        a hare

Story 15:   Michael and the Hay

        Harold Bluett, consociate
        Michael, the carthorse, consociate
        Algy May, the storyteller himself

Story 16:   Michael and the Master of Hounds

        Michael, the carthorse, consociate
        Mrs. Moxley
        Harold Bluett
        Mr. Trewillow, Master of Hounds

Story 17:   Not 'Xactly and the Cigarette

        Not 'Xactly, the village idiot, consociate
        Algy May, the storyteller

Story 18:   Not 'Xactly and the Waterbuckets

        Not 'Xactly, the village idiot, consociate
        the villagers of Trelow
        Jean May, the storyteller

Story 19:   Polly and the Runaway Cart

        Polly, the pony, consociate
        Jean May
        Algy May, the storyteller

Story 20:   The Witchcraft-Exorcism Trial

        a man in Leeds, contemporary
        his wife
        the local vicar, Church of England
        the Methodist minister
        the police
        the psychiatrists
        five children
        a dog

Story 23 - 26:   Ferreting

        a Canadian film crew
        David French, present inhabitant
        Algy May, the story teller
        a rabbit
        the ferrets

Story 27:   Sheepshearing

        Marian, Algy's niece, present inhabitant
        the Canadian film crew
        Algy May, the storyteller

Stories 28 - 30: Dog-Training

        John Newton, present inhabitant
        Miles Fursdon, one storyteller
        his dog, Tramp

Wallace, sheepdog breeder
Algy May, the other storyteller
his dog, Bruce
Alec Turner, breeder
Jess Wilkinson, breeder
Algy's dog, The Driver
a Scotty ewe
A lamb

Story 31: The Dog breaks his Neck

Mrs. Howell's greyhound

Story 32: The Tom Sawyer Readings

Katharine, the storyteller
her brother
her father
people on the bus

Story 33: Going Jiggoty

Canon Hall, present inhabitant
a man in Poundsgate, past inhabitant

A neat complementarity now appears between person and place: at the outset, stories are mapped onto Algy's surroundings but they are about other persons; with the twelfth story, they are about himself but mapped onto other places. The thirteenth and fourteenth stories switch back to other persons in a familiar geography, and the fifteenth through nineteenth stories return to the storyteller in an unfamiliar geography. Because stories by other tellers are all seconds, they continue and extend the Taleworld Algy has established and so carry out his designs. Mapping and characterization can be understood to form co-occurrent pairs: if other persons, then familiar places; if unfamiliar places, then oneself. These pairs compose·an alternation set for connecting the storyteller with the stories, through either his place or his person.[16] Pertinence to the storytelling occasion is sustained first by the locality of the Taleworld and later by the appearance in it of the storyteller as a character. Both alternatives support Algy's presentation of self as storyteller by marking the centrality of the self.

The twentieth and last story of Set I breaks the patterns developed in the preceding nineteen stories: the movement of time from the past toward the present, the movement in space from here elsewhere, and the change in characters from others to self. In time, the story shifts into the present, breaking out of the past though continuing the direction of movement forward in time. In place, the story also continues the direction of movement but too far, to Leeds, a large town in the north of England. In person, the story reverses the pattern of movement toward the self by shifting to contemporaries, that is, to persons who live in the same spacetime, but whom the storyteller never sees face-to-face. For the nonce, Algy sets himself outside the Taleworld with the rest of the participants in the storytelling occasion. This closing story is neither an anecdote about other persons nor a story about oneself but the report of an account in the newspaper of a witchcraft-exorcism trial. Its pertinence to the occasion is sustained by time, in a way that is perhaps characteristic of news, its mere currency constitutes its relevance. The trial is not just in the present, it is going on now.

16. Susan Ervin-Tripp, "On Alternation and Co-occurrence", in Directions in Sociolinguistics, ed., John Gumperz and Dell Hymes (New York: Holt, Rinehart, and Winston, Inc., 1972) pp. 213-250.

Witchcraft Exorcism Trial
(Story 20)

Evaluation	A:	But what- about queerness- what about this- this chap who uh
		um
		had been attending black magic- have you read it?
		And
Temporal Orientation		in the last week or so
	K:	O I haven't read it at all.
		What is it- tell me something
[[	A:	Well he- he and his wife were attending witchcraft sessions.
Spatial Orientation	K:	Where?
	M,J:	(He he he)
	A:	Not just here.
Spatial Orientation	M:	Yes Leeds I think.
	A:	Leeds.
	K:	Um.
	A:	All right?
		And uh
Evaluation		then he found that it was getting a bit beyond him.
	MF:	((Clears throat))
		and- a Methodist Chap
		/
		and he said look I am possessed of the devil you better do something about it.
		And they gave him-
		you've read this haven't you?-
		seven hours solid
		in the vestry floor
Evaluation	K:	For God's sake.
	A:	Yeah.
	K:	Exorcising huh?
	A:	Yeah.
Evaluation		But you see it didn't work all that well because he
		got up in a trance at seven o'clock in the morning
		and
Evaluation		went and murdered his wife in a diabolical way
		....

This story evokes more evaluation by both teller and hearers than any other in the story system. Setting the account outside their circle of acquaintance or forebears, and outside their familiar geographies, appears also to set it outside their shared attitudes. Anecdotes assume shared attitudes and go on to disclose information about what has happened whereas what happens in news stories invites disclosure of information about attitudes, including the teller's.[17] Hence, the evaluations. Unlike the other stories, this one is arguably not altogether under the teller's control.

Closure of Story Set I appears to be a result of these breaks in pattern. Up to now it has been clear how Algy and other storytellers might jointly or severally continue to elaborate the Taleworld. But this story draws the Taleworld away in person and place from the realm hitherto elaborated. So conversationalists appear to have difficulty finding stories which are continuations of that Taleworld and also second or serial to this story. Instead, they go on to discuss and evaluate witchcraft, psychaitrists, seances, drugs, to do other readings, and to look at photographs and artefacts over the next half hour. During this period two brief and isolated anecdotes, (numbers twenty-one and twenty-two) are recounted, these remaining subordinate to the ongoing talk. (Figure 20 shows the patterns of person, place, and time in Story Set I.)

17. This suits Basel Bernstein's distinction between restricted and elaborated code speakers. News stories address a broad audience whose values are not known; anecdotes come up in small groups already drawn into some relation. Bernstein, "Social Class, Language and Socialization" in Language and Social Context, ed., Pier Paolo Giglioli (Middlesex, England: Penguin, 1972), pp. 157-178.

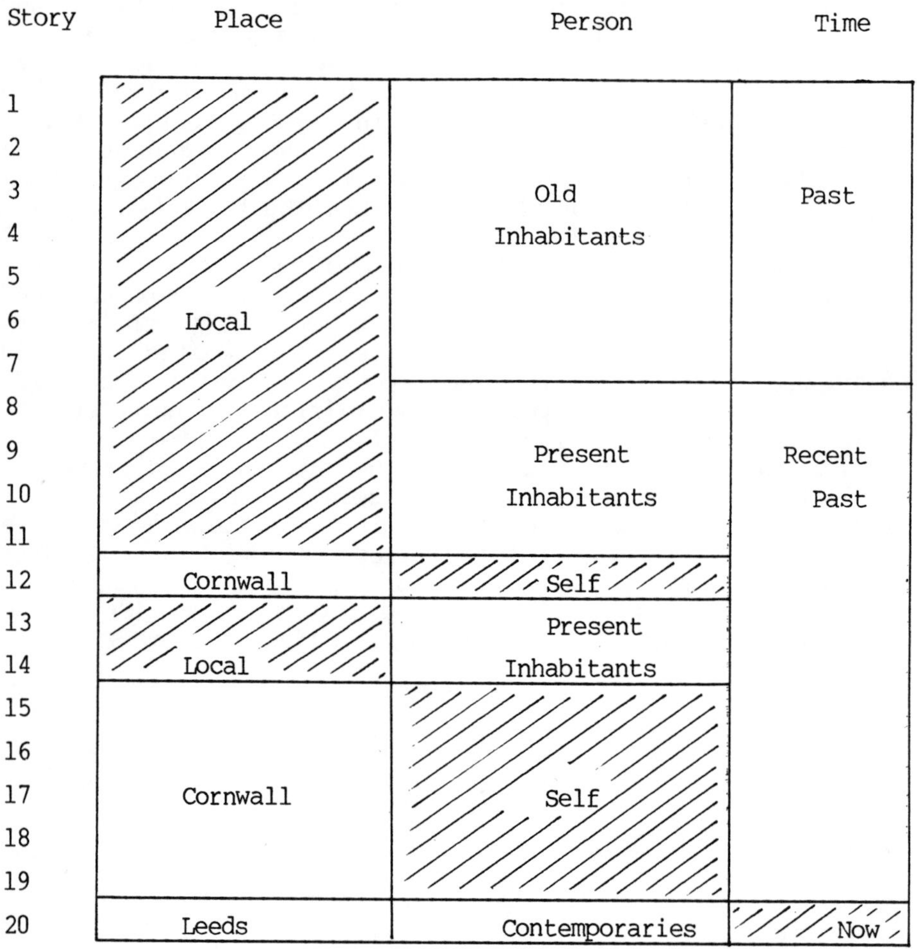

Story	Place	Person	Time
1			
2			
3		Old	Past
4		Inhabitants	
5			
6	Local		
7			
8			
9		Present	Recent
10		Inhabitants	Past
11			
12	Cornwall	Self	
13	Local	Present	
14		Inhabitants	
15			
16			
17	Cornwall	Self	
18			
19			
20	Leeds	Contemporaries	Now

Figure 20: Patterns of Person, Place, and Time in Story Set I.
(Shaded sections sustain relevance.)

Story Set II: Presentation of Character as Self

The stories in Set II start off with the self, here, and now. Algy tells a story in four episodes about helping a Canadian film crew make a film about ferreting: the art of catching rabbits by putting a ferret in one hole in the warren and netting the rabbit (and the ferret) as he comes out another.

Ferreting
(Stories 23-6,
2 of 4 episodes)

Personal/ Spatial Orientation	A:	We never told you about the Canadian film unit that came here to take- well first of all they came to take um country scenes and rabbiting was one of them- ferreting.
	K:	Um.
	MF:	Yeah.
Personal Orientation	A:	And I said to David French for God's sake get a rabbit before you come
	MF:	Um.
	A:	Because um
Temporal Orientation		I said we don't want to mess about in the winter-
Temporal Orientation		there weren't all that number of rabbits in those days.
	MF:	Yeah.
	A:	And he said right I will of course the so and so didn't on the morning of the film he came empty-handed with the ferrets and the nets.
	MF:	Mm.
	A:	Well we tried all the way uphill No rabbits. and it twas getting late and we
Spatial Orientation		went up the road beyond- as you come down- beyond Rowbrook House.
	MF:	Um.

Spatial
Orientation

A: And there's a ground belly there
and I said well try here
and everyone walked over it.
MF: Tss.
A: All of about twenty-five of this film unit.
MF: Yeah.
A: I said to the chap- director chap I said
waste of time
no rabbit's ever going to bolt from there
now.
M: (Ha ha ha)
K: (He he)
A: With all these people walking on it.
M: (He he)
A: And he said O-
well he said that's bad luck
They'd netted up- put the ferrets in out
came the rabbit.
And of course the camera man had been
poised for at least two hours.
M: (Ha)
A: Every time the ferret came up on the high
ground-
came to a net
chap had the camera all ready for the
rabbit you see and he-
he was so bored and-
and with a-
not with it that when the rabbit did come
out
[[MF: [he was nowhere near it.]
       [He wasn't ready.]
A: David French ran down the hill
caught the rabbit in the net
He went about twenty yards down the hill.
And-
and the chap said O- the cameraman-
please put it in again.
MF: (Ha ha ha) Nice.
K: ((Chuckle))
A: Can you imagine.
Yeah.
Please put it in again.
MF: ((Laughs))
A: I said don't be so bloody stupid you-
it'll never come out again.

All: ((Laughter)
  A: Well you can imagine a rabbit bolting twice
    (Ah ha)
    I said if you want to take it
 MF: ((Chuckles))

Spatial
Orientation   A: come down the road
    nearer the farm
    and

Spatial
Orientation   there's a pipe under the road
    and
    net it up both ends
    put the rabbit in- the ferret- and you
       might get a shot you see.
 MF: Tss.

Spatial
Orientation   A: Sure enough at Rowbrook House gate they did
       this
    and-
    actually what happened was
 MF: (he he)
  A: that chap with the camera
    poised
    net
    over one end
    David at the other end
    with the rabbit
    he held the rabbit cause he'd still got it
       in his arms you see.
    He put the rabbit in
    reached back for the ferret and the bloody
       rabbit came out
    and into the net and the
    cameraman only just got it there ((chuckles)).
 MF: ((He he he))
  A: Because it twas so quick.
    (Ha)
 MF: ((Chuckles))
  A: Let's see it-
    this is true-
    let's see it hop to freedom.
    They- we must have a film of it
    hopping to freedom.
    Well I said if you want that come out in
    the middle of

```
Spatial
Orientation              the plain field up there.
                         They you can see it
                         hopping
                         to freedom.
                         O no the stupid bugger said
                         put it down where we are.
                         I said you mean it really.
                 MF:     (Ha ha ha)
                  A:     I had the rabbit then.
                 MF:     (Ha ha ha)
                  A:     Yes drop it down Mr. May.
                 MF:     (Ha ha)
                  A:     Put it down.
                 MF:     ((Chuckles))
                  A:     Ooo I said are you sure-
                         bloody cameraman-
                         I put it down and it shot there like that
                 MF:     ((Chuckles))
                  K:     (Ha ha)
                  A:     Went straight into a gorse bush that was
                            the last [we saw of it. ]
            [[MF,M:                  [((Laughter)) ]
                  A:     Absolutely true.
                         [(Ho ho)          ]
            [[   MF:     [((Laughs))]
            [[    A:     [I swear it's perfectly true. ]
                         We got a fiver for that.
```

The presentation of self as storyteller in Set I underpins
the presentation of a character in Set II who is himself, a
self appearing in his own time and place. Framing this second
presentation as storytelling, not self-description, insulates
it from imputations of immodesty. The storyteller achieves
license to talk about himself in the guise of telling stories.
Two presentations of self at what Alfred Schutz calls different
degrees of directness are thus laminated together.[18] The

18. Schutz, p. 190.

inner lamination of self as character in the story sketches in the possibilities for a broader presentation, but one only indirectly available through the medium of the story. The outer lamination of self as storyteller is a narrowly specified presentation but one directly available to the storytelling occasion. The set-up permits the storyteller to elaborate a second self in a realm over which he has considerable demesne.

The half hour hiatus between the first story set and the second supports the view that the second set is not a continuation of the first but a next move. The patterns of persons and time continue in the directions suggested, presenting a self in the present, but the pattern of place reverses, moving back here from elsewhere. Place in the first of these stories is not just local, it is Algy's own farm, Rowbrook, and the place remains the storyteller's own farm, even when Algy is not the storyteller, for nine stories. The tenth is also the storyteller's own place but the place is California and the time has switched back to the recent past. It is an anecdote I put in about my own family to offer a realm I felt to be roughly commensurate with the ones Algy and the other storytellers were presenting.

Algy inserts the last story of Set II after farewells have begun to be taken. Its introduction after storytelling might have been supposed to be over is indicated and excused by what Sacks and Shegloff call a misplacement marker.[19] This arrangement, they suggest, achieves for an utterance so placed the status of an afterthought.[20] So it is told with the intention of making it the closing story on this occasion.

Going Jiggoty
(Story 33)

```
Misplacement
Marker          A:   I know what I meant to tell you Miles
Personal/             You know where the- you- you saw canon Hall
Spatial                    ┌there in-
Orientation  ⌈⌈ M:      ⌈(                              )⌉
```

19. Emmanuel Schegloff and Harvey Sacks, "Opening up Closings", in Ethnomethodology ed., Roy Turner (Middlesex, England; Penguin, 1974), p. 258.
20. Schegloff and Sacks, p. 260.

```
                          A:   in the hall.
Temporal                  A:  ⌈Yesterday.
Orientation      [[      MF:  ⌊Yeah ((chuckles)).⌉
                          J:  ⌈(                              )⌉
                 [[       A:  ⌊Well
                 [[           ⌊his best story I didn't tell you.⌋
                         MF:   O good.
                          K:   Um.
                          A:   No
Personal                       this is really true and he's probably the
Orientation                         only man
                               that could- well not the only one cause
                               there're
                               others- but there're very few people that
                               know the
                                    meaning of it.
                               Um
                 [[       J:  ⌈(    )
                          A:  ⌊He met⌋somebody
Spatial                        in Poundsgate.
Orientation                    Just coming into Poundsgate
Temporal                       many years ago.
Orientation                    And well he said Jan or whatever his same
                                    was
                               what have you been doing today.
                               O he said uh
Spatial                        took bullocks down to S- uh Stokingham.
Orientation                    Uh it's forty miles away I think.
                         MF:   Yeah.
                          A:   Yeah.
                               Ho um
                               yes and-
                               and I've just come back jiggoty.
                         MF:   Jiggoty.
                          A:   Yeah and uh
                               Canon Hall said
                               O what's that.
Temporal                       And this is
Orientation                    some years ago mind.
                               He- he said you know jiggoty pole.
                               And apparently
                               what they do is
```

in all the roads they were
travelling you see
and you had this pole
and its like a scout's
staff
and you
do a little run and you go round it.
So really you- you're doing a-
you do about four- five yards at a time

Spatial
Orientation

and you can come back from Stokingham
jiggoty.
And still be in quite good fettle to
talk to Canon Hall (He he he)

K: (Ha ha)

Temporal
Orientation

A: in the evening.
Yeah.

K: That's extraordinary.

A: Come jiggoty.
And I mentioned this to somebody- no Canon
    Hall told me-
and they said O yes but-

Personal
Orientation
Spatial
Orientation

um somebody else told me this-
um Farmer Norrish
over at S- uh Middle Stoke-
he was the last man that went jiggoty to
    Ashburton Fair.
Yeah.
So it twas quite a-
a means of going about.

[[MF: Yeah.

K: Sounds really lovely.

A: Apparently you
run round it-
well you've seen kids play haven't you.

K: No

[[A: I haven't
    Haven't you? I have I've seen

Temporal
Orientation

at- I remember as a boy seeing
children sort of getting a pole and running
    on it but
it was a means of transport.
It helped you along- well I can see that
because

```
              when you think you see you
              put it down and you do two little steps and
                  you
    MF:  ((Clears throat))
     A:  land about 0
          quite a bit further on.
          I suppose your arms get tired.
          Anyhow you come back jiggoty.
       J:  (                     )
  [[       [                        ]
       A:  (                     )
     K:  Hm.
     A:  You don't remember that old
          nursery rhyme
          to market to market
          to buy a fat pig
          home again home again
          jiggoty jig.
    MF:  Unhuh.
     A:  Have you heard that one?
    MF:  No.
     A:  Well
          I think you'll find it's the same thing.
```

The story, "Going Jiggoty", reverses two patterns, person and time, and retains the third, the geographical locality on which its continuity depends. Such reversals are characteristic of closing stories of both sets. The reversals are accomplished by layering together the present, Miles and my meeting with Canon Hall, the recent past, Algy's meeting with Canon Hall, and the past, Canon Hall's meeting with the man who went jiggoty. These meetings link ourselves with a consociate and him with a predecessor. The layering thus gives the story almost the temporal depth and personal breadth of the story system, while containing that system in space. Instead of being related to an adjacent story, this one harks back to and reiterates what its teller perceives as thematic to the storytelling occasion. One speculation suggests itself: was Algy searching for something to offer which he would regard as folklore, namely, the nursery rhyme, and along with it an etiology I might not otherwise come across?

Story II picks up and plays out two of the patterns unfolded over Set I, a self in the present, but reverses the direction of place, moving back not only into local geography but onto his (or the other storytellers') own place. In the end, the self as character appears in a Taleworld that is here and now. Figure 21 shows patterns of person, place, and time in Story Set II.)

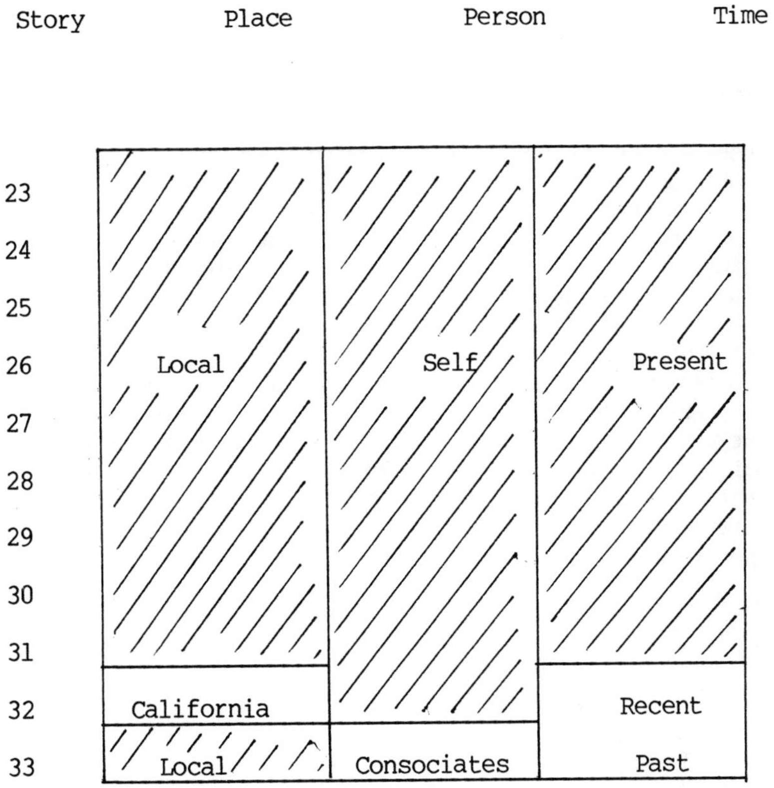

Story	Place	Person	Time

23			
24			
25			
26	Local	Self	Present
27			
28			
29			
30			
31			
32	California		Recent
33	Local	Consociates	Past

Figure 21: Patterns of Person, Place, and Time in Story Set II.
(Shaded sections sustain relevance.)

Despite their transformations of pattern, the two story sets operate together as a system that unfolds a self. The perspective of the self on the events in the Taleworld shifts systematically over the course of the storytelling occasion. Evidence for the events in the first seven stories is hearsay and hearsay at several removes from the storyteller. He was, that is, not only not present to the events, but also not present in the world in which those events transpired, though his predecessors purport to have been present. He has heard stories about these events and these are his retellings. Evidence for the next four stories and for stories thirteen, fourteen, and twenty, is also hearsay but a degree more direct: the events transpire in a spacetime the storytellers actually inhabit though they were not present at the time. They hear the stories about them from persons who were present. Evidence for the twelfth story, and for stories fifteen through nineteen, is eye-witness evidence. The storyteller is present to the events he or she recounts. This contrast between hearsay and eye-witness evidence in Set I is transformed in Set II into the first moves of a more delicately differentiated series of modulations of perspective. Evidence for the events in stories twenty-three through thirty-one is of a third kind, it is direct: the storyteller enacts the events. The character of the stories shifts from what can be called tales (1-7) through anecdotes (8-11, 13-14, 20, 33) to personal experience narratives (12, 15-19, 23-32), with these changes of perspective. (Figure 22 shows shifts of genre.)

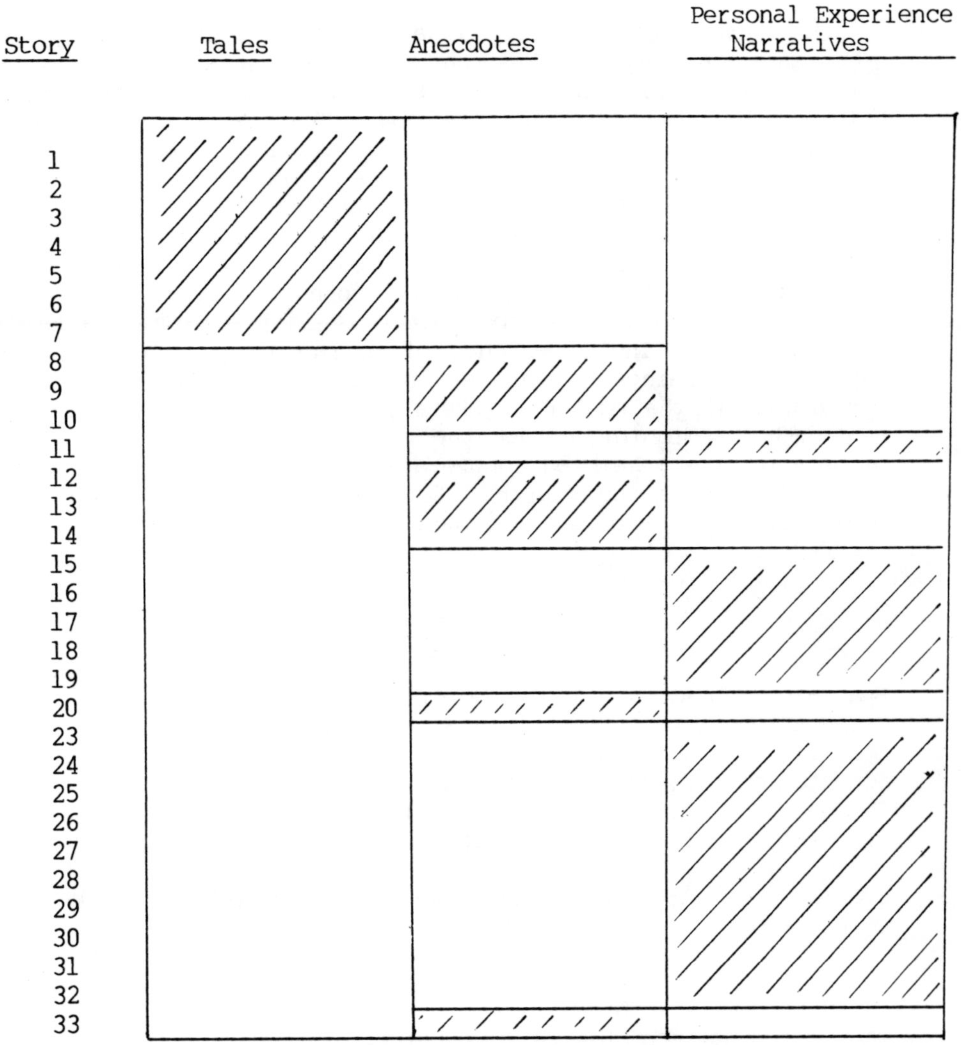

Figure 22: Genre Shift over Story System.

The Trickster Cycle

The presentation of self as a character is informed by the appearance the story takes on of a trickster cycle.[21] The first half dozen stories are set in a preternatural world before things were as they are now. That world opens with a cosmic catastrophe, the lightening striking, continues with curious food, snails, and the prince's dalliances. Supernatural beings appear in the fourth story in the form of pixies who enchant a young lad and turn him into stone, the result of this transformation remaining in a local rock formation. The fifth story is also connected in a legend-like manner to the local geography but only in the form of a name: Hangman's Pit. The appearance of extraordinary, magical, and supernatural beings culminates in the sixth story with the appearance of the master trickster, the Devil himself. In the year 1638, lightening struck the village church killing several members of the assembled congregation, an event attested to by a placque inside the church. It came to be supposed that the Devil had come to collect his own.

The Devil at Tavistock Inn
(Story 6)

Spatial Orientation	A:	You know the story about the thunderstorm at Widecome don't you.
Spatial Orientation	[[J: K:	[Yes] [At the church.
Temporal Orientation	[[A: K:	Sixteen[thirty-eight.] [Yeah.
		Yeah.
Spatial Orientation	A:	Chap called down here at Tavistock Inn do you know?

---

21. For a description of the trickster cycle see Paul Radin, The Trickster (New York: Schocken Books, 1972). For the extent of its applicability here I am indebted to an insight of Brian Sutton-Smith's. See his and David M. Abrams, "The Development of the Trickster in Children's Narratives", Journal of American Folklore 90 (1977), p. 30.

```
            Did you know that.
            Devil?
    MF:     Before he went.
     K:     O did he.
            O I didn't know that.
     A:     Course he did.
    MF:     Um.
     A:     Called there for a drink.
    MF:     On the way
     K:     O.
     A:     up there and he asked
            can you-
            do you know the way to Widecombe?
            Bloke called yeah.
            Straight on there Master.
            He was on a horse you see and-
            black cloak and everything.
            He paid for the drink
            and um before-
            O he drank it up and there was a sizzling
                noise.
   All:     ((Laughter))
     A:     Then he paid for it
            and rode off.
```

Personal
Orientation
```
            When the landlady-
            Mrs. Foley- ((the present proprietress))
   All:     ((Laughter))
     A:    .Mrs. Foley's relation
   All:     ((Laughter))
     A:     picked the money up-
            twas a bundle of leaves.
            In the-┌in the┐saucer.
[[    K:         └Aaah.┘
     A:     Um.
            And then the thunderstorm started....
```

Folktale-like motifs give these stories their preternatural character: the killing of one of three brothers sleeping all in a row, the malevolence of cosmic forces like lightening, the old women surviving on unnatural food, the young woman confined to her cottage to protect her virtue, the magical transformations, the gypsy's trick, the drink sizzling in the Devil's throat and his money turning to leaves. Such a world is properly inhabited by tricksters in the form of preternatural forces, witch-like women, princes and maidens, the piskies, the gypsy, and the Devil.

As the Taleworld moves forward in time, this preternatural
realm gives way in a trickster cycle to a world that is
ordinary but perverse. The trickster figure in the next
fourteen stories becomes, fittingly, the victim or dupe of a
world out of control, like the school teacher in the seventh
story whose minute salary is docked by the inspector for
whimsical infringements. The trickster-as-dupe is personified
by Foxy, the eccentric vicar, introduced in the eighth story:
he casts the ashes from his first cremation into the air over
the churchyard but the wind blows them out onto unconsecrated
ground; he hitches his surplice to the roof of his Bentley and
drives off wearing a deerstalker but the wind snatches the
surplice up and blows it away onto the moor; in honor of an old
ritual, he rolls a cartwheel off the top of a tor into the
river but it is crushed by new trees before it ever gets there;
he tries to fix a generator in the church but the flywheel
comes off, strikes him in the head and knocks him out cold. It
is in the story following on from this one that Algy first
appears as a character, but one peripheral to the events. He
and his wife, Jean, are in a sunken lane in Cornwall when the
flywheel comes off a tractor, skims over the lane, and just
misses their heads, thus providing another class of perversity
tale: narrow escapes. He is here using a version of Sacks'
rule that a second storyteller examine the character in a first
story, then find a second story in which he appears as the same
character.[22] In the next story Bill Hamlyn drops a giant
spool of telephone cabling off the top of a hill and in the
fourteenth story Bill Hamlyn's father chases off after a hare
on his tractor, ruining the furrows he has spent the day
plowing. Here, the hare may foreshadow the reappearance of the
trickster figure in the fifteenth story in the person of
Michael, the carthorse.

Michael and the Hay
(Story 15)

	J: Tell them about um mm Harold
Spatial	Bluett darling in Cornwall
Orientation	and uh-
	[[A: [Yes.] and Michael the horse.

22. Sacks (1970), Lecture 5, p. 16.

J: Um.
   (They'd like to know.)
A: This is true.

Spatial
Orientation

There was a great big carthorse in Cornwall
got out on the common.
Can you help me catch my horse yes I said I
will.
Caught it
brought it in.

Temporal
Orientation
Temporal
Orientation

This is about um April I should think.
Or May perhaps.
About May.

MF: ((Clears throat))
A: He says I'm going to-
   be making hay you see?
   I don't want any trouble with him catching
        him
   he says I'm going to keep it in now.
   Well as it happened ((chuckles)) to be a
        very wet summer.

Personal/
Spatial
Orientation

Now I used to take the milk up from our farm
up to
outside Harold Bluett's place
where
Michael was.
And (he he he) I see
Bluett coming down with a
sack of grass on his back every morning you
     know-

MF: Ha.
A: toiling down
   to feed Michael.
K: ((Chuckles))
A: And that wasn't the only time of the day he
        used to
   do it about three times a day.
   And he mowed
   this-
   mowed the grass

Temporal
Orientation

with a scythe of course in those days there
        was nothing new in

        mowing grass with a scythe.
        He mowed this
        grass
        loaded it into a sack and took it down to
            Michael.
        Twas a very wet summer.
        And
        May went down.
        June went- June came p- ((chuckles)) past
        still no bloody hay weather.
        Michael was still in the stables
        Bluett scything like a
    MF: (He he)
     A: stupid bugger every day or
        three times a day
        feeding Michael he'd mowed the first field
  MF,K: ((Chuckle))
     A: without making hay at all.
     K: Ho no.
     A: Feeding Michael.
        No it's absolutely true.
     K: (Ha ha)
     A: There wasn't a blade of grass on this.
        And
        he'd fed it to Michael to help
        pull the hay wagon what?
     K: (Ha ha)
    MF: ((Chuckles))
     J: He was a lovely horse wasn't he.
     A: Great big fat horse hm.

Algy re-enters this story as witness to these events, his ongoing presence lending credence to the absurdly elaborated labors of the farmer to feed the horse he might, had he but known, have left to crop the field for himself. The sixteenth story is about a similarly mischievous piece of Michael's behavior, if it is possible to attribute such an intention to a horse. The next two stories introduce as trickster an idiot called "Not 'Xactly", whose nickname means not exactly right in the head. The first story shows his odd incompetence with a cigarette and the second his equally odd skill at conveying village gossip. The trickster figure in the nineteenth story is a pony called Polly who runs away with Jean in a trap over rougher and rougher ground and through narrower and narrower gates until there is nothing left of the trap, though the pony, and her driver, are quite intact. In the twentieth story, the tricksters are the witch and his antagonists, the priests and the psychaitrists. The appearance of these liminal figures as tricksters, the hare, the horses, the idiot, the witch, the priests, and the psychaitrists completes the perversity tales, stories from a world in which objects, animals, and finally, persons behave perversely, the perversity becoming increasingly intentional with the shift toward animacy.

This enhancement of control ushers in the last stage of the trickster cycle in which the trickster tames chaos. In the twenty-third story, the trickster takes on his final transformation, as the culture hero, the man of special knowledge and power in his world, a world now known, controlled and accountable. In the four episodes about ferreting, a contrast is set up between natives and foreigners. The natives appear skilled, knowledgeable, and clever while the foreigners are ignorant, inept, and stupid. The animals, especially the rabbit, still retain a trickster-like perversity. The locals, especially Algy, display native shrewdness, while the Canadian film crew appear as city bumpkins. The twenty-seventh story, about Marian shearing a sheep, has the same distribution of values except the animal trickster disappears, heightening the contrast between the clever countrymen and the city bumpkins. The culture hero's control over the natural world culminates in a set of three stories about handling dogs, the animals who have been tricksters now being mastered. The stories consist of a good deal of dog-training lore attached to brief incidents, both displaying the teller's mastery.

Excerpt from Dog-training Stories
(Stories 28 - 30)

A: And I've had all sorts a-
this isn't a bad dog you just (hold) him
here.

Personal
Orientation

We call him The Driver you can't go anywhere
unless he sits in the landover.
MF: Ts.
A: And uh (he)
(Hm) yeah and when you're not in it he's
out there in it
waiting for you to go somewhere.
MF: Ts.
A: But um-
O he's a useful dog.
But the trouble with (him) is
K: ((Chuckles))

```
              A:   if you're going to get a dog
                   hard enough to stop a Scotty ewe
        [[ MF:   Yeah. ]
        [[  A:   [or a ]lamb[for ]that matter he's too hard
           MF:        [Yeah]
              A:   to be any good you see.
              A:   These all retreat.
             MF:   Yeah.
              A:   And a bloody good thing they do.
Spatial            Took ages up there tonight trying to catch
Orientation          a-
                   a lamb that was out over the fence.
                   And uh
                   only because the dogs wouldn't stand.
             MF:   Yeah.
              A:   I had
                   three dogs
                   wouldn't stand.
                   Every time the lamb approached them
                   they just parted or ran away you see and
                       the lamb went on
                   But um
                   if you got a dog hard enough to stand
                   for a
                   sheep or a lamb
                   then he's not much bloody good because he's
                       too rough you see
                   That's the thing.
             MF:   Yeah.
```

The trickster cycle can be seen as the acquisition of control over preternatural chaos. (Figure 23 shows the Trickster Cycle.)

Story	Action	Character	Genre
1	Catastrophe-Natural	Human Victims	Preternatural Tales
2			
3	Perversity	Supernaturals	
4	Magic	Supernatural Trickster	
5	Perversity	Gypsy Trickster	
6	Magic	Supernatural Trickster	
7		Trickster as Dupe	
8			
9			
10			
11	Narrow Escapes		
12			
13			
14			
15	Perversity		Perversity Tales
16			
17			
18			
19	Narrow Escapes		
20	Catastrophe-Unnatural	Supernatural Trickster	
23			
24		Trickster as Hero	
25	Mastery of Animal World		
26			Tales of Mastery
27			
28			
29			
30			
31	Perversity		
32	Mastery of Social or Natural World		
33			

Figure 23: The Trickster Cycle.

Algy's presentation of self as character lies along the contours of the trickster cycle in such a way that his appearance as an actor in the stories coincides with the emergence of the culture hero.[23] In the preternatural world, he does not appear at all. In the world of liminal beings, he appears as a peripheral character. And in the world of power, he appears as a central figure, the character of Algy thus taking color from his appearance as and with the trickster as culture hero.

Of course, a story system that takes on the appearance of a trickster cycle is idiosyncratic to this occasion. What might be regarded as generic is the development of the self as a character over the course of a storytelling occasion, rather than in a single story, and, as a consequence of this extended development, a character that modulates and changes. The possibilities for presentation of self as character are enriched by its evolution over a storytelling occasion.

The organization of this presentation of self parallels the pattern of breaks and continuities at other levels of analysis in the stories. Person, place, and time, genre shift, and the unfolding trickster cycle are similarly punctuated. The seventh story about the inspecter and the school teacher is the pivotal story in the shift from past to present and from predecessors to consociates, from tales to anecdotes and from the preternatural world to the perverse. The twelfth story, "Algy and the Flywheel," marks the shift from a local geography to Cornwall, from others to self, and from anecdotes to personal experience narratives. The twentieth story, about witchcraft and exorcism, loses both geographies, switches to contemporaries, the present, and reports of written narratives. The twenty-third story, opening the second set, regains a local geography, recovers a self, returns to personal experience narrative, and presents the culture hero. The thirty-third and closing story retains its local geography and shifts to anecdotes, other people, and the recent past, this constituting the last appearance of the culture hero. The formal characteristics of the storytelling occasion inform its content. (Figure 24 relates patterns of breaks and continuities at different levels of analysis.)

23. See Alan Dundes, "Texture, Text, and Context", <u>Southern Folklore Quarterly</u> 28 (1964), pp. 215-265, p. : "The structure of the context (social situation) ....is paralled by the structure of the text used in that context."

Story	Place	Person	Time	Genre	Prospect
1					
2					
3					
4					
5					
6		Predecessor	Past	Tale	Preternatural Perversity
7		Consociate	Recent Past	Anecdote	
8					
9					
10	Local				
11	Cornwall	Other		Anecdote	
12		Self		Personal Experience Narrative	
13					
14					
15					
16				Personal Experience Narrative	
17			Recent Past		
18		Self			
19	Cornwall	Other	Now	Report	Perversity
20	Elsewhere	Self		Personal Experience Narrative	Mastery
23	Here				
24					
25					
26					
27					
28					
29					
30			Present	Personal Experience Narrative	
31		Self	Recent Past		
32		Other	Past	Anecdote	
33					

Figure 24: Pattern of Breaks and Continuities at different Levels of Analysis in Story System.

The self being presented by the story system is laminated inside the Taleworld. However, by a series of local modulations, each having its own significance, the Taleworld arrived at by the second story set is not far removed from the world of everyday life.[24] The likenesses between the Taleworld and the ordinary one "...allow meaning to leak from one context to another along the formal similarities that they show," writes Mary Douglas.[25] They permit the insertion of a self in one realm via its insertion in the other. The self laminated in the story leaks into the situation so that although that self can be detached from its presenter, it cannot be altogether disclaimed. And, in this instance, the laminated self is not only claimed but celebrated.[26]

The Storyrealm has also become pervious to the conversation in which it is an enclave. The multiple frames of both Taleworld and Storyrealm which set off the stories at the outset have been attentuated over the course of the occasion so that by the dog-training stories near the end, these realm-status markers have almost disappeared, and storytelling has become almost indistinguishable from conversation. Both Taleworld and Storyrealm have thus become transparent to the world of everyday life. I have spoken as if the storytelling occasion were a single realm. In fact, it consists of a cluster or array of realms which partially coalesce: the Taleworld, the Storyrealm, the conversation itself, its geographical setting, its historical period, in short, the unfolding world of everyday life, of which conversation is an aspect. Hence, Algy May's status as a character in the stories enhances his status as a storyteller on the occasion, and both of these enhance his status as a person in everyday life. Multiple selves, laminated together during storytelling, thus come to affect each other.[27] Interrelated presentations appear in disparate realms.

24. See Georges, p. 319, on "the significance of discernible correspondences and noncorrespondences that can be said to exist between the whole storytelling event or any one or more of its aspects and the total social structure or any one or more of its aspects ...."
25. Mary Douglas, Rules and Meanings Middlesex, England: Penguin, 1973), p. 13.
26. Peter Seitel devises a related three-realm analysis for proverbs consisting of 1) the occasion on which the proverb is used, 2) the imaginary situation presented in the proverb, and 3) the social situation to which the proverb refers. Seitel, "Proverbs: A Social Use of Metaphor", Genre 2:2 (1969).
27. See Georges, p. 318, on multiple social identities.

CHAPTER FOUR

JOINT STORYTELLING:
Discourse and Interaction*

The analysis of narrative at the level of discourse, that is, relationships among words, can be contrasted and related to the analysis of narrative at the level of interaction, that is, relationships among participants in the storytelling occasion. Both analyses are concerned with aspects of the Storyrealm. Such an approach to narrative analysis moves away from performance theory to develop a systemic model out of interaction theory. Arrangements by storytellers in conversation to take an extended turn at talk in order to tell a story have been supposed to result in continuous narration by a single narrator. Hence, the attraction of the performance model. However, it turns out that narration is not continuous nor are narrators singular. Instead, a story transfix at the level of discourse holds across the story's mutual construction at the level of interaction.

Performance Theory

Performance theories of folklore regard stories as situated communication.[1] The story or text is taken as an aspect of discourse framed as performance, and the storytelling event is taken as an aspect of interaction enacted by a performer.

* A version of this paper was given at the 1977 American Folklore Society Meetings in Detroit, Michigan. I would like to thank Dell Hymes for an acute critical reading of that version which helped me re-see and re-write it, and at the same time to absolve him of responsibility for the result. The paper was published in Cahiers de Litterature Orale 15 (1984).

1. Richard Bauman, in "Context in Contemporary Folklore", Unpublished Lecture at the University of Pennsylvania (Philadelphia: 1978) calls texts the "thin and partial record of deeply situated human behavior."

Because the story is part of discourse and the storyteller a participant in the conversation, some of the organization of the story must be directed to its performance in conversation.

Conversation is organized around turntaking.[2] A turn typically consists of a single utterance at the completion of which other participants are entitled or expected to take a turn. An utterance is a complete spoken unit which can be, but is not necessarily, a complete grammatical sentence. In conversations involving more than two persons, the mechanics of turntaking can be quite complex, but in principle each participant is equally entitled to take a turn. Between two persons, again with qualifications, turntaking is in principle even-handed. For storytelling, some transmutation of these egalitarian expectations occurs. Stories consist of at least two necessarily sequenced clauses.[3] For that reason, they take more than one utterance to complete.[4] However, other participants expect to take their turn on completion of a single utterance. So storytellers must arrange to take an extended turn in order to tell a story. This adjustment at the discourse level can be described at the level of interaction as a shift from mere participant in the conversation to "the specialized and functionally differentiated role of raconteur and storyteller", as Erving Goffman expresses it.[5] It is

2. For a close description, see Emmanuel Schegloff and Harvey Sacks, "Opening up Closings", Ethnomethodology, ed. Roy Turner (Middlesex, England: Penguin, 1974), p. 236. Also Harvey Sacks, Emanuel Schegloff, and Gail Jefferson, "A Simplest Systematics for the Organization of Turntaking in Conversation," Language 50 (1974), pp. 696 - 735.
3. William Labov, "The Transformation of Experience in Narrative Syntax", Language in the Inner City (Philadelphia: University of Pennsylvania Press, 1972), p. 360: "With this conception of narrative, we can define a minimal narrative as a sequence of two clauses which are temporally ordered: that is, a change in their order will result in a change in the temporal sequence of the original semantic interpretation."
4. Harvey Sacks, Unpublished Lectures (Irvine: Spring, 1970) Lecture Two.
5. Erving Goffman, Frame Analysis (New York: Harper and Row, 1974), p. 438.

these arrangements that have been supposed to result in
continuous narration by a single narrator. Consider in this
light the following instance of storytelling in conversation.

I am spending Wednesday afternoon, the 26th of March, 1975,
with Florence Brown at Dunstone Cottage, one of a cluster of
cottages near the village. Mrs. Brown is seventy-seven, short,
round-bodied, round-faced, and merry. She and her husband,
Jack, also short, merry, and apple-cheeked, with a round belly
and bandy legs, are still living in the cottage in which they
raised their eleven children. One of the children was named
after the nephew of a farmer called Alford Bickle, for whom Jack
worked as a young man. She has been telling me about Alford
Bickle's suicide. The transcription comes in on her acount of
his first suicide attempt, followed by the story of the suicide
itself. In the middle of that story her husband, Jack, comes
home. He says something at the cottage door, calls to his wife,
then registers my presence in the shadowy kitchen by saying,
"Well landsakes." During all this Mrs. Brown is trying to tell
her story. The next two minutes of joint interaction are of
interest here. In story and conversation, Mrs. Brown calls her
husband "Father." (In the transcription, "B" is Mrs. Brown, "K"
is myself, and "J" is Jack Brown.)*

```
     B:  Well Father went in
         he said on the day or day after.
         Father was out having his dinner.
         He thought he heard somebody up over in the loft
  5      and he went up.
         There was the old man with a mm rope
         in he's hand he was looking about for a place to hang up
              this-
         put this rope up
 10      to hang heself.=
     K:  Heaven's sake.
     B:  Yes we got un down he said look- look he said you-
         you got to stay with you-
         come on he said you go on in with your sister.
 15      So he goes in and he said to her-
         to his sister he said-
         he said you keep your brother in he said
         he isn't fit to be out he said
         he's gone in the loft
 20      and uh
```

*See transcription devices in appendix.

```
            just took away a rope from him.
            O dear dear she said come in Alford come in you mustn't
                 do that= well we went but-
            we come but a day or two after
   25       uh Father went down to the farm
            so he said uh
            heard this gun go off.
            I went and I looked at those little (            ).
            So anyway come up the road ┌and I ┐
   30 ⌈⌈J:                              └(    )┘ bloody secret.
      ⌈⌈B: ┌come up┐the road hey?
        J: └Here. ┘
        B: come up the road
      ⌈⌈J: ┌Well landsakes        ┐
   35 ⌈⌈B: └and on the road┘right there was old man with his face
                 blew away.
      ⌈⌈K: For heaven's┌sake.┐
        B:            └Yeah.┘
            Wasn't he Father.
   40 ⌈⌈    ┌I was right wasn't I.          ┐
        K: └What an extraordinary thing.  ┘
        B: Don't ye remember.
        J: Hoos hoos.
        B: Ooo Lordy won't hurt for a day or two.
   45 J: No ain't going to hurt anything I hope it twon't hurt
                 me.
        B: (Ha ha) Well?
        J: Well the bugger he sat- he sat on an hedge in the garden
            and he pushed the trigger with a forked stick.
   50 K: Really.=
        J: He missed himself the first time
        B: and he reloaded the gun.
        J: He took that cartridge out of the gun
            put it┌in his mouth┐
   55 ⌈⌈K:      └Heavens.    ┘
      ⌈⌈J: ┌and he      ┐
      ⌈⌈B: └put the┘cartridge in his┌mouth
        J:                          └put another cartridge in┘
            and he found the gun again-
   60       and that cartridge-
            he was buried with that one in his skull.
        K: For heaven's sake=
        J: Yeah.
        K: And the- he'd had one in his mouth and so that one
   65          exploded did it?
        J: Well it didn't- well no you see that was the one- the
      ⌈⌈      case┌of the one that exploded.┐
        B:       └Fired you see.            ┘
```

```
       K: [Well   ]
70 [[ J: [That ]he missed himself with.
       B: He missed hisself with the first one[so he reloaded.   ]
   [[ J:                                       [Twas just the case.]

       So he took him out=
    K: O I see.=
75  J: put it in his mouth
       and uh then fixed the trigger- fired the other trigger
       and then he[blew      ]his face right up.
   [[ K:          [Amazing.  ]
       B: And do you know he had to[leave the]
80 [[ J:                           [Well     ]
       the man's mad at that time[he must be ]gone wasn't him.
   [[ K:                         [Absolutely.]
       Yeah.
       J: [He was]mad then wasn't he.
85 [[ B: [Yeah. ]        [          ]
                          Well and then Father lived with the
              sister right on?
    K: Yeah.
    B: She only farmed about three months after.
90 [[   [and uh       ]
       J: [Three months]from this accident.
    B: Twelve months eh?
    J: Three months?
    B: How long did her carry on after you.
95  J: I was there four years.
    B: O yes course four years after.
       Then in the end her ha- hung herself.
```

Interaction Theory

Analysts of storytelling continue to be influenced by the expectation that narrators will be singular and texts discrete. William Labov devises an account of what he calls personal experience narratives which uncovers and elucidates the structure of apparently unstructured anecdotes.[6]

6. Labov, with Joshua Waletzky, "Narrative Analysis: Oral Versions of Personal Experience", Essays on the Verbal and Visual Arts, ed. June Helm (Seattle and London: University of Washington Press, 1967); Labov, Language in the Inner City; and Labov and David Fanshel, Therapeutic Discourse (New York, San Francisco, London: Academic Press, 1977).

(Footnote 6 Continued on Next Page)

However, the analysis excludes stories (like the one given) with interpositions not considered part of the narrative structure, and it excludes stories (again like that one) in which part of the narrative structure is contributed by others. A shift from performative to interactional accounts of the structure of stories discloses another perspective. Stories are mutually constructed by participants in the storytelling occasion.[7] Splitting these participants into teller and hearer disguises the systemic character of storytelling. As Ray Birdwhistell argues:[8]

> Whether studied from the point of view of the performance of a single actor or from the equally atomistic position of those who conceive of the world as made up of people who alternately speak and listen or move and watch, focus upon the actor and the reactor serves only to obscure the systematic properties of the scene.

Edward T. Hall considers this sort of atomism characteristic of western analysts.[9]

> Western culture has a habit of artificially separating events that really belong together. Talking and listening is just one example, for the two processes are intricately intertwined.

On an interactional analysis, the roles of teller and hearer are understood to be distributed among participants in the

(Footnote 6 Continued from Previous Page)

> Labov's intention to elicit the ordinary language of a given speaker skewed his original collection of narratives so that the analysis then devised for them retains some of the flaws of the elicitation procedure. Specifically, he preferred discrete texts by single narrators.

7. See Charles Goodwin, "The Interactive Construction of the Sentence Within the Turn at Talk in Natural Conversation", given at the American Anthropological Association Meetings in San Francisco (December, 1975), for an exquisite dissection of the influence of other participants on the speaker's utterance.
8. Ray Birdwhistell, Kinesics and Context (Philadelphia: University of Pennsylvania Press, 1970), p. 98.
9. Edward T. Hall, Handbook for Proxemic Research (Washington, D.C.: Society for the Anthropology of Visual Communication, 1974), p. 103.

storytelling, not uniquely lodged in any one of them. Robert
Georges describes the resulting storytelling system thus:[10]

> Once the storyteller begins to receive and decode the
> responses of the story listener and to interpret and
> respond to them as feedback, the storyteller and the
> story listener begin to shape the message jointly.

If the story is regarded as mutually constructed at the
level of interaction, at the level of discourse the story can
be seen as a transfix with multiple contributors. The framing
of discourse as narrative, that is to say, can hold for a span
of discourse even when it is formed by the interaction of
several participants. Narrative texts are not necessarily
discrete from the context of discourse. Rather, despite their
indiscreteness, spans of discourse can still be transfixed by
story frames. The analysis undertaken here will therefore
address both the designs that make the story hold together as a
transfix, and the differential contributions that articulate
its internal structure. Texts are embedded in contexts and
tellers implicated with hearers in a communication system. The
estrangement of text from context and teller from hearer is a
special -- and characteristically literary -- modulation of the
possibilities of storytelling.

Story Analysis I: Interaction

Since stories are worked into conversation as extended
turns, it might appear that taking any other turn during a
storytelling is, of its nature, an interruption. Despite this
appearance, stories told during conversation are, as Roger
Abrahams notes, peppered with utterances by other persons.[11]

10. Robert Georges, "Toward an Understanding of Storytelling
     Events", Journal of American Folklore 82 (1969), p. 322.
11. Roger Abrahams, "The Play of Worlds in Story and
     Storytelling," Unpublished Manuscript (University of
     Texas, Austin: 1977) pp. 24 and 25. See also Harvey
     Sacks, Unpublished Lectures on Storytelling in
     Conversation, Lecture VIII (Irvine, California: 4 June
     1970), p. 1: "Now it will radically mis-formulate what
     happens in stories to not appreciate both the fact that
     listeners do talk up in stories and that they may talk up
     in stories." Also Sacks, Lecture VII, part 2 (1970), p.
     8: "that people interrupt in a story, make comments, make
     sarcastic possibilities, make queries about the thing,
     etc., are not evidence of their trying into heckle down a
     story; they're evidence of the fact that they're
     listening."

Incidental utterances consist of parenthetical remarks or asides occurring during the course of the story or alongside remarks directed to it. For instance, after Jack Brown comes in, Mrs. Brown tries to engage him in the story she is telling by saying, "Don't ye remember", and Jack brushes her off with, "Hoos hoos", meaning something like "hush, hush". She takes him to be putting her off on account of a specific difficulty he has been having with his head and says, "Ooo Lordy won't hurt for a day or two", and he says, "No ain't going to hurt anything and I hope it twon't hurt me". Then she says, "Well?", and Jack picks up the story with

A: Well the bugger he sat- he sat on an hedge in the garden and he pushed the trigger with a forked stick.

The pair of utterances,

Aside   B: Ooo Lordy won't hurt for a day or two.
Aside   J: No ain't going to hurt anything and I hope it
             twon't hurt me

are asides, before and after which the story continues to unfold. These are understood to have no bearing on the narrative. They are enclaves of a different ontological status within the realm of the story.

Brief interpositions like 'hm' or 'yeah' uttered in the course of the story are clearly directed to it. Of these Goffman writes,[12]

> ....finding himself with a conversational slot to fill, the individual will often find that all he can muster up is a grunt or a nod. Timed and toned correctly, such a passing over of an opportunity for speech will be organizationally quite satisfactory, equivalent syntactically, in fact, to an extended utterance....

Passing over an opportunity to speak at length may, in fact, be requisite during storytelling. Brief interpositions are designed, Goffman continues, as forms of "encouragement, demonstrations of attentiveness, and other 'back channel' effects,":[13] these attention markers not being intended to

12. Goffman, p. 502.
13. Goffman, p. 509.

disrupt the flow of narrative. "Really" (line 50) registers awareness of what is going on and encourages its continuation. "Absolutely" (line 82) and "Yeah" (lines 83, 85, and 88) support the interpretation of the suicide (offered in lines 81 and 84) and so sustain the narration. Goffman describes these as back channel cues to speakers to keep going, which happen to have surfaced verbally.[14] Supportive communications of this kind can be non-verbal. Such cues, then, are to be understood as metacommunications about the story that is unfolding, not part of the story itself. How is it, though, that such remarks can be interposed in the storytelling without constituting an interruption?

Interruptions are of two orders: technical interruptions, that is, remarks which cut in on another speaker's utterance whether they count as interruptions or not, and thematic interruptions, that is, remarks which count as interruptions even if they do not cut in on another speaker's utterance. Technical interruptions are of three types: 1) premature starts, 2) simultaneous starts, and 3) mid-sentence starts. Premature starts are failures to observe the obligatory pause at the end of a turn, and include running over the tail of the previous utterance. (These are marked in the transcription by equal signs where the pause should have been.) For instance, as I finish speaking Jack Brown is already acknowledging my response (lines 62 and 63):

```
            K:  For heaven's sake=
Pre-start   J:  Yeah.
```

Pre-starts are designed to assure their user the next turn at talking, either in order to fit a remark into an ongoing discourse (as in line 10):

```
            to hang heself.=
Pre-start   K:  Heaven's sake.
```

or to recover the floor after such an interposition (as in line 46):

```
            K:  Really.=
Pre-start   J:  He missed himself the first time.
```

Successful pre-starts can exclude the utterance they would interrupt by cutting in ahead of it.

14. Goffman, Forms of Talk (Philadelphia: University of Pennsylvania Press, 1981), p. 28.

Simultaneous starts are failures to agree on whose turn it is to speak. Co-starts result in simultaneous speech in the course of which one or another speaker breaks off, thus according the other the floor. (Simultaneous speech is marked on the transcription by brackets.) For instance, Mrs. Brown asks her husband a question at the same time that I comment on her story (lines 37, 38, and 39). Since the remarks are simultaneous, one or both of them may be lost to hearers. Mrs. Brown corrects for this possibility by appending another question to engage her husband's attention, though, since her first question may nonetheless have been heard, not in the same words.

```
                [[B:  [I was right wasn't I                 ]
Co-starts         [K:  [What an extraordinary thing.]
                B:  Don't ye remember.
```

Later, when I find Jack Brown has started to speak at the same time I have, I break off (lines 69 and 70):

```
Co-starts [[K:  [Well ]
          [J:  [That ]he missed himself with.
```

Mid-sentence starts, starting to speak during someone else's turn, are of four kinds. The first, overlaid speech, consists of utterances inset to run after the start and before the end of the utterance they overlay. For instance, my evaluation overlays Jack's clarification of the mechanics of the suicide (lines 77 and 78):

```
            J:  and then he [blew his ]face right up.
Mid-start   K:            [Amazing. ]
```

These mid-starts can thus do registerings or appreciations without taking up a turn. The second kind of mid-start consists of brief utterances completed within a mid-sentence pause, thus showing attention or appreciation without either taking up a turn or overlaying speech. For instance, I catch on to Jack's explanation of the suicide method before he quite finishes it, and let him know (in lines 73 to 75):

```
            J:  So he took him out=
Mid-start   K:  O I see.=
            J:  put it in his mouth
```

Conversationalists can evidently attend to brief overlaid words or phrases even if they are talking themselves, but not to extended overlaid utterances. The third sort of mid-start consists of initiating longer utterances in the middle of another turn, especially by misusing the mid-sentence pause as an end-pause. For instance, Jack Brown goes on with his own explanation in the middle of one his wife is already offering, her's following on from his earlier explanation (lines 65, 66, and 67). The mid-start is fitted into the juncture between clauses:

```
            J:  That he missed himself with.
            B:  He missed hisself with the first one
                      ┌so he reloaded      ┐
Mid-start[[J:         └Twas just the case. ┘
```

Later, Jack Brown starts an evaluation in the middle of Mrs. Brown's account of Jack leaving the farm (an utterance she picks up again later) causing her to break off in mid-sentence (lines 79, 80, and 81):

```
            ┌┌B:  And do you know he had to┌leave┐the
Mid-start[[ └J:                           └Well ┘
                  the man's mad at that time he must be gone
                  wasn't him.
```

This trick can be reversed by treating one's own end-pause as a mid-pause and creating a run-on sentence, or skipping one's own end-pause to start a new sentence, both resulting in keeping the floor. For instance, Mrs. Brown goes from the attempted suicide story to the suicide story without a break between sentences (lines 51 and 52):

```
            B:  O dear dear she said come in Alford come in you
Mid-start       mustn't do that = well we went but-
                we come but a day or two after
```

A fourth mid-start consists of utterances started by one speaker and completed by another, called chime-ins by Harvey Sacks (lines 47 and 48):[15]

15. Sacks, Lecture VI (1966), p. 16. According to Emanuel Schegloff, chime-ins are one of a class a phenomena more commonly referred to by Sacks (and others) as "collaborative productions" or just "collaboratives" (sometimes also as "joint productions"). As with the term "collaborative narration," these usages presuppose something about the intention of the producer which is called into question here. Personal Communication (1984).

```
        J:  He missed himself the first time
Mid-start  B:  and he reloaded the gun.
```

Whether this, or any other technical interruption, counts as thematic depends, not on its success or failure, but on what Barbara Kirshenblatt-Gimblett has called the culture of interruptability.[16] She contrasts cultures where attentiveness is marked by chipping in to cultures where attentiveness is marked by silence. Thematic interruptions are interpositions felt to interrupt the speech event or thematic continuity of the story even though they may be fitted into the discourse at technically appropriate junctures. They may either interrupt the story event without interrupting any of the utterances that constitute it, or they may interrupt the story by interrupting its constitutive utterances. It might be supposed that the interpositions and asides mentioned here qualify as thematic interruptions even when they are not technical interruptions. Afterall, they do not carry forward the story line. The fact of the matter is that, for the most part, not even the technical interruptions so qualify.

The interpositions in question are sprinkled throughout the story so that they appear to break up the narrative line. They take the form of artefactual turntaking, thus retaining during storytelling one of the patterns of conversation, but in an abbreviated form. The teller's claim to the floor remains unimpaired. A disadvantage of artefactural turns lies in either teller or hearer treating one as a full turn, that is, one across which the storyteller does not hold the floor. Is Mrs. Brown's chime-in on Jack Brown's story (lines 47 and 48) intended to be an interruption or a continuation, and does Jack regard it an an interposition through which he holds the floor or a takeover by which he loses it?

```
        J:  He missed himself the first time
Chime-in   B:  and he reloaded the gun.
```

The turntaking form of interpositions is directed to conversation, aligning the story with surrounding talk. The fact that conversational anecdotes are peculiarly pervious to interpositions tends to support this interpretation. The content of the interpositions, however, is directed to the story. They are, that is, attention-markers, supportive utterances, appreciations, and evaluations of the story,

16. Barbara Kirshenblatt-Gimblett, Personal Communication (Philadelphia: 1978).

metacommunications about the kind of story it is and how hearers are responding to it. They attend to stories as a different order of event from the conversations in which they are enclaves. The story as transfix, then, is sustained across artefactual turns. The turntaking still involves hearers in the mutual construction of the story.

Some of the interpositions in this story are evaluative in the sense that they reveal attitudes toward or feelings about the story. Labov's well-known analysis of evaluation addresses only evaluations by the narrator in the course of the narrative:[17]

> The evaluation of a narrative is defined by us as that part of the narrative which reveals the attitude of the narrator towards the narrative by emphasizing the relative importance of some narrative units as compared to others.

Labov's view disregards storytelling as communication, as if stories were stored inside individuals and reeled off whenever they were appropriately triggered by circumstances. In fact, evaluative work can be done by other participants, and located outside as well as inside the boundaries of the story. Indeed, in conversation some evaluation by others is expected. In the course of the story these can take the form of appreciations which make it clear that the hearer is attending to the story (line 11):

    B: ... he was looking about for a place to hang
             up this-
         put this rope
         to hang heself.=
Evaluation: K: Heaven's sake.

After the story, evaluations express an attitude towards the story as a whole (line 62):

    J: and that cartridge-
        he was buried with that one in his skull.
Evaluation: K: For heaven's sake.

They can be expressed by teller (line 81) as well as hearer (line 78).

17. Labov and Waletzky, p. 37.

```
              ┌─ J:  and then he┌blew his┌face right up.
Evaluation:│ │ K:          └Amazing.┘
          ┌ │  B:  And do you know he had to┌leave the┐
          │ │  J:                           └Well      ┘
Evaluation:   the man's mad at that time he must be gone
                      wasn't him.
```

Labov claims evaluations are typically suspended between what he calls the complication and resolution of the narrative proper.[18] The evaluation so positioned in this story happens to be by a hearer, not a teller (line 55):

```
              J:  He took that cartridge out of the gun
           ┌┌     put it┌in his mouth┐
Evaluation:│ │K:         └Heavens.     ┘
              J:  and he
```

Some evaluations are located near the part of the story they intensify (line 50):

```
              J:  and he pushed the trigger with a forked stick.
              K:  Really.=
```

Others (like lines 78 and 81 above) can turn up anywhere and comment on the story as a whole. Evaluations are not necessarily sequenced in the sense Labov mentions, that changing the order of the clauses changes the inferred order of the events.[19] But they can be closely attached to a narrative element that is sequenced or they can be loosely associated with the narrative sequence as a whole. Though not part of that sequence, Labov justly regards evaluations as crucial to the story. They transform it from a series of events that happen one after another into a series of events that follow on from one another, from the consecutive to the consequential, from "so what" to "just so" stories, to borrow a phrase coined by Amy Shuman.[20]

18. Labov, p. 369.
19. Labov and Waletzky, p. 21.
20. Amy Shuman, Personal Communication (Philadelphia: 1979).

Prefaces and codas precede and follow the story, initially introducing it into the conversation and finally linking it back on to the conversation. The term "preface" is used by Harvey Sacks to mean conversational devices designed to get their speaker the floor for an extended turn at talk in order to tell a story. Hearers then provide a response which licenses the storytelling.[21] A hearer's invitation to tell a story can combine in one utterance the function of preface and response. (Such an invitation by interviewers preceded the stories Labov collected for his analysis.) Prefaces and invitations can take the form of abstracts, brief summaries of the story which appear to offer hearers information about how to monitor the story for its end, namely, the completion of the action outlined in the abstract. Abstracts can also appear, as Labov argues, as the beginning of the story.[22]

In the absence of prefaces or invitations, it may still be possible to trace what Labov calls the originating function of the story, that is, the remark or topic of conversation that precipitated it.[23] It is never clear beforehand which remarks will trigger a story though often clear afterwards which remarks have. On this occasion, Mrs. Brown and I have been talking about her children, some of whom have unusual names. One of them, Albany, was named after Alford Bickle's nephew. In talking about this nephew, Mrs. Brown offers an abstract of what will later be the suicide story.

```
             B:  Course Albany uh- when his uncle died
                 he came over here
                 uh
Abstract         to stay with his aunt cause his uncle wa- shot
                    himself.
Abstract         And my husband found him
                 when he shot himself.
                 So they had Albany    come    back here and stay
                    with his auntie
        [[ K:                               [ Really!]
             B:  (for a while-) she was an old maid.
```

21. Sacks, "An Analysis of the Course of a Joke's Telling in Conversation," Explorations in the Ethnography of Speaking, Richard Baumen and Joel Sherzer, eds. (London and New York: Cambridge University Press, 1977), pp. 337 - 353, pp. 340 - 341.
22. Labov, p. 363.
23. Labov and Waletzky, p. 41.

This abstract might have been the beginning of the suicide story or a preface to it, licensed by the response, "Really", except that Mrs. Brown regards it as an account of how they came to meet the nephew, Albany, and so came across the name. She continues:

```
        B:  And he used to come to get away from his aunt
            cause she was a bit (batty)
            He used to come down to our house for the
            evening and
                  stay you know (     ) an hour or two.
        K:  Isn't that interesting.=
        B:  and (    ) and=
        K:  Does sound like the family might have been a
            bit batty
                  doesn't it.
        B:  Hm?
        K:  The family might have been a bit batty=
        B:  Well they were very wealthy=
        K:  Were they.
        B:  I mean whether twas the money went to their
            head or what
                  it twas I don't know.
Invitation:  K:  Why did the father shoot himself- the- the
            uncle- in
                  this country.
         B:  O
            course he was funny for a long time he um
            just went out one day and did it.
            And his father
            drowned himself.
         K:  My heavens.=
      [[ B:  It was like a family (trait).
         [ K:                    [ Yes.        ]
            (                          )
         B:  Uh and his fa- his father
            drowned himself in the same yard
            where this fellow (went)
            in a- in a trough of disinfectant.
```

Mrs. Brown goes on to describe the queer behavior of Alford Bickle leading up to his first suicide attempt: the occasion on which he was looking about for a place to put up a rope to hang himself. Mrs. Brown uses the story of the attempted suicide as prologue to the story of the suicide itself, the story her husband walks in on. Mr. Brown in turn uses her last line as preface to his own telling of the story:

End/   B: and on the road looking right there was old man
Preface   with his face blew away.
                  . . . . .
           J: Well the bugger he sat- he sat on an hedge in
                  the garden
                  . . . .

    Codas allude to events sequential but not consequential to those that happened in the story. Labov writes: "Codas close off the sequence of complicating actions and indicate that none of the events that followed were important to the narrative."[24] The events that followed serve to reconnect the events in the story with the present situation by filling in the interval between. "These codas have the property of bridging the gap between the moment of time at the end of the narrative proper and the present. They bring the narrator and the listener back to the point at which they entered the narrative."[25] Codas can be contributed by hearers only if they share knowledge of the Taleworld. Mrs. Brown, for instance, offers a coda to Jack's version of the suicide story (line 80).

Coda   B: Well and then Father lived with the sister
                  right on?

Such an offering is apparently subject to correction by the teller (lines 91 to 93).

Coda   B: She only farmed about three months after.
                  [And uh
           [[J: [Three months]from this accident.
           B: Twelve months eh?
           J: Three months?
           B: How long did her carry on after you.
Coda   J: I was there four years.

24. Labov, pp. 365-366.

The coda spins out events from the story, in this instance, leading to another suicide (lines 94 and 95).

Coda: B: O yes course four years after.
                  Then in the end her ha- hung herself.

This coda picks up and substantiates an earlier topic of conversation, suicide as a family trait, thus circling back to the preceding conversation. The coda also traces out events subsequent to the story which provide a perspective on persons present to the storytelling occasion. This coda also becomes an abstract for the story of the sister's hanging herself later in the conversation.

Orientations to stories are designed to provide information regarded as necessary in order to understand what is transpiring in the story, and at just that juncture where the information is likely to be required.[26] They are not themselves sequentially organized but are directed to what is. Characteristically, according to Labov, orientations precede the narrtive sequence and "serve to orient the listener in respect to person, place, time and behavioral situation."[27] Jack Brown's opening line sets the scene for the suicide (line 48):

Orientation: J: Well the bugger he sat- he sat on an hedge in
                  the garden

Mrs. Brown can depend on her earlier descriptions of the family queerness, a story about Alford Bickle's supernatural strength ("O he had the strength of Old Nick he said."), and the story of his suicide attempt to orient hearers to the background of the suicide. Corrections, clarifications, and explanations in

25. Labov, p. 365.
26. Sacks, Lecture VII (1970), p. 10: "What we have is a sense of context being employed by the teller, which involves fitting into the story, in carefully located places, information that will permit the appreciation of what was transpiring which is not information which involves events in the story sequence at that point."
27. Labov and Waletzky, p. 32.

the course of the story can be regarded as orientations in the sense that they, too, provide information necessary to understand what is transpiring. In this vein, when Mrs. Brown sees by my response that I have supposed Jack to say that Alford Bickle put the gun in his mouth, she makes it clear that what he put in his mouth was a spent cartridge (lines 49 to 52):

```
               J:  He took that cartridge out of the gun
                   put it ┌in his mouth┐
               K:         └Heavens.     ┘
                ┌┌J: ┌and he           ┐
Clarification:  └└B: └put the┘cartridge in his mouth
```

When it is clear to Jack Brown that I have not quite understood the story (line 64), he does a rerun in which further explanations and clarifications are contributed by both the Browns (lines 66 to 77):

```
               K:  And the- he'd had one in his mouth and that
                        one
                   exploded did it?
Explanation:   J:  Well it didn't- well no you see that was
                   the one- the case┌of the one that┐exploded
Clarification: ┌┌B:                 └Fired you see.  ┘
               ┌┌K: ┌Well┐
Clarification: └└J: └That┘he missed himself with.
Explanation:   B:  He missed hisself with the first one
                   ┌so he reloaded.┐
Clarification:     └Twas just the  ┘case.
Explanation:       So he took him out=
               K:  O I see.=
Explanation:   J:  put it in his mouth
                   and uh then fixed the trigger- fired the
                   other trigger and then he blew his face
                   right up.
```

Joint Storytelling

The contribution of asides, interpositions, evaluations, prefaces, codas, and orientations to stories by hearers as well as tellers evidences the mutual construction of the story. The teller's performance is guided, punctuated, supported, and elaborated by others. On this understanding, what appears to some analysts not to be a story, or to be one riddled with interruptions, is seen to be a transfix with multiple contributors. A radical instance of the mutual construction of stories remains to be considered, one in which the teller's contribution cannot be technically distinguished from the hearers', and that is joint storytelling: the contribution by different persons of the narrative clauses which carry forward the plot. In this instance, hearer becomes teller.

The fundamental structure of the story is a series of necessarily sequenced narrative clauses which recount a series of temporally unfolding events.[28] The disclosure and characterization of this fundamental structure in personal experience narratives is one of Labov's notable contributions to narrative analysis. On his analysis, the narrative moves from the orientation through a series of complicating actions toward resolution (dots indicate elisions):

		. . . .
Orientation:	B:	we come but a day or two after
Complication:		uh Father went down to the farm
		so he said uh
Complication:		heard this gun go off.
Complication:		I went and I looked at those ( )
Complication:		So anyway come up the road and I
		((Jack enters))
		. . . .
		come up the road- hey?
		. . . .
		come up the road
		. . . .
Resolution/		and on the road looking right there there
Abstract		was old man with his face blew away.
Orientation:	J:	Well the bugger he sat- he sat on an hedge
		in the garden
Complication:		and he pushed the trigger with a forked
		stick.
		. . . .
Complication:		He missed himself the first time
Complication:	B:	and he reloaded the gun.
Complication:	J:	He took that cartridge out of the gun
Complication:		put it in his mouth

28. See Labov and Waletzky, p. 21.

....
Complication: and he ... put another cartridge in
Complication: and he found the gun again-
                   and that cartridge-
Resolution: he was buried with that one in his skull.

Performance theorists describe storytelling on a two-party model, a model that neatly lodges performing in one person and audiencing in the other. This approach moves away from the even narrower literary habit of considering just the detached text as the storytelling event only to arrive at the difficulty of third persons. Maintaining the two-party design in the presence of three persons requires a redistribution of the roles of teller and hearer. Three possibilities present themselves. One is the creation of a co-present nonparticipant status, an arrangement characteristically made for children, these being regarded as only tangentially attentive to adult conversations. In fact, because the requirements for conversation can be sustained by two persons, a third can all too easily find himself out of it. For this reason, Sacks argues, there is some obligation upon conversationalists to keep third persons in.[29] A second way to maintain the two-party design with three persons is to align third persons with one of the two primary roles, in the way, it may be, that wives are supposed to align themselves with husbands.[30] For storytelling, this results in one teller with multiple hearers or multiple tellers with one hearer. A third solution, the one pursued here, is to redistribute the properties inherent in telling and hearing over more than two persons. The

29. Sacks, Lecture VII (1970), p. 26: "Three people are locked together; one can leave to be sure, and the conversation continue, but that one can't go into another conversation, and can't get another conversation off of that one. So the problem of speakers to keep a third party in is less than in a four-party conversation which, if it turns into a two-party conversation permits the others to drop out, so that some amount of talk is designed to keep people who are not talking, in.
30. Sacks, Lecture VII (1970), p. 25: "three couples could still be something like a three-party conversation if a rule which assigns women the job of laughing and not talking were preserved."

storytelling is then regarded as a communication system in which telling and hearing are not so discrete as the two-party model for conversation implies. Nonetheless, modes of participation in the system can be differentiated.

Utterances in conversation have been seen by analysts as moves in a game. Harvey Sacks describes the way participants monitor conversation for sequentially relevant next moves as floor-seeking, as if getting the floor were their intention in talk.[31] By contrast, I suggest, floor-avoiding might be used to describe the way participants whose intention is not to get or hold the floor monitor conversation for sequentially constrained next moves. These differential descriptions could then apply respectively to storytellers and story hearer on this occasion. Their modes of participation can thus be discriminated but not contrasted. Performing and audiencing are not complementary elements in a matched set but the extremes of a more finely differentiated range of participation modes.

Story Analysis II: Discourse

If the notion of joint storytelling solves a puzzle at the level of interaction, the puzzle of how to distribute two roles, teller and hearer, among three people, it creates a puzzle at the level of discourse, the puzzle of who gets to tell which part of the story when. On this occasion, Mrs. Brown has been doing serial storytelling, serial stories being runs of stories by one teller loosely tied together thematically.[32] Some of these stories show a kind of end-linkage in which one story serves as prologue for the next. For instance, a story about Alford Bickle's supernatural strength prologues the story of his suicide attempt, foreshadowing his death, and providing a hint of his unnatural state of mind.

Beginning: B: And they was going threshing
                  and they got their own thresher you see
                  and the belt slipped.
                  And Father said Coo you never saw the
                       strength of that man.

31. Sacks, Lecture VI (1967), p. 10: "It's if you can't decide what sequentially relevant next action is being done, that you can't make a move."
32. For an account of serial storying see Chapter Two.

```
                    You see the blinking uh belt come off
                    and he never stopped the thresher
End:                he went and he pulled the belt around the um
                    wheel you know-
                    round the thing that was going.
Evaluation:    [[   Well he said[anybody else would]have done
Evaluation:    [[K:              [For heaven's sake.]
              B:    would have killed himself.
              K:    Yes.
              B:    He said and
Evaluation:         he- ha- O he had the strength of Old Nick
                      he said.
                    So he said I said to him it's about time he
                      said you go in and rest up
                    Boss he said.
Coda:               Go in with your sister and sit down for
                      awhile.
                    You uh shouldn't be out here.
                    O I'm all right I'm all right
                    Well you go in and sit down he said
                    and have your dinner.
                    So off he went.
Beginning:          Well Father went in
                    he said on the day or day after
                    Father was out having his dinner.
                    ....
```

Here, where storytelling is well established, using one story as prologue for the next pre-empts the requirement for a preface, permission to take an extended turn being, perhaps, implicit in the framework of the occasion. The attempted suicide is itself elegantly related to the suicide as prologue to story. However, Mrs. Brown also runs the last sentence of the prologuing story into the first sentence of the suicide story and skips the obligatory pause between (lines 22 to 23):

```
Coda:         B:    O dear dear she said come in Alford come in
Coda/                     you mustn't do that=well we went but-
Beginning:          we come out a day or two after
```

Since storytellers can be expected to relinquish the floor on completion of a story and sentence ends signal possible completions, Mrs. Brown thus assures herself the floor. Into the middle of this story so carefully engineered to keep her the floor comes her husband, Jack Brown. Mrs. Brown and I are sitting in the kitchen. Mr. Brown says something at the front door, comes on down the hall talking, turns the corner into the kitchen, sees me and says, "Well landsakes". His first remark runs over the end of Mrs. Brown's utterance (lines 27 and 28)

$$[[\begin{matrix} \text{B:} \\ \text{J:} \end{matrix} \quad \text{So anyway come up the road} [\begin{matrix} \text{and I} \\ (\quad) \end{matrix}]$$

bloody secret.

So she repeats that remark at the same time that Jack calls down the hall. She reruns the remark a third time and then Jack arrives at the doorway into the kitchen and says (line 32),

J: Well landsakes.

At this point in the conversation Mrs. Brown can foresee three problems. The first is greetings. Greetings are fixed exchanges or utterance pairs done, it at all, at the beginning of an encounter.[33] Jack Brown and I have not seen each other yet on this occasion. However, to permit us to greet each other would require Mrs. Brown to relinquish the floor for at least two turns right in the middle of her story. The possible consequence, then, is that her turn will be interrupted. A second problem is rehearings. Storytellers are meant to be attentive to whether or not their listeners have already heard a story. "Effective performance", writes Goffman, "requires first hearings, not first tellings."[34] Clearly, Jack has heard the story before, in fact, it is one he has told. Spouses are routinely expected to politely tolerate or even encourage the telling of stories they have already heard, but they are not required to do so. The possible consequence of this is that Mrs. Brown will have to abandon her turn. The third problem is what Harvey Sacks calls "entitlement".[35] Mrs. Brown has a claim to the story in virtue of having started it but Mr. Brown has a claim, too, in a sense usually given priority in talk, that he experienced the events in it. And

33. Sacks, "Everyone has to Lie", Lecture (1967), p. 17: "If greetings do occur, they occur at the beginning of a conversation."
34. Goffman, Frame Analysis, p. 508: "Effective performance requires first hearings, not first tellings."
35. Sacks, Lecture IV (1970).

the possible consequence of that is that Mr. Brown will take
over her turn. Mrs. Brown solves all three of these problems
in one move: she jumps to the end of the story (lines 33 and
34):

```
[[ J:  [Well landsakes.]
   B:  [and on the road]looking right there was
              old man with his face blew away.
```

This quick conclusion is intelligible because of the
prefatory remarks earlier in the conversation about Jack Brown
finding the old man after he shot himself and the prologuing
story of the attempted suicide. It accomplishes three things.
It pre-empts the position in which greetings would have taken
place if they were going to, it cues Jack Brown as to which
story is being told, and, at the same time, it finishes the
story. I pronounce astonishment and Mrs. Brown goes on to
invite her husband to address himself to the story, thus neatly
acknowledging his provenance (lines 39 to 42):

```
[[ K:  For heaven's[sake.]
   B:            [Yeah.]
       Wasn't he Father.
[[    [I was right wasn't I.          ]
   K: [What an extraordinary thing.   ]
   B:  Don't ye remember.
```

Jack Brown puts her off a moment and then produces what
appears to be a continuation of her story (lines 48 and 49):

```
J:  Well the bugger he sat- he sat on an hedge in the garden
    and he pushed the trigger with a forked stick.
```

However, this piece of the story fits into the sequence before
the piece Mrs. Brown has already given. In fact, it begins a
retelling, not a continuation of her story. The two pieces are
not presented as one story and so are not, in that sense, joint
storytelling. Jack's story transforms the end of Mrs. Brown's
story into an abstract for his own. Getting Jack to tell the
story himself solves the problem of entitlement. It also
affords him entry into the conversation in a way that may make
up for skipping greetings.

Jack Brown continues his story with a sentence he starts and Mrs. Brown finishes (lines 47 and 48):

J: He missed himself the first time
B: and he reloaded the gun

Any contribution to the story by participants other than the teller makes it an instance of mutual construction. This, however, is an instance not just of mutual construction but of joint storytelling: the mutual construction of the narrative clauses that carry forward the plot.

Whether joint storytelling is what has been called collaborative narration is another question.[36] Joint storytelling can just as well be the result of competition as collaboration. To count as collaborative narration, both storytellers' utterances must not only be essential to the story in the technical sense that they carry forward the sequentially organized story line, but also they must be intendedly mutually constructed. Consider this utterance closely. It consists of two narrative clauses separated by what Labov calls temporal juncture, that is, it represents two events necessarily sequenced in time:[37] The clause, "and he reloaded the gun" necessarily comes after "He missed himself the first time". However, Mrs. Brown's chime-in does not really complete Jack Brown's sentence. What appears as completion is really the transformation of a possible complete sentence, "He missed himself the first time", into an independent clause. The initial sentence, that is to say, does not invite a chime-in, unlike, Sacks speculates, broken-off sentences might.[38]

A chime-in is neatly designed to cut in on the storyteller's turn without cutting off the story. This presents the possibility of inserting a continuation into the

36. Kirshenblatt-Gimblett introduced the study of collaborative narrative in "Personal Experience Narrative as a Primary Form," given at the American Folklore Society Meetings in New Orleans (1975).
37. Labov, pp. 360 and 361.
38. Sacks, Lecture VII (1966), p. 16, "what we have is something produced which by itself is not a sentence which, what it does is, its user makes his piece of talk a dependent clause and makes the prior piece of talk an independent clause and not a sentence. I.e, he hooks his statement onto the previous one."

story but it also presents the possibility of attempting a takeover of the story, an arrangement that uses the machinery of the story to take it away from its teller. However Mrs. Brown intends her chime-in, Mr. Brown interprets it as a takeover attempt. To evade that, he backs up and reruns her section of the story by inserting events which necessarily precede the one she has just recounted (lines 51 to 61):

```
     J:  He missed himself the first time
     B:  and he reloaded the gun.
     J:  He took that cartridge out of the gun
         put it in his mouth
[[                 [
   K:             Heavens.          ]
   [J:  and he             ]
[[  B:  put the cartridge in his mouth
[[  J:                    [put another cartridge in]
         and he found the gun again-
         and that cartridge-
         he was buried with that one in his skull.
```

Jack's rerun of Mrs. Brown's chime-in at once chides her, recovers him the floor, and fits in information about the spent cartridge in Alford Bickle's mouth which sets up the end of the story.

Natural ends: death, sleep, departures, farewells, and other completions; will be taken as story ends unless some other indication is provided.[39] The obvious completion of the utterance, "and he found the gun again-", would be, "and shot himself". Jack knows I have been monitoring the story for just this outcome. And so has his wife. However, he wants to insert further information about the cartridge before closing. To achieve this, he re-starts the end three times, manipulating the grammar to suit his design (lines 59-61):

```
End        J:   and he found the gun again-
Re-start        and that cartridge-
Re-start        he was buried with that one in his skull.
```

He shifts "that cartridge" from subject to object and arrives at the end by synecdoche, the substitution of the aftermath, burial with the cartridge in his skull, for the graver event

39. Sacks, "On the Analyzability of Stories by Children," in Directions in Sociolinguistics: The Ethnography of Communication, John Gumperz and Dell Hymes, eds. (New York: Holt, Rinehart and Winston, 1972), pp. 325-245, p. 342.

it presupposes, death by suicide. This structure, devised to hold on to my attention and, conceivably, to hold off his wife's contributions, gives the story the sophisticated turn that makes it ironic or macabre.

Chiming in to complete another person's utterance, whether competitive or collaborative, discloses shared understandings. Goffman writes: "During a performance it is only fellow performers who respond in this direct way as inhabitants of the same realm; the audience responds indirectly, glancingly, following alongside."[40] The Browns on this occasion take up the same alignment toward the events in the story, as privy to that realm, in contrast to my own attitude as an outsider. The production of a joint story is a neat way to show a foreigner, in the local sense of someone from outside the shire, that these two are a group.[41] Of course, the foreigner's utterances contribute to the shape and articulation of the storytelling, if not the story, in that respect constituting all three of us a group.[42]

Levels of Analysis

Stories can usefully be analyzed at two levels: the level of discourse, relationships among utterances, and the level of interaction, relationships among persons on occasions. Labov's analysis works at the discourse level, disarticulating stories into their constituent elements. One limitation of his analysis is its failure to give an account of what holds stories together when they are not discrete from surrounding conversation. In this story, brief utterances which are incidental to the story turn out to be non-interruptive whereas the one essential utterance giving the appearance of collaboration, the chime-in, is treated as an interruption. Despite differential contributions of either sort, the story frame transfixes a span of discourse, sustaining its

40. Goffman, Frame Analysis, p. 127.
41. Sacks, Lecture VI (1966), p. 15: "Now there's an obvious thing that such a production might be seen to do, is of course it's perhaps as neat a conceivable means as you could have for showing the new guy that this is a group."
42. Dell Hymes, Personal Communication (Philadelphia: 1979). Hymes suggested that if the two storytellers make a group, so, in another way, do the three conversationalists.

ontological status as narrative. Sacks, by contrast, works at
the level of interaction, relating utterances to each other.
The notion of turns makes it clear that utterances are
understood to be implicated together in a system.[43] The
virtue of his analysis is its elucidation of the bearing of
relationships among participants on the structure of
storytelling. At the level of interaction, it turns out that
the role of narrator is shared for this story but the floor is
disputed. Entitlement to the story is re-negotiated over the
course of the telling. The mutual construction of the story
sustains the turntaking pattern of conversation. These two
systems, the system of discourse and the system of interaction,
appear to cut across each other in the story, the
differentiation of roles at the level of interaction breaking
up the discretion of the story at the level of discourse. In
reality, the story as transfix holds across its mutual
construction.

This inquiry investigates the interplay between the
Storyrealm and the realm of conversation to disclose how
relationships at both the level of discourse and the level of
interaction shape the story. Stories in conversation have been
regarded as tracings of an individual which can be hunted out
and mounted up for analysis. On the contrary, stories, like
other turns at talk, are mutually constructed, contributions by
hearers at the least guiding and punctuating the teller's
narration. So stories must be analyzed as mutual
constructions. Joint storytelling presents a radical instance
of the mutual construction of stories in the form of one story
told by two persons. In light of this, the story is seen not
as continuous narration by a single narrator but as a transfix
with multiple contributors.

43. Schegloff and Sacks, "Opening up Closings."

CHAPTER FIVE

STORYABILITY AND EVENTFULNESS:
Beyond Referential Theories of Narrative*

A story is <u>made out of</u> events to the extent that plot
<u>makes</u> events <u>into</u> a story.

Paul Ricoeur[1]

The relationship between the Storyrealm and the Taleworld
is commonly presumed to be referential. The presumption of
referentiality is enhanced in anecdotes whose Taleworlds can
easily be supposed to be real. The story is then understood to
be shaped by, and in turn to direct attention to, aspects of
reality. The fallacy of this presumption can be brought out by
examining the relationship between Storyrealm and Taleworld
where the Taleworld is not real but fictive. The sense in
which fictions refer to anything at all is unclear. In
considering the relationship between the Storyrealm and the
Taleworld, then, it will be revealing to see whether the
constitution of the Taleworld, the relationship between the
Taleworld and the Storyrealm, and the relationship between the
Taleworld and the real are the same or different for fictions
and true stories. The traditional move in narrative theory has
been to locate the difference between the fictive and the real

* The argument for stories as reconstitutions was first given
as a paper called "Against Referentiality in Storytelling" at
the 1977 California Folklore Society Meetings, Pitzer College,
California. This became part of a later version called
"Storyability and Eventfulness," given at the 1981 American
Folklore Society Meetings, San Antonio, Texas.

1. Paul Ricoeur, "Narrative Time", <u>Critical Inquiry</u> 7, #1,
(Autumn 1980), pp. 169-190, p. 171.

in the constitution of the Taleworld: imaginary realms yield fictions; real ones yield true stories. This move is confounded by two difficulties: one, the sense in which realities do not yield true stories; and the other, the sense in which imaginary realms do not yield fictions.

The Ontological Status of Taleworlds

The sense in which realities do not yield true stories begins to come out in what might be called ontologically mixed Taleworlds. Legends taken as fictions are mapped onto the geography of the ordinary; anecdotes supposed to be true turn out to be jokes; fictional characters occupy real settings; stories told as fictions turn out to be true: realities are embedded in fictions and fictions in realities. To sort out the fictive from the real in such instances, it might be useful to invoke what Marie-Laure Ryan economically calls the principle of minimal departure.[2]

This principle states that we reconstrue the world of a fiction and of a counterfactual as being the closest possible to the reality we know ... It is by virtue of the principle of minimal departure that hearers are able to form reasonably comprehensive representations of foreign worlds created through discourse, even though the verbal description of these worlds is always incomplete. Without the principle, interpretation of verbal messages referring to private mental or non-existent worlds would be limited to the extraction of semantic entailments.

To operate here, the principle would have to be applied backward, not to claim that everything in the Taleworld is to be taken as like the real one unless otherwise specified, but to claim that if anything in the Taleworld is not like the real, that realm is fictive. To detect fictions, the principle would have to be enforced absolutely: any divergence from the real would qualify a Taleworld as fictive. On this criterion, all the instances mentioned would be fictive or, at most, the last, stories told as fictious which turn out to be true, could be said to modulate from fictive to real. There are, however, some difficulties with this solution.

2. Marie-Laure Ryan, "Fiction, Non-factuals, and the Principle of Minimal Departure," Poetics 9 (1980) pp. 403 - 422, p. 406.

An initial reluctance to use the principle of minimal departure to discriminate fiction from reality arises from the suspicion that the principle imparts plausibility, not truth value. Lodging fictive elements in real worlds or real ones in fictions lends those Taleworlds realism, not reality. The deeper difficulty lies in the implication that truth value depends on the fit between the Taleworld and the real one. This view relies on the assumption that referentiality is a relation that holds between two realms of events of different ontological statuses rather than, as is usually supposed, between a realm of discourse and a realm of events. If this view held, some Storyrealms would refer to Taleworlds which would refer to real ones. Occam's razor might be invoked here to proscribe interposing an extra lamination between the realm of discourse and the realm of events. That excision lays the groundwork for an alternative solution. If the difference between the fictive and the real is not located in differences among kinds of Taleworlds, or between the Taleworld and the real one, it may be located in differences among kinds of realities. On this view, it is not that Taleworlds are mixed but rather that realities are multiple.

Ontological Geographies

Moving around in the course of everyday life, persons experience transitions from one set of ontological assumptions about the nature of reality to another, or what is called here realm-shift. But one realm, the realm of the ordinary, the commonsense world of everyday life, is the one that is unreflectively called reality. Alfred Schutz describes this as the paramount reality, the realm to come back to, touchstone of other realms.[3]

These other realms are separated from the ordinary by borders, barriers, interstitial spaces which are also thresholds to another world. Heda Jason describes the sorts of spatial barriers that lie between the ordinary world and the world of the numskulls: a path, a road, wilderness, barren regions, walls, a gate, a yard, a street, the fringes of settlements, desert.[4] Other realms are accessible only

3. Schutz, p. 253.
4. Jason, p. 210.

through altered states: time travel, space travel, changes of class or ethnicity, sleep, trance, fantasy, memory, hallucination, mediatation, magical transformation, death. The realm of the dead, to take an example, is supposed to be contiguous at some points with ordinary reality and passages between the two realms are supposed to be possible, through such passages usually require radical changes of state. The loss of animacy or bodily incarnation are generally requisite for passage to the realm of the dead, and returning from that realm entails extreme attenuations of substance, resulting in visitants who are barely visible and faintly tangible, though occasionally quite audible. Having arrived, ghosts and spirits become enclaves in the ordinary. As Erving Goffman remarks about such ontological complexities, "once the realm of the literally real is left, great license is to be expected."[5] The space or condition between realms can be perceived as dangerous, vulnerable, or magical for realm travelers. Its interstitial character invites consideration as a rite of passage.[6]

Other realms are more or less akin to the ordinary. The realm of the past and the realm of the future are removed from the ordinary along a temporal dimension. The realms of the exotic and the extraterrestrial are removed along a spatial dimension. Among present realms, the miniature and the gigantic shift away from the ordinary along a physical dimension. And perhaps the realms of the supernatural, the demonic, the angelic, the ghostly, and the dead could be said to remove themselves along a metaphysical dimension. The arrangement of realms according to their kinship with the ordinary suggests hierarchies or fields of realities distributed from the familiar to the fabulous to create, as it were, an ontological geography.

5. Goffman, p. 256.
6. The notion of interstitial categories has been extended from Arnold Van Gennep's work by such practicioners as Mary Douglas and Victor Turner. Arnold Van Gennep, The Rites of Passage (Chicago: University of Chicago Press, 1960); Mary Douglas, Purity and Danger (Middlesex, England: Pelican, 1970); Victor Turner, The Forest of Symbols (Ithaca and London: Cornell University Press, 1970).

Some realms are considered to border on the ordinary. Fairyland, for instance, lies alongside the ordinary world while the realms of the gods and the demons lie above and below it, sometimes in many-layered heavens and hells.[7] Other realms overlay the ordinary. Children's games occupy and adopt some of the features of ordinary space. Ordinary realities are themselves multiple. The realms of work, play, thought, and talk are each entered into as paramount realities. Still other realms lie inside the ordinary as stories do in conversation. Thus the realm of conversation and its enclave, stories, can be seen as aspects of the ordinary. The distribution of other realms along the boundaries of the ordinary can be seen to define what ordinariness is. In that respect, alternate realities have an affinity with each other: "The alien, the strange, the pathological, the demonic, the freakish, and the hellish may be analogical possibilities we come to by way of the outskirts of the familiar," writes Maurice Natanson.[8]

The spatial metaphor employed here suggests that multiple realities constellate around the ordinary as their centrality. Here again it is tempting to locate fictive realms by the principle of minimal departure from the realm of the ordinary. To do so, however, is to misunderstand the experiencial nature of reality. Any realm, whether ordinary or extraordinary, insofar as it engages participants in their reality,[9] though knowledge of other realms persists to define its limits. There is no absolute disjunction between our experience of the fictive and the real: which realm is fictive depends on the epistemology of its perceiver. To regard any realm as inherently fictive or inherently real is to make a contrast of the fine discriminations among their ontological statuses. It is in this sense that realities do not yield true stories.

7. See Jason, p. 208 and elsewhere.
8. Natanson, The Journeying Self (Reading, Massachusetts; Menlo Park, California; London; Don Mills, Ontario: Addison-Wesley, 1970), p. 37.
9. Alfred Schutz, On Phenomenology and Social Relations, Helmut R. Wagner, Tr. (Chicago and London: University of Chicago Press, 1973) p. 254. See also Nelson Goodman, Ways of Worldmaking (Indianapolis: 1978) p. x, on the general intellectual movement away from assumptions of "a world fixed and found" to the recognition of "a diversity of .... versions or worlds in the making."

The Ontological Status of Storyrealms

A sophisticated alternative to reckoning the realm status of stories from the constitution of either the Taleworld or the real one has been proposed by Barbara Herrnstein Smith. She relocates the difference between the fictive and the real in the Storyrealm. "For the essential fictiveness of literary artworks is not to be discovered in the unreality of the characters, objects, and events alluded to, but in the alludings themselves."[10] To do this Smith distinguishes between two kinds of discourse: fictive discourse and natural discourse.[11]

Briefly, then, by "natural discourse" I mean all utterances that are performed as historical acts and taken as historical events. If one asks what other kind of discourse there is, the answer is simple: there is no other kind; natural discourse is discourse. There are, however, other verbal structures which constitute, in themselves, neither historical acts nor historical events, but rather representations of them and, as such, are understood not be governed by the same conventions that obtain for natural utterances: and these verbal structures I refer to as fictive utterances.

Fictive utterances, Smith argues, are representations of natural utterances. Natural utterances, in turn, are a class of event. "A fictive utterance consists entirely of a linguistic structure, unlike a natural utterance, which consists of a linguistic event occuring in a historical context."[12] Some natural utterances are then presumably representations of events. The pivot of her analysis is the contention that some utterances (natural utterances) count as events. That is, they convey or conceal information; they influence or are influenced by contexts; they constitute, say, a slap on the back or a slap in the face. This nodus of event and utterance is also the source of the difficulty with Smith's

10. Barbara Herrnstein Smith, On the Margins of Discourse (Chicago and London: University of Chicago Press, 1978), p. 11.
11. Smith, p. 84.
12. Smith, p. 30.

theory. Fictive utterances which occur in the realm of discourse are representations of natural utterances which are a kind of event and so part of the realm of events. Natural utterances, themselves in the realm of discourse, are in turn representations of events in the realm of events. And the events represented by natural utterances are secretly supposed to be real ones, so that the realm status of stories is afterall contingent on the realm status of the events they are about. The difficulty with this formulation may be clearer in a figure.

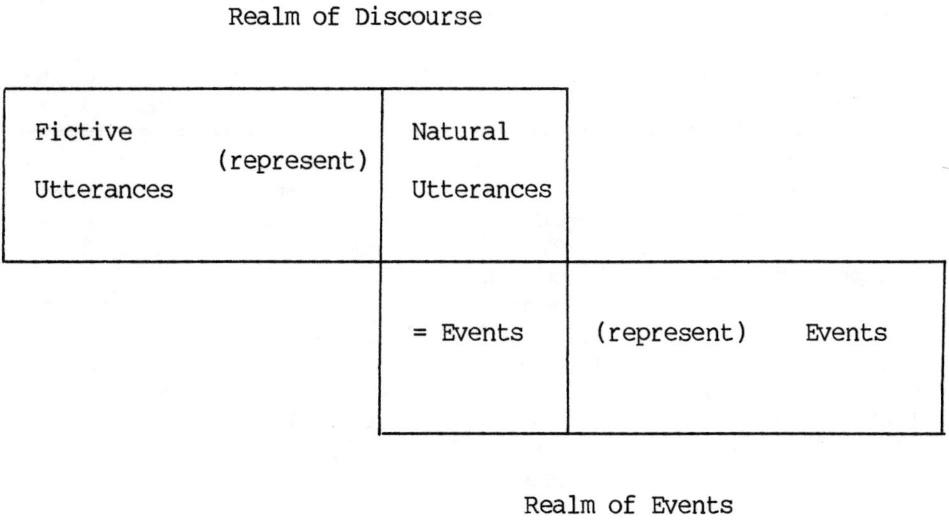

Realm of Discourse

Fictive Utterances	(represent)	Natural Utterances	
		= Events	(represent) Events

Realm of Events

Figure 25: The puzzle of Natural Utterances as Events.

One way to locate this difficulty is to notice that "utterances" occurs both in the realm of discourse and the realm of events and so does "events." In classifying some utterances, like anecdotes, as events and regarding fictions as representations of these, Smith excludes as fictions other representations of events, again like anecdotes, when the events represented are not utterances. Puzzles about the nature of fictions vanish only to reappear as puzzles about the nature of utterances and events.

This difficulty can be brought out with respect to anecdotes in conversations. Anecdotes can be regarded as instances of natural utterances. If, on Smith's analysis, fictive utterances fall clearly into what I would call the Storyrealm, and events fall clearly into what I would call the Taleworld, where do natural utterances fall? Their realm status is ambiguous. Insofar as anecdotes are framed as discontinuous with their contexts, so that they do not count as conversational acts or events, they can be seen as fictions; insofar as they are implicated in those contexts as acts and events, they can be supposed to lose their realm status as stories. Anecdotes do in fact partake of the nature of both fictions and events. To call them natural utterances is to miss their fictive qualities and to call them fictions is to miss their status as events. Collapsing the previous figure back into two realms schematizes the solution to this puzzle.

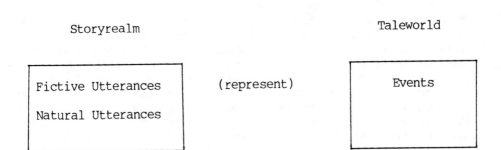

Figure 26: The Relationship between the Realm of Discourse
         and the Realm of Events.

If the boundary is not drawn between fictive and natural utterances but between stories and events, it is possible to investigate whether, when, and how stories, whether fictive or true, are protected from or susceptible to their contexts (a variation within the Storyrealm); and, as a separate undertaking, to see whether, how, and to what extent events in the Taleworld are connected or disconnected to realities (a variation within the Taleworld).[13]

References and Inferences;
Recoveries and Reconstitutions

The notion underlying both the attempt to locate the distinction between the fictive and the real in the Storyrealm and the attempt to locate it in the Taleworld is referentiality. In the first instance, the distinction depends on whether the Storyrealm refers to natural utterances or to events; in the second, it depends on whether the Taleworld referred to is real or imaginary. In both instances, the direction of influence is supposed to run from Taleworld to Storyrealm. The uneasiness of either of these formulations becomes apparent when the puzzle of how to constitute a story out of "private mental or nonexistent" realms of events is considered. The puzzle appears to be a version of the metaphysical problem of how to create something out of nothing.

13. Smith, p. 29. Another and powerful reading of this argument is Ryan's, adapted from John Searle: people telling fictious are people pretending to be people telling true stories, in what Searle distinguishes as pretending to refer as opposed to referring seriously. Both intend to move away from supposing that fictions refer to imaginery events and both run into similar difficulties with, among other things, the proliferation of theoretical entities and the ontological ambiguity of anecdotes. They make a move toward the theory I propose, though, in shifting the locus of the distinction between the fictive and the real from the Storyrealm to the intentionality of the tellers or hearers: the notion of pretending to be somebody else, or what Ryan calls substitute speakers. Ryan, pp. 412 - 413; John Searle, "The Logical/Status of Fictions," New Literal History 6 (1975). pp. 319 - 332.

The solution I propose reverses the direction of influence: stories are not constituted out of events, events are reconstituted by stories. Taleworlds are realms of events as they are conjured up by Storyrealms. For persons on storytelling occasions, these Taleworlds have no prior or separate existence, even when they are among those realms we call realities. Or, more properly, tellers and hearers have no access to such a prior or separate existence on the occasion of the storytelling. Each Taleworld is constituted by tellers and hearers out of an array of available sources in the story, themselves, and their experienced, recollected, and imagined realms. Once it is seen that Taleworlds are made up by stories, and not the other way around, it is possible to look at how stories use or instruct hearers to use other realms, both fictive and real, to make them up out of. And here, the principle of minimal departure can be elegantly invoked (as it is by Marie-Laure Ryan).

Stories, then, are not constituted out of imaginary events, imaginary events are reconstituted by stories. Taleworlds, whether fictive or real, are brought into being, sustained, and banished by the attention of tellers and hearers as it is composed by stories on storytelling occasions. In that sense, all Taleworlds are imaginary. And that, of course, is the sense in which imaginary realms do not yield fictions.

The distinction between the fictive and the real is not in the constitution of the Taleworld any more than it is in the constitution of the Storyrealm. Seen from inside or as if from inside, as entered into and inhabited, all Taleworlds are real. (Sophisticated characters in literary genres sometimes step out of frame to comment on their realm, the gesture at once pointing up and flouting its conventional framings.) To suppose that fictions can be reckoned from a locus in the Taleworld is to suppose, paradoxically, that in fictions this locus vanishes.[14] The resultant temptation to shift from a foothold in the Taleworld for true stories to a foothold in the Storyrealm for fictions has clouded analysis. Seen from inside

14. See Raymond Williams, Marxism and Literature (Oxford: Oxford University Press, 1977), pp. 147-148: "there was a falsification—a false distancing—of 'fictional' or the 'imaginary' (and connected with these the 'subjective'). And there was a related suppression of the fact of writing—active signifying composition—in what was

(Footnote 14 Continued on Next Page)

the Storyrealm, all Taleworlds are imaginary, brought to mind by acts of the mind.

To see the Taleworld properly as fictive or real is to draw away from it in order to reckon its realm status from outside, that is, to frame it. (Such a frame might, of course, be mentioned in the Storyrealm.) Apprehensions of the ontological status of Taleworlds as fictive or real are anchored in the perceptions and attitudes of participants in storytelling occasions. These attributes are not inherent in Taleworlds but modes of attention to them. Taleworlds framed as realities direct tellers and hearers to look to their past experience in reconstituting those realms. Fictive frames cut away this directed looking: a fictive Taleworld is not intended to be netted into persons' constantly reconstituted realities.

Still both realms are reconstitutions. As Roger Abrahams notes, "we are reminded repeatedly that telling the truth involves us in just as formulaic an enterprise as engaging in fantasy."[15] It would be possible to make a case for seeing that stories reconstitute fictive realms and find the case was open to the objection that true stories do not work in the same way. For that reason, I shall pursue the ontological constitution of anecdotes. If even true stories can be seen as reconstitutions, then clearly fictions can be so seen.

Anecdotes appear to be designed to recover past events. But the past is eerie philosophically; it is at once fixed and lost. What storytellers and hearers have access to is not the

(Footnote 14 Continued from Previous Page)

distinguished as the 'practical,' the 'factual' or the 'discoursive.' These consequences are profoundly related. To move, by defintion, from the 'creative' to the 'fictional', or from the 'imaginative' to the 'imaginary', is to deform the real practices of writing under the pressure of the interpretation of certain specific forms. The extreme negative definition of 'fiction' (or of 'myth')—an account of 'what did not (really) happen'—depends, evidently, on a pseudo-positive isolation of the contrasting definition, 'fact.'"

15. Roger Abrahams, "The Play of Worlds in Story and Storytelling", chapter of unpublished work-in-progress tentatively titled Goings On: Between Acts and Enactments (University of Texas, Austin), p. 41

past but traces and recollections, artefacts and mentafacts, out of which they might reconstruct the past. As Maurice Natanson writes: "When we distinguish between the event, its trace, and the historian's attempt to reconstruct events through the study of traces, we suggest, really, that there is a major problem with respect to the reality of which events are a part."[16] The events alluded to by the story are not the past but what can be inferred about it from the telling. Stories are not referential but inferential. They are not recoveries of the past but reconstitutions in the present.

As such, stories display affinities with the occasions on which they are told as well as with the events they are about. They are coded not only for reconstituting the past but also for gearing into the present. Attitudes toward the events, and the relationships among them presented by the story, inform hearers' sense of the past. If events are fixed and lost, stories are flexible and available. It is not so much that stories cannot change events as it is that events cannot change stories.[17] Stories create their Taleworlds, including the realm of the past. So stories are not second-order events but events in their own right, occasioned events with an insertion in the ongoing present as Storyrealms.[18] The events they are about do not constitute stories; stories reconstitute events.[19]

Stories, Storytellers, and Storytelling Occasions

One virtue of reconstituting past realms is the lodgement they offer past selves. Such an alternative lodgement may be especially attractive to old people whose presentations of self in everyday life may come to seem to them circumscribed.

16. Maurice Natanson, Literature. Philosophy and the Social Sciences (The Hague: Mouton, 1962), p. 193.
17. Samuel Butler is supposed to have remarked that God can't change history, historians can.
18. Contrast John Austin, How to do Things with Words (New York: Oxford Uuniversity Press, 1965), p. 22 on etiolations of language.
19. See Jonathan Culler, "Fabula and Sjuzhet in the Analysis of Narrative", Poetics Today 1 #3 (1980), pp. 27-37, p.33, on the recurrent opposition between "the priority and determining power of events and the determination of events by structures of significantion".

Stories about the past reconstitute for them a realm of events in which they were livlier than they are now. And one over which they exercise a far more delicate and absolute control than they ever did when they inhabited it. Its insertion in the present provides them the foothold for an alternative mode of presentation.

Florence Brown and her husband Jack are both seventy-seven when they tell the story of Alford Bickle's suicide, examined in Chapter Four. The Taleworld created by that story turns out to be a realm of the past which the Browns inhabited some fifty years ago. It lies in the same geographical region the storytellers and hearer now inhabit, farming country in Devon. This overlay of the terrains of the Taleworld and the real permits the storytellers the more smoothly to move into the Taleworld as characters. Their presence in that realm brings up an ethical puzzle: why did Jack Brown not intervene in or prevent the suicide: he had intervened in the earlier suicide attempt. Was this one different? If, as I suppose, it is not that events are captured by stories but that stories conjure up events, will it be possible to figure out this puzzle by investigating not the events but the story? Or, to put it another way, if stories are not referential just how is it that events are accessible through them?

Perspectives

The investigation of the story as a sequentially organized event suggests that there is only one story to which participants in the storytelling contribute different parts. Actually, there are two stories, one by each teller, and these are partially interlaced. Jack Brown's contribution proves not to be a continuation but a retelling. More precisely, there are two perspectives on the events which take the form of stories.

The first perspective is introduced by Mrs. Brown in her story of the suicide attempt followed, without a break, by her story of the suicide. Jack Brown finds Alford Bickle looking about in the loft of a barn for someplace to put up a rope "to hang heself". ("Heself" is Devon dialect for "himself".) Jack rescues him and returns him to his sister, warning her about his intentions. But only a day or two later, Jack goes down the road to the farm, hears a shot and comes upon the old man "with his face blew away". In the middle of her telling of the suicide story, her husband, Jack, comes home. In order to finish the story, she repeats one line three times where his entering remarks overlap her storytelling, "come up the road", and then goes straight on to the end: " and on the road looking right there was old man with his face blew away". After that, she invites Jack to address himself to the story in three queries: "Wasn't the Father", "I was right wasn't I", and finally, "Well?".

Jack Brown then tells his own version of the story from a second perspective, that of Alford Bickle himself. The old man sat on "an hedge". (Hedges in Devon can consist of low stone walls which are sometimes built up higher with shrubs or trees.) He works the trigger of a long rifle with a "forked stick", misses himself the first time and, Mrs. Brown chimes in, reloads his gun. Jack explains that first Alford Bickle took the spent cartridge out of the gun and put it in his mouth, that is, Mrs. Brown makes clear, he "put the cartridge in his mouth", he fires again, not missing this time, and is buried with that cartridge in his skull. The perspective has shifted between the two tellings, from Jack Brown's to Alford Bickle's.

Neither story is strictly what William Labov calls personal experience narrative.[20] If Alford Bickle told the story himself, it would be. Jack Brown is at best only witness to these events. Mrs. Brown knows the story at second-hand. I know it at third-hand and you at fourth. These orders of evidence can be sorted into what Goffman has called "laminations" away from the event.[21] The first lamination consists of central figures or actors in the events. The second consists of recipients of direct information about the events, or witnesses. The third and subsequent laminations consist of recipients of indirect information, or hearsay, in various degrees. Perspectives on the events shift with the storyteller's role as the person who enacts the events, sees them, or hears about them, directly or indirectly, in whatever degree.[22]

20. William Labov and Joshua Waletzky, "Narrative Analysis: Oral Versions of Personal Experience: in June Helm, ed., Essays in the Verbal and Visual Arts (Seattle and London: University of Washington Press, 1967).
21. See Goffman, pp. 156-157.
22. Labov has been exploring the legal notions of eye-witness and hearsay evidence with respect to narrative. Unpublished Lectures (University of Pennsylvania: 1979).

Strategic claims are based on these laminations. The closer the teller is to the innermost lamination, the more authoritative the telling. In light of this, it is possible to interpret what has happened here. Each narrator has shifted the telling one lamination closer to the events than he or she really was. Mrs. Brown tells the story from the point of view of Jack's witnessing of the events. Jack Brown tells the story from the perspective of Alford Bickle's experience of the events. In reality, Jack was not there. He came upon the old man, just as Mrs. Brown says, "with his face blew away". Everything about the acts leading to the suicide is induced from the position of the body near the hedge, the presence of the forked stick, the condition of the gun, the location of the discharged cartridge, and so on. So Jack Brown could not have intervened in the suicide. He was not there when it happened.

Storyability and Eventfulness

The Browns' shifts of perspective move hearers nearer to the event. Labov argues that eventfulness is in events and that is what makes them reportable or tellable. The sense of eventfulness is expressed in evaluations in the story. "Evaluative devices say to us: this was terrifying, dangerous, weird, wild, crazy; or amusing, hilarious, wonderful; more generally, that it was strange, uncommon, or unusuall--that is, worth repeating. It was not ordinary, plain, humdrum, everyday or run-of-the-mill."[23] Labov's criterion for tellability is uniqueness. On the contrary, while Harvey Sacks agrees that only some events are tellable or what he calls storyable given "the restricted storyability of the world under a competent viewing of it," his criterion for storyability is ordinariness.[24] "A kind of remarkable thing is how, in ordinary conversation, people, in reporting on some event, report what we might see to be not what happened, but the ordinariness of what happened."[25] Events are conventionalized, typified for stories, fitted into the frameworks of anonymous reality.[26] Accidents, fights, journeys, adventures, misadventures, crimes, deaths; such

23. Labov, "The Transformation of Experience in Narrative Syntax" in his Language in the Inner City (Philadelphia: University of Pennsylvania Press, 1972), p. 371.
24. Harvey Sacks, Unpublished Lecture Notes (University of California, Irvine: 1970), Lecture III, p. 12.
25. Sacks (1970), I, p. 3.
26. See Natanson, The Journeying Self, p. 25.

events undergo a kind of "epistemological domestication", in the phrase of Maurice Natanson, wherein what might be mysterious is rendered unproblematic, mundane, ordinary.[27] For instance, "a startling feature of mundanity is its incorporation of death as a typified event."[28] Recognizing typified events as storyable is part of our cultural competence, even so recognizing them in the course of experiencing them.[29] A particular person's experience of such an event may be unique to him; nonetheless, it is storyable in virtue of its ordinariness.

Suicides are in this sense storyable. They are among the sorts of events persons can figure are stories, or possible stories, if they come across one. Suicides, but not suicide aftermaths. Sacks, discussing automobile accidents, elucidates this matter: "Whereas people collect serious wrecks, it doesn't strike us that people collect types of wreck aftermaths. And of course if you start now to see that the tellable parts of an event have a tellability so restricted, and begin to get an idea then about how it is that not anything is a story, and that people don't figure anything's a story, and see that even in a scene where there is a story it's not any story that could be made out of it. So you get back to, in some ways the theme of the first lecture having to do with the restricted storyability of the world under a competent viewing of it."[30] Indeed, the display of competence in selecting typified events for stories is so compelling that storytellers like the Browns use aftermaths to recover deaths.

Jack Brown's story might nevertheless have recounted the suicide by recounting his discovery of it, working inductively from results to cause.[31] In fact, Labov argues, such inversions of sequence never occur in conversational anecdotes.[32] The sequential order of the story replicates the temporal order of events. An account of this is suggested by Goffman's contention that the engagement of hearers in stories is contingent on the management of information states, for "suspense is to the audience of replayings what being

27. Natanson, The Journeying Self, p. 27.
28. Natanson, The Journeying Self, p. 16.
29. Sacks (1970) I, p. 8.
30. Sacks (1970) III, p. 12.
31. See Sacks (1970) III, p. 20.
32. Labov, Language in the Inner City, p. 359.

lodged in unforetellable unfoldings is for participants in real life."[33] So storytellers return hearers to the information state or horizon that obtained at the outset of the events, regardless of their own order of discovery. The characteristic shift of stories into the present tense reflects this lodgement.[34] The effect of this arrangement is to imply the presence of the storyteller on the occasion of the suicide. In recounting the suicide, however, each storyteller has withdrawn himself from the story, modestly providing an account of what happened and not an account of his or her experience of what happened.

Stories make what Sacks calls "selections among alternatives".[35] Not only do they select what events to tell but they also select what to tell about the events, since "even for some things that bear telling, not anything about it may bear telling."[36] Some of the events that happen along with as well as before and after those being recounted are excluded. "For in fact every narrative, however seemingly "full", is constructed on the basis of a set of events which might have been included but were left out; and this is as true of imaginary as it is of realistic narratives," writes Haydon White.[37] The events that are so cut out are also cut up, articulated into segments shaped by discourse, a shaping that comes to influence the perception of events.[38] The selected

33. Goffman, pp. 506-507.
34. Sacks (1971) VI, p. 5: "So in a way a present is designedly isolated. By 'designedly' again, I mean to point up that the pasts before that present are set up to arrive at that as a present, and that present is used, then, to project futures. So it has this fine temporal organization to it, in which a range of tenses are manipulated to isolate a present. The present that's isolated is itself used as a platform for projecting futures."
35. Sacks (1968) Topic, p. 2.
36. Sacks (1970) III, p. 11.
37. Hayden White, "The Value of Narrativity in the Representation of Reality", Critical Inquiry 7, #1 (Autumn 1980), p. 14.
38. See Amy Shuman, "Retellings: Storytelling and Writing among Urban Adolescents" (Philadelphia: Ph.D. Thesis, University of Pennsylvania, 1981), p. 246. She distinguishes between events and experiences, arguing that "events are categories of experience, not to be confused with the experiences themselves."

events are then tied together to produce a causally related
concatenation of events that follow along from and are directed
toward each other. This condition of mutual implication makes
the last event appear to be what the first event was orienting
to all along. So, events in stories seem to come with
beginnings and ends, but there are no such boundaries in the
Taleworld. There, events are ongoing.[39] Stories cut out,
cut up, bind together, and bound off events. It is the
sequence so devised by stories that yields a sense of
eventfulness. If ordinariness provides storyability; stories
impart eventfulness.

Referentiality

The supposition that eventfulness is lodged in the
Taleworld is rooted in referentiality, the notion that events
inform stories as reality informs language. Insofar as the
theory of referentiality assumes that the shape of discourse is
informed by the shape of the events it is about, and not the
other way around, it is apparent that the linguistic model does
not suit narrative. The relationship that holds between
Storyrealm and Taleworld is not properly referential. In fact,
within linguistic philosophy attention to the relationship
between language and reality has shifted from matching words to
things, as in the early Wittgenstein, to regarding language as
a map of reality.[40] The underlying notion now is that the
map is designed, as Abraham Kaplan writes, "to direct attention
to certain resemblances between the theoretical entities and
the real subject matter."[41] The map must then be accompanied
by instructions about how to use it to look at the territory,
instructions in the form of what Gregory Bateson calls
metacommunications or frames:[42]

> Language bears to the objects which it denotes a
> relationship comparable to that which a map bears to a
> territory. Denotative communication as it occurs at the
> human level is only possible after the evolution of a
> complex set of metalinguistic (but not verbalized) rules
> which govern how words and sentences shall be related to
> objects and events.

39. See White, p. 26, on closure.
40. Ludwig Wittgenstein, Tractatus Logico-Philosophicus, ed.
    Bertrand Russell (London: Routledge and Paul, 1933).
41. Abraham Kaplan, The Conduct of Inquiry (San Francisco:
    Chandler, 1964), p. 265.
42. Gregory Bateson, Steps to an Ecology of Mind (New York:
    Ballantine, 1972), p. 180.

Language does not mirror reality. Linguistic philosophers since the later Wittgenstein have come to think of language as a separate universe of discourse whose import is not contingent on its correspondence with reality.[43]   Indeed, Edward Sapir and Benjamin Lee Whorf hypothesize that the contingency may be reversed so that, at least in some instances, language informs reality.[44]   So I am concerned to bring out the way in which the shape of the events is informed by the shape of the discourse.   The notion of stories as reconstitutions provides an account of why the organization of a story is not exhausted by the organization of the events it is about: influence runs from stories to events as well as from events to stories. Hence, Marie-Laure Ryan's "two seemingly incompatible attitudes toward the fictional text: viewing it as a world-reflecting as well as a world-creating utterance; taking the fictional world to exist independently of the narrator's declarations, while using these declarations as material for construing this world."[45]

Sequence, Time, and Consequence

The puzzle of eventfulness is hidden in the relation of sequence to time and consequence.   Sequence is the convention for time in stories.   Paul Ricoeur writes: "I take temporality to be that structure of existence that reaches language in narrativity and narrativity to be the language structure that has temporality as its ultimate referent."[46]   However, in the realm of events, one thing happens after another whereas in the realm of the story, one thing follows on from another.   That is, writes Haydon White: "The events must be not only registered within the chronological framework of their original occurrence but narrated as well, that is to say, revealed as

43. Wittgenstein, Philosophical Investigations, G.E.M. Anscombe, tr. (New York: Macmillan, 1953).
44. Benjamin Lee Whorf, Language, Thought and Reality (Cambridge: M.I.T. Press, 1969), p. 214: "We are thus introduced to a new principle of relativity, which holds that all observers are not led by the same physical evidence to the same picture of the universe, unless their linguistic backgrounds are similar, or can in some way be calibrated."
45. Ryan, "The Pragmatics of Personal and Imperrsonal Fiction," Poetics 10 (1981), pp. 517 - 531, p. 530.
46. Ricoeur, p. 169.

possessing a structure, an order of meaning, which they do not possess as mere sequence."[47] Sequence for stories is ontologically distinct from time for events. Harvey Sacks says: "Now, I separated temporal from sequential organization which is something separate from a temporal organization by virtue of what a sequential organization is; i.e., such an organization as for each point in it that is subsequent to some other point, an appreciation of that point turns on an appreciation of its position."[48] Stories do not consist of discrete consecutive events; the events are consequentially related. Sequence might be said to be informed by time in the Taleworld, and by consequence in the Storyrealm. Eventfulness is not located in the temporal relationship between events, the way they fall out over time, but in their consequential relationship, the way they engender significance in each other.

Sequence forms the bridge across which eventfulness travels from the Storyrealm to the Taleworld. The consequential relations between consecutive events in stories imputes to them a causality, a consequentiality, an eventfulness they may not natively possess. The sequential consequentiality of life is an interpretation forwarded by (among other things) stories. Life does not merely provide raw events for transformation into scriptings, Goffman argues, it is conceived of in a way that makes such transformations possible.[49] In his lecture on the theatricality of talk, Goffman claims that talk devises for itself appearances of linked, mutually influenced, sequenced, climaxed, or otherwise intentionally sorted material as eventful.[50] What Dell Hymes has called "narrative thinking" is one among many "renderings of experience," in Amy Shuman's suggestive phrase.[51] Other renderings, history, memory, humor, complaint, explanation, confession, invest their own structures in events. To discover these structures of narrative in life is to confuse Storyrealm with Taleworld. "What wish is enacted, what desire is gratified, by the fantasy

47. White, p. 9.
48. Sacks (1971) IX, p. 5.
49. Goffman, pp. 550 and 557.
50. Goffman, Unpublished Lecture (University of Pennsylvania, 1973).
51. Dell Hymes and Courtney Cazden, "Narrative Thinking and Storytelling Rights: A Folklorist's Clue to a Critique of Education", Keystone Folklore 22 #1 and 2 (1978), p. 26.

that _real_ events are properly represented when they can be shown to display the formal coherency of a story." Haydon White continues:[52]

> I have sought to suggest that this value attached to narrativity in the representation of real events arises out of a desire to have real events display the coherence, integrity, fullness, and closure of an image of life that is and can only be imaginary. The notion that sequences of real events possess the formal attributes of the stories we tell about imaginary events could only have its origin in wishes, daydreams, reveries. Does the world really present itself to perception in the form of well-made stories, with central subjects, proper beginnings, middles, and ends, and a coherence that permits us to see "the end" in every beginning?

The segmentation and concatenation of events into stories creates the logical sequence which appears to refer to the chronological sequence. It is across the bridge of sequence that the notion of time enters the Storyrealm. Once this equivalence is established, the next move is the reduction of the chronological to the logical, as Paul Ricoeur explains.[53]

> The segmenting and concatenating of functions thus paved the way for a reduction of the chronological to the logical. And in the subsequent phase of structural analysis, with Griemas and Roland Barthes, the search for the atemporal formula that generates the chronological display of functions transformed the structure of the tale into a machinery whose task it is to compensate for the initial mischief or lack by a final restoration of the disturbed order. Compared to this logical matrix, the quest itself appears as a mere diachronical residue, a retardation or suspension in the epiphany of order.

On this argument, sequence is illusory. The logical organization of the story is merely the surface manifestation of its deep structure. Sequence, the reflection of time in linguistic analysis, becomes in structural analysis a transformation of structure. Sequence appears on the first

---

52. White, pp. 8 and 27.
53. Ricoeur, p. 184.

analysis to be bound to time and on the second to be severed from it. The phenomenological perspective on the relationship between Taleworld and Storyrealm invoked here suggests an understanding of these two apparently incompatible possibilities.

Sequence and Structure in Context

The Storyrealm is oriented in two directions, toward the events it is about and the occasion on which it is told. To see the Storyrealm in the context of the Taleworld is to attend to sequence, the aspect of narrative that draws stories toward events. Seen so, sequence is the armature along which narrative is constructed. And movement through the sequence is, as Victor Turner argues, transformative.[54] Seeing the Storyrealm in the context of the storytelling occasion draws attention to its structure, the relations between elements in the sequence and their bearing on the occasion. Consequentiality is consequentiality for tellers and hearers as well as the consequentiality of events.

Stories are neither simply sequential nor simply structural, to the exclusion of the other. If the sequential axis is split off on the one hand and the structural framework is precipitated out on the other, the resultant syntagm directs attention to the relationship between stories and the events they are about and the resultant paradigm directs attention to the relationship between stories and the occasions on which they are told. Stories shift between structural and sequential presentations as tellers and hearers shift between contexts of interpretation. Ricoeur writes:[55]

...every narrative combines two dimensions in various proportions, one chronological and the other non-chronological. The first may be called the episodic dimension, which characterizes the story as made out of events. The second is the configurational dimension, according to which the plot construes significant wholes out of scattered events.... I understand this act to be the act of the plot, as eliciting a pattern...a configuration from a succession.

Paul Ricoeur

54. Victor Turner, "Social Dramas and Stories about them," Critical Inquiry 7 #1 (1980), p. 161.
55. Ricoeur, p. 178.

If the story is taken to be referential then it is merely a mode of access to the Taleworld and so, as Richard Wollheim notes, "ultimately expendable or throwaway."[56]   If, on the other hand, the Storyrealm is regarded as a reconstitution, not only does it conjure up the Taleworld, but also, it orients that realm to the occasion on which the story is told.   The Storyrealm becomes the pivot between the Taleworld and the real.

56.   Richard Wollheim, Art and Its Objects (New York, Evanston, London: Harper and Row, 1968), p. 75.

CHAPTER SIX

ONTOLOGICAL PUZZLES ABOUT NARRATIVE*

Stories present themselves in three realms. They can be seen as an aspect of conversation, part of the occasion on which they are told and continuous with it. In this presentation, their designs must be reckoned from their connections with other aspects of the occasion. They appear in the realm of conversation. Or, stories can be seen as an enclave within conversation, framed off from it as a different order of discourse. In this presentation, their designs must be reckoned from connections among elements within the story. They appear in the Storyrealm. Or, stories can be seen as a realm of events not present to the storytelling occasion at all but conjured up for that occasion by the story. In this presentation, their designs must be reckoned from connections among the events they are about. They appear in the Taleworld. These three realms are laminated together in the storytelling occasion. The outermost or surface lamination is the story as conversation; the next or underlying lamination is the story as narrative; and the innermost or deepest lamination is the story as events.[1]

* This paper was first presented at the American Folklore Society Meetings in Salt Lake City, Utah, in 1978, under the title, "Lineal and Nonlineal Codifications of Narrative". A later version was given at the Modern Language Association Meetings in Los Angeles, California, in 1982, under the present title and was subsequently published in Poetics 13 (1984) pp. 239 - 259 in a shorter form. Barbara Kirshenblatt-Gimblett's critical reading transformed some of the obscurities of the earlier versions for this extended analysis.

1.   See Erving Goffman, Frame Analysis (New York: Harper and Row, 1974), p. 82 on lamination and framing.

This chapter considers a story in each of these realms in order to discover the presentation it makes from all three perspectives. Seeing the same story in different perspectives affords understandings not apparent in any perspective taken separately.[2] Understandings attained from one perspective angle into and inform understandings from another. The chapter then follows frame shifts over the course of a single storytelling to disclose the perspectives from which the story is seen as it unfolds. These inquiries bear on a consideration of genre.

The story was told in the course of another evening's conversation with Algy May in the spring of 1975. I have come with two friends, Miles Fursdon and Peter Martin, a young farmer and a young forester, to visit Algy, Jean, and Marian. We talk, as usual, in the kitchen of the old farmhouse. After greetings, Algy teases me about having the tape recorder again, ascertains that it is on, and embarks on his first story of the evening.*

```
     A:  I like the story about
            a
[[ K:  [ Ha ] see?
        He always tells a story=
     A:  No go on
        (give him)
    MF:  ((Chuckles))
     A:  When  ((chuckles))
[[ K:         [  ((chuckles)) ]
     A:  Is it on?
     K:  Of course it's on let's see.
     A:  All right I'll- this is my
        final thing.
        I was
        had a drink or two and I was walking back from Newton
            Abbot to Ashburton.
        /
```

*See appendix for transcription devices.

2. See Gregory Bateson, <u>Mind and Nature</u> (New York: E.P. Dutton, 1979), p. 21, "... two or more information sources come together to give information of a sort different from what was in either source separately."

And-
in the wintertime.
/
And I was tired
I thought I saw a car coming.
In fact it did come.
Slowly.
Overtook me.
I thought
I don't know it's got no lights.
Anyhow
opened the door jumped in.
Passenger side.
Thought
um anything special in the thing?
And
sat there you see and when we got to a corner great
      hairy hand comes round
K: Hm.
A: moves the steering wheel and
on we go.
K: ((Coughs))
A: Then I nodded off- went to sleep.
Stopped at the
A-38 or no- Eastern Garage-
whatever it was
and
woke up suddenly you see
thing had stopped
and there was this chap
getting petrol
to be
put in the car.
(With the attendant and that?)
So I got out.
And the
owner of the car said
where've you come from?
Well I said I
saw the car coming along and I
just stepped in
he said you bugger you know I been pushing this car
      for the last five miles
[[K: [((Laughs))]
  MF:[((Laughs))]
  A: And there was I pushing you as well.

[[All: [((Chuckles)) ((Laugh))]]

A: He'd run out of petrol.
((Laughs))
Stupid story.
It's true actually
yeah.
((Laughs))
S- he had on a- a leather uh hairy gauntlet you see you-
right on the steering wheel.
Push push.
((Laughs))
K: ((Laughs))
A: Quite a good story isn't it really.

A Little Nap, a Little Mystery

The little nap makes a little mystery. Conditions in the Taleworld appear to be unpropitious for taking a nap. It is late at night, Algy is walking back home, alone, a lonely road, a long walk, in wintertime. This is clearly the set-up for some ominous event. And, indeed just such an event seems to transpire. A car comes along, no lights, no driver, Algy gets into it on the passenger side, a hairy hand grasps the steering wheel--and he falls asleep. However, some of the incidents that make Algy's behavior puzzling could also account for it. He had had a drink, it was late, he had a long way to go on a lonely road, it was cold, he was tired, and a rare car appears. So he slips into it and nods off. There is, then, a relationship between preceding and subsequent events, one that appears to be causal. The puzzle is that contradictory causes seem to produce the same consequence.

The Sequential, the Consequential, and the Consecutive

Relationships between events in the Taleworld can be reinvestigated as relationships between elements in the Storyrealm. Puzzles about mystery in the realm of events are thus transformed into puzzles about mechanics in the realm of narrative. The appearance of causality is enhanced by the sequential arrangement of events by the story. "For us," writes Dorothy Lee, "chronological sequence is of vital importance, largely because we are interested, not so much in the event itself, but rather in its place within a related series of events; we look for its antecedents and its consequences. We are concerned with the causal or telic

relationship between events or acts."[3] Sequence invites us
to monitor events for causal relations. "Indeed", writes
Roland Barthes, "there is a strong presumption that the
mainspring of the narrative activity is to be traced to that
very confusion between consecutiveness and consequence,
what-comes-after being read in a narrative as
what-is-caused-by."[4] Causality is not inherent in events but
imputed to them by stories. Sequencing in the Storyrealm
creates the presumption of causality in the Taleworld.

The relationship between elements in the Storyrealm is not
causality but mutual implication: a first element implies and
is entailed by a next.[5] In this story, for instance, the car
comes and Algy gets into it. The appearance of the car implies
a chance of getting into it and getting into it entails the car
having come. Mutually implicated elements, which Barthes calls
"cardinal nuclei," can be strung together to form the
syntagmatic axis of the story.[6] The sequence of elements
including the nap might be described thus: a car comes, Algy
gets into it, encounters danger, and falls asleep. Elements in
the sequence are not only mutually implicated but also directed
toward climax, here, the consequence of the appearance of the
hairy hand. In this story, the nap now appears in the place of
the climax. What leads hearers to expect a climax is clearer
if the sequence is represented, following Claude Bremond, as a
series of binary choices:[7]

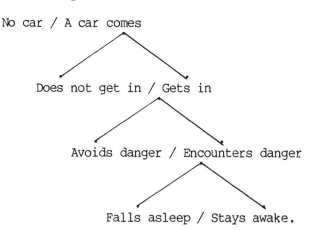

No car / A car comes

Does not get in / Gets in

Avoids danger / Encounters danger

Falls asleep / Stays awake.

3. Dorothy Lee, <u>Freedom and Culture</u> (Prentice-Hall, 1959), p.
    94
4. Roland Barthes, "An introduction to the Structural
    Analysis of Narrative", <u>New Literary History</u> 6 (1974-75),
    pp. 237-272, p. 248.
5. Barthes, p. 253.

Either a car comes or it does not come. When it comes, he either gets into it or not. By getting into it, he either encounters danger or avoids danger. But having encountered danger, Algy might be expected either to succumb or escape. Instead, he falls asleep. Is the nap the climax?

The nap appears to be the climax on account of its position. However, the next element after an antecedent is not necessarily its consequence, even if, perhaps especially if, that consequence is the climax. Within the story sequence, a distinction must be made between the consequential and the merely consecutive. Consequential elements are mutually implicated to form the plot. Consecutive elements come after but do not follow on from the consequential ones. They spin out the span between. Several consecutive elaborations intervene between the initial appearance of the car and Algy's getting into it.

Consecutive:	I thought I saw a car coming
Consequential:	In fact it did come
	Slowly
Consecutive:	Overtook me.
Consecutive:	I thought
	I don't know it's got no lights.
	Anyhow
Consequential:	opened the door jumped in.

Consecutive elements set the rhythm of storytelling. Barthes writes that such an element, which he calls "catalysis", "precipitates, delays, or quickens the pace of the discourse, sums up, anticipates, and sometimes even confuses the reader."[8] In this story, consecutive elaborations draw out the episode of the car, rendering each move in slow motion, dreamlike, thus enhancing the hallucinatory or legendary effect of the story.

The suspension of action, especially the suspension of action just before climax, creates suspense. Indeed, the distribution of suspense in a narrative roughly locates its climax by preceding and delaying it. If the nap is a consecutive element, it creates suspense where it is most

6. Barthes, pp. 247–248.
7. Claude Bremond, "Morphology of the French Folktale", Semiotica 11 (1970), pp. 247–276.
8. Barthes, p. 253.

indicative, just before the climax. By this strategy, the position where climax can be expected is filled by an element designed to defer its appearance while sustaining the anticipation of it. However, the nap is clearly not the consequence of the appearance of the hairy hand. Barthes explains that "a sequence is a logical string of nuclei, linked together by a solidarity relation: the sequence opens when one of its terms is lacking an antecedent of the same kin, and it closes when another of its terms no longer entails any consequent function."[9] The nap and the hand are not of the same kin. Even if the hand is antecedent to the climax, the nap is not its consequence. So the nap is not the climax, either by position or implication.

However, the nap is still consequential to the story provided it is consequent on or antecedent to something else. The story sequence consists of strings of elements of the same kin, each containing at least two elements, so arranged that the opening element of one string may be lodged between elements of another, thus forming an interlocking series.[10] For instance, it is possible to sort out the string of elements pertaining to the car as follows: a car comes, Algy gets into it, the car goes on, stops, and Algy gets out. Between going on and stopping, Algy falls asleep. Between stopping and getting out, he wakes up. The nap can be seen, then, to consist not of a single element but of a string of two elements of the same kin. Falling asleep is antecedent to the consequence of waking up. The nap is not consecutive but consequential, not a suspension of action but an extension of action. It must be regarded as one of a potentially unlimited set of consequential and inconsequential elements that intervene between the appearance of the hairy hand and the consequences of that appearance. The extension of action projects the hunt for climax beyond the nap into the second half of the story.

9.   Barthes, p. 270.
10. See Barthes, p. 270: "Narrative thus appears as a succession of tightly interlocking mediate and intermediate elements ..."

Sequence and Frame

A distinction must be made between the sequential and nonsequential aspects of the story. The sequential aspect, consisting of both consequential and consecutive elements, is so ordered that, as William Labov points out, inverting the order of elements in the Storyrealm inverts the inferred order of events in the Taleworld.[11] The drink, the long walk, alone, on a lonely road, in wintertime, and being tired are in this sense nonsequential. Though these elements precede the nap in the story, they are not necessarily sequenced, only incidentally sequentially deployed. They could be inserted in any order and in several places in the story without altering the sequence of events. Clustered at the beginning of the story, they form what Labov calls an orientation section.[12] Labov regards the orientation as the background against which the story sequence proper unfolds. This understanding relies on a sequentiality that does not obtain for orientations. An orientation is neither the cause nor the background of what follows, but the frame.

Frames consist either of bits of information, which Barthes calls "informants" or of disclosures of attitudes, which he calls "indices". They indicate the character, atmosphere, mood, or motivation that informs elements or sequences of elements, thus indexing the relationships among elements. The orientation counts as one of the class of frames which "provide pure, locally relevant data" about what is transpiring.[13] This is not merely information deemed necessary in order to understand what is transpiring, as Harvey Sacks describes it, but information that suggests or supports

11. William Labov, "The Transformations of Experience in Narrative Syntax" in his Language in the Inner City (Philadelphia: University of Pennsylvania Press, 1972), pp. 354-396, pp. 359-360.
12. Labov and Joshua Waletzky, "Narrative Analysis: Oral Versions of Personal Experience", in Essays on the Verbal and Visual Arts, ed. June Helm (Seattle and London: University of Washington Press, 1962), pp. 12-44, p. 32.
13. Barthes, p. 249.

an interpretation of it.[14] Frames can include explicit clarifications and explanations as well as predisposing and counterposed conditions.

Sequences, then, display relations among elements at the same level of analysis; frames indicate relations between elements at different levels of analysis.

The theory of levels (as enumerated by Benveniste) provides two types of relations: distributional (if the relations belong to the same level) and integrative (if they straddle two levels). It follows that distributional relations alone are unable to account for meaning. Thus, in order to carry out a structural analysis, it is necessary first to distinguish several levels of description (instance de description) and to place these levels within an hierarchical (integrative) perspective.[15]

Sequence provides plot; frames provide meaning. Thus, frames bear on but do not engender sequence. They might be said to make sense of sequences, sense being a relation between two levels and sequence being the relationship within a level.

Lineal and Nonlineal Codifications of Narrative

Seeing frames at a different level of analysis from sequence entails a shift from lineal to nonlineal codifications, to adopt Dorothy Lee's terminology.[16] Codifications mold understandings of the events they codify.

14. Harvey Sacks, Unpublished Lectures on Storytelling in Conversation, Lecture VII (1970), p. 10: "What we have is a sense of context being employed by the teller, which involves fitting into the story, in carefully located places, information that will permit the appreciation of what was transpiring which is not information which involves events in the story sequence at that point."
15. Barthes, p. 242 (his parentheses).

To select a codification is to move toward analysis bound by the perspective it affords. Lineal codifications foreground the sequential organization of stories. They segment stories into elements and deploy them along an axis. Analysts of this ilk tend to regard the necessarily sequenced elements as the syntagmatic axis of the story and to fit the nonsequential elements in and around that axis. For this reason, Labov assorts narrative elements according to their relative fixity of position.[17] An artefact of this codification is that unsequenced elements appear peripheral to analysis. At its extreme, lineal codification suppresses or excludes consideration of elements whose properties are not sequentially determined, or forces such elements into spuriously sequential arrangements. Nonsequential elements are properly understood as frames of sequential elements, not merely aspects of sequence.

Switching from lineal to nonlineal codifications foregrounds the structural framework of stories. Nonlineal codifications sort elements into sets and array them in a framework. Analysts of this persuasion tend to set up a paradigm for the story which masks its sequence. An effect of this codification is to render sequence irrelevant or trivial to analysis. This is the seed of the structuralist insight that sequence is only one mode of access to the formal organization of the story. At its extreme, nonlineal codification contrives to banish sequence as an accident of the unfolding of structure over time.[18]

16. Lee, "Codifications of Reality: Lineal and Nonlineal" in her Freedom and Culture pp. 105-120. Criticisms of Lee in terms of the actualization of these systems of codification in various cultures does not impugn the theoretical discriminations she puts forward.
17. Labov and Waletzky, 12 - 44 and elsewhere.
18. Claude Levi-Strauss says: "The chronological order of succession is reabsorbed by an atemporal matrix." Quoted by Cluade Bremond, "Le Message Narratif," Communicatiore 4 (1964). Also Victor Turner, "Social Dramas and Stories about them", Critical Inquiry 7 (1980), pp. 141-168, p. 161: "Here I would query the formal structuralist implication that sequence is an illusion and all is but a permutation and combination of rules and vocabularies already laid down in the deep structures of mind and brain."

On a lineal codification, this story transforms one configuration of events into another. On a nonlineal codification, alternate configurations are laminated into the story at different levels of analysis. Nonlineal codifications can be taken as transformations of the lineal. "To understand a narrative", writes Barthes, "is not only to follow the unfolding of the story but also to recognize in it a number of 'strata', to project the horizontal concatenations of the narrative onto an implicitly vertical axis."[19] Henry Glassie argues that alternative codifications capture the same event from different perspectives.[20]

> The alternative of a one dimensional field has been offered... but, in fact, neither a field nor a hierarchy is discontinuous..., and, either is reduced practically to the dichotomy of object and environment for study; the incorporative moves laterally or vertically can yield the same result. In either case, the system can be shifted to any object, from the smallest to the largest, so that a complete description can be produced. One of the object's components can be selected as an object with its own compositional and relational aspects, or all of the object's relations can be bundled into a new object so that what were formerly relations become components and a new field of relations is opened for examination. The whole system can be moved upward and downward to connect all of the cosmos, atomistically and holistically.

In a sense, however, different codifications reify different events. The story reified by a lineal codification draws in the events the story is about as a context of interpretation. Sequence relates consequence in the Storyrealm to time in the Taleworld. The story reified by a nonlineal codification draws in the occasion on which the story is told as a context of interpretation. Frames afford perspectives on the events and the story for persons on storytelling occasions.

19. Barthes, p. 243.
20. Henry Glassie, "Structure and Function: Folklore and the Artifact", Semiotica 7 (1973), pp. 313-351, p. 316.

However, the lineal and the nonlineal might be seen not as alternative codifications but as aspects of narrative. Stories are layered together structurally as well as unfolded sequentially. A shift in codifications does not necessarily descry two mutually exclusive sets of elements, the structural and the sequential. Some elements figure in both sets. If the sequential aspects are precipitated out as one level of analysis, the nonsequential elements can be laminated onto the sequence as frames. On this analysis, sequentiality is revealed as a kind of relationship, not mere succession. Frames, in turn, are not taken simply to lie along the edges of the events or realms of events they enclose. They are understood to span and transfix the events they bear on. They work not just to shift realms but to pervasively qualify them. Layering displays differences among the levels of analysis at which frames occur as well as differences among the orders of the events they frame. On this understanding, frames themselves are disclosed as events whose realm status can be investigated.

What on sequential analysis appeared to be a cause turns out on structural analysis to be an account. The account forwarded is not in the frame but in the relationship between the frame and the element or sequence of elements on which it bears. The nap reveals the significance of the drink, the long walk late at night on a lonely road in wintertime, and being tired. The same frame considered in relation to a different element takes on a different significance. In this instance, the same frame supports alternative interpretations. What might be seen as counterconditions for taking a nap, namely, being alone late at night on a lonely road, can also be seen as conditions for the appearance of the hairy hand. The frame indexes not only both of these elements but also the relationship between them and the relationships among them and the element that precedes them in the sequence, the arrival of the car. Indexing is what renders relationships among elements more than sequential.[21] In light of this frame, the car appears as rescue, on the one hand, from feeling tired, the possibility realized in the nap; and on the other hand, from mysterious dangers, the possibility realized in the hairy hand.

21. See Barthes, p. 247.

The tension between these two possibilities is sustained through the appearance of the hairy hand by the alternative interpretations the frame supports.[22] If the hand is imaginary, the drink, the late night, the cold, and the tiredness index hallucination due to sleepiness, and the hand is congruent with the nap. Hence, the nap's plausibility. If the hand is real, the long walk alone on a lonely road late at night indexes vulnerability, and the hand is contrasted to the nap. Hence, its mystery. Hallucination is appropriate to sleepiness as vulnerability is to alertness. Falling asleep in the presence of a real severed hand is the possibility that foils interpretation and feeds interest. The suspense that leads hearers to expect something to happen becomes mystery about what has happened already.

Suspense and Mystery

Suspense and mystery have been taken as aspects of the same phenomenon. Actually, suspense is a property of the sequential unfolding of stories. It is generated by spinning out the hiatus between mutually implicated elements of the plot so that hearers are suspended between expectation and satisfaction. Mystery is a property of the structural layering of stories. It is created by withholding the proper framework of interpretation from the plot sequence to which it applies so that hearers are mystified. Suspense comes to a climax: the appearance of the anticipated event. Mystery comes to a resolution: the disclosure of an interpretation. In stories, mystery is usually grafted onto suspense so that resolution accompanies or closely follows climax. Thus, the tension generated by deferred completion at the level of sequence attaches to deferred interpretation at the level of structure, and the puzzlement engendered by withheld interpretation, in

22. See Susan Stewart. "The Epistemology of the Horror Story", Jounal of American Folklore 95 (January 1982), pp. 33-50, p. 35: "The sign's referent is clouded in an ambiguity which we cannot decipher, and interpretation is deferred until the narratives's resolution." And, p. 4: "The hesitation experienced by the reader or audience in this type of story is one of being in between interpretations, in between states of being."

turn, enhances the suspended climax. In this story, the relationship between suspense and mystery appears to have broken down. What looks like suspense turns out to be mystery. At the juncture where climax might be expected to occur, Algy takes a little nap. The nap at once puts off climax and eludes interpretation. The hunt for climax finds instead resolution. But the resolution works a transformation: it turns the Taleworld into a different ontological realm.

The nap takes on a different status in the Taleworld from the one it holds in the Storyrealm. The nap continues the story but splits the events the story is about into two realms. Before the nap, events occur in the realm of the extraordinary; afterwards, they occur in the realm of the ordinary. The nap becomes a pivot between realms. The capacity so to shift realms is inherent in sleep. Sleep is itself an altered state of consciousness, shifting from the waking world to the realm of sleep and thence to dreams. Here, that realm-shift is used to provide passage to a different waking world, one bearing the earmarks of the ordinary. Because realm-shift is from the extraordinary to the ordinary, Algy can be supposed to wake up figuratively as well as literally, to wake up in the sense of come to or catch on. By this ontological transformation, the nap splits and bridges the two realms of events.

So divided, events attain an ontological neatness. They are not contradictory or incongruous aspects of the same realm but suitable constituents of two different ones. The contrast between these two realms is delicately indexed by two frames of the kind Barthes calls "indices".[23] These are distinguished from informants in providing, not information or understandings, but apprehensions and attitudes. Informants index relationships among elements in the story; indices proper index relationships between the story and the storyteller or hearer. They imply "a deciphering activeness and consequence".[24] In this, they resemble Labov's evaluations.[25] The contrasting indices are "slowly" and "suddenly". "Slowly" frames the arrival of the car in the realm of the extraordinary.

23. Barthes, p. 249.
24. Barthes, p. 249.
25. Labov and Waletzky, p. 33.

Consecutive	A: I thought I saw a car coming.
Consequential	In fact it did come.
Index	Slowly
Consecutive	Overtook me.
Consecutive	I thought
	I don't know it's got no lights
	Anyhow
Consequential	opened the door jumped in
Informant	passenger side.
Consecutive	Thought
	um anything special ( )?
	And
Consecutive	sat there you see and when we got to a
	corner great hairy hand comes round
	K: Hm.
Consecutive	A: moves the steering wheel and
	on we go.
	K: ((Coughs))
Consequential	A: Then I nodded off- went to sleep.

The slow rhythm indexed here is sustained throughout the episode of the car by the consecutive elements interposed to spin out suspense between consequential ones. By these devices, the passage takes on an air of unreality, hallucination, vision, legend; of other-worldly experience. Algy's awakening in the realm of the ordinary, by contrast, is framed by "suddenly". Commensurately, a quick pace is produced by paring down consecutives. These devices create an air of reality, factuality, ordinariness; of down-to-earth experience.

Consequential	A: Stopped at the
	A-38 or no- Eastern Garage-
	whatever it was
	and
Consequential	woke up suddenly you see
with Index	(thing had stopped)
Consequential	and there was there was this chap
	getting petrol
	to be
	put in the car.
	(With the attendant and that)?
Consequential	So I got out.

Though reframed, the events transpiring in the realm of the ordinary are still sequential to those is the realm of the extraordinary. Following out the sequence leads to two enclaves embedded in the ordinary. The enclaves are set off from that realm by the laminator verb "said".[26] Laminator verbs frame enclaves as a different order of event from the events around them and marks one boundary of the events so framed.

```
                    A:    And the
Lamination                owner of the car said
                          where've you come from.
Lamination                Well I said I
Consequential             saw the car coming along and I
Consequential             just stepped in.
```

Within the enclave, Algy's story is all consequential, as if he provides in a second realm the deep structure of his own story in the first. The driver's story, likewise laminated in an enclave, also consists of consequential elements, but his are laced with indices like "you bugger" which disclose his attitude.

```
Consequential   A:  he said you bugger you know I been pushing
                          this car for the last five miles
                    ...
Consequential           and there was I pushing you as well.
```

As Barthes writes, "when a single sequence involves two characters--it is the normal case--the sequence implies two perspectives......what it comes to is that each character, even a secondary one, is the hero of his own sequence."[27] Here, these two perspectives are explicit. The two characters themselves provide reruns of the same sequence of events from different perspectives. The distribution of knowledge between characters is differential. Some aspects of the events are hidden or partially hidden from one or the other until this moment of disclosure. It is this differential that permits the initial understanding of the events as extraordinary. The two reruns fitted together then compose a second and ordinary account.

26. See Goffman, p. 505.
27. Barthes, p. 257.

The enclaves themselves have two ontological presentations: one, as a pair of little stories laminated in the story and, two, as a rerun in the second half of the story of events transpiring in the first. The enclaves as stories are sequential but not consequential to the story. The telling of these little stories is what happens next but what the stories tell is not. Stories within a story suspend their framing story whole they are being told. They count as events, specifically as tellings, but not as the events they recount. The enclaves as events, by contrast, are consequential but not sequential to the story. They are reruns of events that have already transpired in the other realm. Rerunning the same events in a different realm implicitly constitutes an explanation or resolution of the mystery in the first run. Resolution is thus substituted for climax in the story sequence.

Puzzles about Frame

The resolution is supported by the relationship between the sequence of events inside the reruns and their frames. The events in Algy's rerun are consequentially related to each other through not consequent on what precedes them. The motive for stepping in is located in the cluster of frames that make up the orientation at the opening of the story. Taken in relation to this sequence of events, that frame indexes getting into a moving car with no driver as the result of tiredness, cold, drink, and so on, and not as a foolhardy invitation to the extraordinary. The driver's rerun provides an account of the appearance of a moving car with no driver. This account, itself a frame, is indexed by the following frame about running out of petrol as innocent and ordinary, not some sort of supernatural act or trick. A third frame directs attention back to the first run of these events. In it, the hairy hand is reframed as a fur glove, not one of the legendary hairy hands. Tinkering with frames in this way appears to be designed to make sure the resolution fits. The frames themselves lie either along the edges of the events they frame, where they also serve as boundaries, or elsewhere in the story, and occur either before or after the events they frame so that they work both frontwards and backwards. The third frame explicitly extends the explanatory range of the resolution arrived at in the second half of the story back over the first half.

The events in the first half of the story turn out likewise to be laminated, not in stories but in thought. To laminate events in thought is to constitute them impressions or images, casting doubt on the experience of them. They are rendered dubious, unreliable, suspect, and therefore vulnerable to reframing. The substantiality that appears to be claimed for them can easily be disclaimed. Sleep itself can be regarded as an extension of thought, a further attentuation of Algy's lodgment in reality. The laminator verbs in the second half resituate events in reality by transforming the status of knowledge: "thought" becomes "said"; "I thought I saw a car coming" becomes "I said I saw a car coming"; "I thought I don't know" becomes "he said ... you know". This second lamination reframes the passive and impressionistic as active and precise, thus shifting from illusion to reality. The epistemological priority granted what is said over what is thought gives weight to the reframe.

The ontological complexities alluded to here can be schematized as follows. A story is itself an enclave in the realm of conversation, one that evokes another realm of events called here the Taleworld. Among the events in that Taleworld are two more enclaves, the thoughts of one character and the stories of both, each of which conjures up its own Taleworld. The twist here is that the events in one of these Taleworlds are the same as the events in the other. So the system does not become an infinite regress of stories within stories but something more paradoxical, a feedback system that loops back on itself to transform what has already transpired.

Lamination protects enclaves from some of the assumptions that hold for the realm in which they are embedded. The enclave in the first half of the study shares sequencing but not, it turns out, ontology with the enclosing realm. Though they happen one after another, the events in the framing story are ordinary whereas those in the enclave are extraordinary. The second pair of enclaves shares ontology but not sequencing with its enclosing realm. Both realms are ordinary but sequentiality breaks off at the enclaves. This double lamination permits the reversal of interpretation. In the first half of the story, laminating events in the realm of the extraordinary lends them the appearance of legend without claiming they are legendary. They remain vulnerable to reframing as ordinary. In the second half of the story, laminating events in stories prevents them from counting as part of the sequence of events, thus rendering them interpretations. The first lamination suspends interpretation, to be provided by the second; the second lamination suspends the flow of events, directing the interpretation back to the events in the first. The second half of the story repeats and transforms the events in the first half so that the narrative is recursive, at once returning to and extending understanding of already unfolded events.

Puzzles about Perspective

Persons present on storytelling occasions can disattend the story while still attending the conversation, for instance, by monitoring other persons' interest in the story, or they can attend the story as conversation, for instance, by reckoning whose turn is next or what response will be appropriate. Or they can attend the story and disattend what it is about, for instance, by assessing how it is told. Or they can attend what the story is about (disattending both story and conversation) in different realms, for instance, as extraordinary or ordinary. These, among other ontological possibilities, are immanent in the storytelling occasion, drawn out by the frames brought to bear by persons on that occasion. The multiple framings and resultant presentations of any story to a person on an occasion remain for the most part unrecoverable. However, among the discourse on a storytelling occasion are frames designed to direct attention to one realm or another. These provide, as it were, an open reading, a map of the public pathway along which hearers are supposed to move through the realm of the story.

The directions given afford hearers perspectives on the story.[28] Events in the story appear to them from a particular angle in a particular realm. These perspectives may or may not be those from which the teller sees the events. To move along the unfolding of the story is to move through realms of events. This chapter lays out the system of perspectives for hearers on this occasion insofar as these are sustained by the frames given.

28. See Boris Uspensky, A Poetics of Composition, tr. Valentina Zavarin and Susan Wittig (Berkeley, Los Angeles, Londo: University of California Press, 1973), p. 126 on nonconcurrence of points of view of author and reader, and p. 130 on external and internal view points.

Persons are initially present to the occasion as co-conversationalists, implicitly egalitarian roles in which turntaking is even-handed. Occasions to speak and listen are interchanged among participants. Algy May's allusions to my tape-recorder shift the occasion from conversation toward performance, a realm in which attention is directed not so much to whatever events are recounted as to the recounting. In this vein, Algy's opening frame directs attention to the Storyrealm, not the Taleworld.

A: I like the story about

With that first frame, Algy discriminates himself as storyteller from the rest of us as hearers, these being asymmetrical roles in which the storyteller is dominant and turntaking is in abeyance. It may be that the presence of the tape-recorder can be regarded as an open invitation to tell stories so that the customary conversational preface to elicit permission an reserve an extended turn is not requisite. So Algy tries to embark forthwith on an opening frame: "When". However, I construe his opening as a preface and interpose a response designed (among other things) to grant him an extended turn in which to tell a story.[29]

K: Ha see?
   He always tells a story.

This remark, Algy's subsequent check to see that the tape-recorder is going, and his allusion to his performance as "my final thing", all heighten the reframing of the occasion as performance. These remarks can be regarded as an enclave of conversation within the Storyrealm after which Algy shifts to the Taleworld. The story proper then begins.

   I was-
   had a drink or two and I was walking back from
   Newton Abbot
   to Ashburton.

29. Harvey Sacks, "An Analysis of the Course of a Joke's Telling Conversation," in Explorations in the Ethnography of Speaking, Richard Bauman and Joel Sherzer, eds. (London and ivd.: Cambridge Univ. Press, 1977) pp. 337 - 353, pp. 340 - 341.

And-
in the wintertime.
/
And I was tired.

The use of "I" operates as a pivot between realms to insert the storyteller in the Taleworld as a character. The teller may then be expected to unfold that realm from the perspective of the character he is. In reality, the teller initially gives a description of the character who happens to be himself from the perspective of an outside observer present, invisibly but omnisciently, in the Taleworld, the same description he might have given in the third person. Hearers are invited to take up the teller's perspective on himself as a character so that the perspectives of teller and hearers are aligned as against that of the character.

The first lamination, inside thought, inserts hearers in the awareness of the character. Hearers no longer perceive what transpires but how he sees what transpires. The Taleworld unfolds from his perspective, hearers move through it inside his body, see it from his position. This phenomenological insertion in the Taleworld supports the partiality of Algy's perception of the hairy hand.

A: I thought I saw a car coming.
     In fact it did come.
     Slowly
     Overtook me.
     I thought
     I don't know it's got no lights
     Anyhow
     opened the door jumped in
     passenger side.
     Thought
     um anything special (in the thing)?
     And
     sat there you see and when we got to a corner great
          hairy hand comes round
K: Hm.
A: moves the steering wheel and
     on we go.

The phrase, "I thought", keeps the perspectives of Algy as teller and his hearers separate from his character's. Within the lamination, though, the teller aligns his perspective and his hearers, with the character's. This alignment is disrupted by the recurrence of the phrase, "I thought", which makes visible the lamination. The frame, "Passenger side", returns teller and hearers briefly to their perspective as outside observers in the Taleworld. And the aside, "you see", and its response, "Hm", transiently resituates tellers and hearers in the storytelling occasion as interlocutors with different perspectives on the Taleworld. Despite these disruptions, the alignment of teller and hearers with the character's perspective holds through the moment the character falls asleep.

While the character is asleep, the teller recounts that the car stopped at the garage. This moves teller and hearers back to the perspective of an observer in the Taleworld, a realm that has now shifted from the extraordinary to the ordinary. Within the realm of the extraordinary, all perspectives are enfolded in the character's. Outside that realm, perspectives begin to split apart.

A: Then I nodded off- went to sleep.
       Stopped at the
       A-38 or no-Eastern Garage-
       whatever it was
       and
       woke up suddenly you see
       thing had stopped
       and there was this chap
       getting petrol
       to be
       put in the car.
       (With the attendant and that)?
       So I got out.
       And the
       owner of the car said
       where've you come from?

Waking up might be perceived by hearers as if from inside the character, or from outside. Tagging "You see" onto this description separates Algy as teller from both hearers and himself as character. From here, the perspective on events is ambiguous. They can be seen to unfold from the character's perspective: he notes that the car had stopped as if he had only just become aware of it, he sees the chap getting petrol "there", seen from here, he moves himself out of the car, and is addressed by its owner. Or these moves might be taken to be unfolded from the perspective of an outside observer for whom Algy and the owner are both characters in the scene.

The owner's remark introduces a third perspective on events, his own. Events in the Taleworld can now be perceived from inside one character, from inside the other character, from outside both characters but inside the Taleworld, or from outside the Taleworld. Algy as teller can be seen to shift between the perspectives of the two characters, presenting, by turns, Algy's innocence and the owner's ire. Or Algy as teller can be understood to recount the whole conversation as if from the perspective of an outside observer. Either of these, Algy's partisanship toward both characters or his detachment from either, loosens his alignment with himself as a character. And, by virtue of that, hearers' alignment with Algy either as teller or character is also loosened. It is no longer clear which perspective is being prescribed here.

```
   A: Well I said I
      saw the car coming along and I
      just stepped in
      he said you bugger you know I been pushing
              this car for the last five miles
      K:  ((Laughs))
[[    MF: ((Laughs))  ]
   A: and there was I pushing you as well.
         ((Chuckles))
[[ All: ((Laugh))    ]
```

Not only do the two characters' tellings unfold perspectives on this conversation in the Taleworld but they also evoke other Taleworlds. Both evoked Taleworlds are ordinary, and both are reruns of the events in the extraordinary Taleworld. Algy's perspective on the rerun purports to be the same as his perspective on the first run. As teller, he recounts the events from his perspective as a character. Yet this telling contravenes the other, leaving hearers skeptical, not only about which telling to subscribe to but about which he subscribes to. The owner makes Algy a character is his story, one seen from his own perspective as a character. The owner's "you know" invites Algy to take up his perspective, to admit shared knowledge. This presents the possibility, not attested to by Algy's own rendering, that Algy played a trick on the owner. His own account is designed to convey the impression that he himself was taken in. And both accounts are presented by Algy as storyteller. What does Algy know, as character or as teller, and when?

The divergent perspectives held by the two characters in their own stories are reflected in the divergent perspectives

shown by each character in Algy's story. As teller, Algy's
perspective flicks from alignment with one to alignment with
the other. Thus, the possible shifts in perspective from
saying to what is said, as from thinking to what is thought,
are doubled by the presence of a second speaker or thinker.
Closing frames withdraw perspectives from inside the Taleworld
out into the realm of conversation.

A: He'd run out of petrol.
     ((Laughs))
     Stupid story
     It's true actually
     yeah.
     ((Laughs))
     S- he·had on a- a leather uh hairy gauntlet
          you see you-
     right on the steering wheel.
     Push push.
     ((Laughs))
K: ((Laughs))
A: Quite a good story isn't really.

The remark about running out of petrol is a clarification
or explanation of events in the Taleworld which support the
owner's perspective on them. The second frame, "Stupid story",
redirects attention to the Storyrealm, inviting hearers to
adopt Algy's perspective on that realm. The frame, "It's true
actually", directs attention back to the Taleworld and invites
hearers to subscribe to Algy's evaluation of it as true.
Insistence on its truth here speaks to hearers' possible
doubt. The next frame, about the leather gauntlet, provides a
clarification or explanation in support of this truth-claim,
this time from Algy's perspective as a character. The last
frame directs attention back to the Storyrealm and suggests
that hearers regard this as a story. So as the story closes,
frames of the Taleworld alternate with frames of the
Storyrealm. Both kinds of frames seem to be designed to patch
up hearers' alignment with Algy, the first, by suggesting that
their alignment with him as a character in the Taleworld can
hold because those events are true, and the second undermining
that by suggesting that even if they are not true, hearers'
alignment with Algy as teller can hold because this is just a
story.

Though invited to look on events as if from other
perspectives, persons on occasions also take up their own
ontological placement in a realm. If a boundary is drawn in

the Taleworld between the extraordinary events and the ordinary ones, the driver of the car is seen to be confined to the realm of the ordinary. The horizons of that realm constitute the limits of his knowledge. From this perspective, it is he who is taken in, having innocently been made to push Algy along with the car he was already pushing. As a character in the Taleworld, Algy has access to both the realm of the extraordinary and the realm of the ordinary. He shifts, over the course of the story, from one to the other. From this perspective, it is he who is taken in, having been led to believe that the ordinary realm was an extraordinary one, possessed of the legendary hairy hand. If a boundary is drawn between the Taleworld and the Storyrealm, hearers are seen to be confined to the Storyrealm. Their only access to the events is through the story. From this perspective, it is they who are taken in, having been persuaded that the legend-like events recounted actually transpired. It is possible for all three parties, the hearers and both characters, to be taken in if the boundaries between the extraordinary and the ordinary, and between those Taleworlds and the Storyrealm, are seen to be peeled away over the course of the storytelling to reveal each possibility in turn. But this is not true of the fourth party. Algy as teller must be presumed to have access to all these realms. As a character, he might have experienced the appearance of the hairy hand either as the legendary hairy hand or the real fur glove, or both, or, as teller, he might have set up this ambiguity solely for his hearers to experience. Since the self secreted in the realm of the extraordinary is not the self who tells the story, some shifts of perspective are requisite.

Shifts of perspective beyond those inherent in the situation turn not only on reframes by perceivers but also on relationships between perceivers. Gregory Bateson writes that frames consist of "all exchanged cues and propositions about (a) codification and (b) relationship between the communicators. We shall assume that a majority of propositions about codification are also implicit or explicit propositions about relationship and vice versa, so that no sharp line can be drawn between these two sorts of metacommunication".[30] Hearers can be given over to the teller's perspectives as long as they are not given grounds for suspicion about what he is up to. The relationship between hearers and teller affects their assessment not only of what events are transpiring in the story

30. Bateson and Jurgen Ruesch, Communication (New York: W. W. Norton, 1968), p. 209.

but also of what genre of story is transpiring. True stories align hearers with teller, other genres split their perspectives.

Puzzles about Genre

Shifting realms resets generic expectations. Heda Jason argues: "Each genre of oral literature has its own world. The world of the fairy tale, for instance, is populated by golden castles and glass mountains, talking animals and flying carpets. The world of legend contains ghostly dark ruins, hidden treasures and curiously formed stones which are in reality sinners who have been petrified for punishment."[31] This story contravenes that argument by either presenting two Taleworlds under one genre or changing genres.

On a structural analysis, genres can be seen as clear-cut but multiple. If genre cues are seen as embedded in the structure of the story, the first enclave can be regarded as a legend on account of its ontological status as extraordinary. On this analysis, the rest of the story can be seen as a coda, to adopt Labov's term, consisting of events that bridge the gap in time and understanding between the legendary events and the occasion on which the story is told.[32] The second pair of enclaves can be regarded as true stories on account of their ontological status as ordinary. On this analysis, the first enclave is a reframe of these, the true events. The framing story must be understood to be about a different set of events from those in the enclaves. It is, that is to say, not about the events themselves, but about perceptions or tellings of them, about what is thought or said, not about what is done. The framing story can be regarded as a true story in virtue of truthfully recounting Algy's impression of what transpired. On this analysis, the enclaves are interpretations.

31. Heda Jason, "Numskull Tales: An Attempt at Interpretation" in her Studies in Jewish Ethnopoetry (Taipei: Orient Cultural Service, 1975), pp. 197-234, pp. 199-200.
32. Labov, "Transformations of Experience in Narrative Syntax", p. 365.

On a sequential analysis, genres are blurred, to borrow a term of Clifford Geertz's.[33] If genre cues are seen as unfolded over the sequence of the story, hearers are led through a series of generic suppositions beginning with an orientation to the extraordinary, but not necessarily supernatural. The story becomes supernatural with the appearance of a hairy hand severed from its proper corporeal lodgment. Susan Stewart argues that this separation of the part from the whole is one of the insignia of legends in which ... "the part has become monstrous and suppressed the whole to which it should belong."[34] This motif makes it possible to know the story alludes to a legend before knowing the legend to which it alludes.

The legend is "The Legend of the Hairy Hands". According to Ruth St. Leger-Gordon, in 1921, a series of accidents, some of them fatal, befell horses, ponytraps, bicycles, cars, and motorcoaches, along a stretch of highroad between the villages of Postbridge and Two Bridges out on Dartmoor. One survivor described a pair of huge hairy hands closing down over his own just before his accident, forcing his motorcycle off the road. This tale gives rise, it is supposed, to the local legend of the hairy hands.[35] In transporting some of the elements of this legend off the moor and onto the main road from Newton Abbot to the edge of Dartmoor, Algy may be supposed to have created a migratory legend out of a local one. But if this is a legend, the threat of the hairy hand is never realized in it. Instead, the legend is demystified: the hairy hand turns out to be a fur glove, attached in the customary fashion to the hitherto invisible driver. What looked extraordinary becomes ordinary.

33. Clifford Geertz, "Blurred Genres: The Refiguration of Social Thought," The American Scholar (Spring 1980), pp. 165-179.
34. Stewart, p. 42. In a sense, as William Westermann points out, the car appearing without a driver partakes of this same metonymy. Personal Communication (University of Pennsylvania, 1984).
35. Ruth St. Leger-Gordon, The Witchcraft and Folklore of Dartmoor (Wakefield, England: E.P. Publishing Limited, 1972), pp, 120-124.

This reversal of circumstances, rendering the extraordinary ordinary, is characteristic of some kinds of jokes, in which the deflation attendant on the reversal constitutes their humor. Here, the driver's remark can be taken as a punchline. Or the joke can be seen as a practical joke or prank, either on Algy by the driver or on the driver by Algy. Indeed, the parity between what turn out to be ordinary circumstances and "The Legend of the Hairy Hands" is so striking as to suggest that Algy is making up a tall tale. Here, the joke is on the hearers who have been led to suppose initially that Algy experienced a legend and subsequently that he experienced real events which happened to be just like a legend. The second supposition is plausible only in comparison to the first. The modulation of ontological assumptions in the second half of the story leaves the legend in the first half intact, though reframed, thus supporting the story's claim to be true. To suppose that the story starts out as a legend and ends up as a joke, prank, tall tale, or true story is to overlook the way the ontology of the first half of the story implies that the whole story will be a legend whereas the ontology of the second half reframes the first as a true story, tall tale, joke, or prank.

The Extraordinary, the Ordinary and the True

Genre might be reckoned from just that realm-shift in the Taleworld, the transformation of the extraordinary into the ordinary by virtue of which truth-claims are sustained or abandoned. True stories can sustain their truth-claims by transforming the extraordinary into the ordinary. Jokes can also transform the extraordinary into the ordinary, but in doing so they abandon their truth claims. Jokes, once caught, are understood never to have happened, however ordinary they may appear. Legends sustain their truth-claims despite the extraordinary character of the events. They are presented as possible realities, as believable if not as believed. Tall tales also sustain the extraordinary but abandon their truth-claims. They are designed to carry hearers along until their increasing preposterousness strains credulity. This story purports to be true at the outset. It loses the appearance of a joke when it sustains that truth-claim; it loses the appearance of a legend when it transforms the extraordinary into the ordinary; and it loses the appearance of a tall tale in doing both. Hence, by the end, the story recovers the truth-claim it started out with and attains the

status of a true story. Yet, these other generic possibilities
continue to color apprehension of the story as it unfolds.

True stories usually have ordinary Taleworlds; legends have
extraordinary ones. Ordinariness makes an implicit claim to
reality whereas extraordinariness raises doubts. Hence, the
problem of belief in legend. In fact, Taleworlds are merely
realms of events, worlds, microcosms, heterocosms that can be
framed as fictive or real.[36] If the Taleworld is framed as a
reality, it will be supposed to have had an instantiation in
space and time. If the Taleworld is framed as a fiction, it
will not. The Taleworld of jokes, for instance, is framed as
fictive. If hearers know before hand that a story is a joke,
they can take up the perspectives it offers without being taken
in by them, even if the joke is told in the first person.

Both extraordinary and ordinary Taleworlds can be framed as
realities. By inserting himself in the Taleworld, Algy so
frames it. However, as the Taleworld becomes extraordinary,
maybe supernatural, his insertion becomes uncomfortable. As
Jason notes: "If a character appears in an unusual place, ...
the respective text does not belong to a clear-cut genre".[37]
In this instance, Algy's appearance in the story introduces,
perhaps designedly, a confusion between true story and legend.
The personal experience of legendary events lends them an
uneasy credulity. Disbelief now impugns not only the Taleworld
but also the teller. It raises the possibility that

36. Compare John Woods' logical solution to the paradox that
    fictional statements are both true and false. As he, too,
    notices: "That we seem ready to acquiesce without
    embarrassment in such apparent contradictions suggests to
    me that they are indeed only apparent and that the
    appearance can be dispatched under posulation of
    ambiguity." In "Animadversions and Open Questions,
    Reference, Inference, and Truth in Fiction" Poetics 11
    (1982), pp. 552-562, p. 553. The issue can be sidestepped
    by treating the truth of fiction as a different order of
    knowledge, namely, aesthetic knowledge as does Gottfried
    Gabriel, "Fiction and Truth, Reconsidered", Poetics 11
    (1982), pp. 541-551, p. 542.
37. Jason, "Jewish-Near Eastern Numskull Tales: An Attempt at
    Interpretation", Asian Folklore Studies 31, p. 19.

Algy may be lying. This shifts attention from the relationship between the Taleworld and other realms to the relationship between the teller and the telling. From this perspective, genre can be reckoned from the ontology of the Storyrealm.

Fictions and realities are frames of the Taleworld; truth and lies are frames of the Storyrealm. If the Storyrealm is framed as true, then it will be understood that Algy was there, that he did experience such events, and that they did appear to be legendary. If the Storyrealm is framed as a lie, then it will be supposed that Algy was not there, that he did not experience such events, or that they were not legendary. A Storyrealm framed as a lie is a tall tale. It purports, falsely, to conjure up a reality. In this instance, it would be a tall tale designed to induce hearers to credit the legend. In revealing the lie, the reframe turns the genre into a prank or practical joke in which the humor consists of disclosing to hearers that they have been taken in. What is at issue is transformed from an existential question: does such a realm as legends conjure exist, to an intentional one: is the storyteller truthful. The suspicion that this story may be a lie is aroused by frames that draw attention to its status as a Storyrealm. Hearers are thereby invited to judge the teller instead of the Taleworld. This shift masks the question of fiction and reality since Taleworlds, whether fictive or real, can be conjured up by Storyrealms framed as true. In both instances, the realms conjured up are what they purport to be in the story. The story truthfully gives the ontological status of the Taleworld. Storyrealms framed as lies, on the other hand, purport to conjure as realities what turn out to be fictions.

Truth and fiction are not "proper nots", to use Susan Stewart's apt phrase.[38] The proper contrast to truth in the Storyrealm is lies; the proper contrast to fiction in the Taleworld is reality. If the Taleworld is framed as fiction, the issue of lying is set aside since that realm never purports to be a reality. (This is so with the curious exception of stories that present as fictions what turn out to be realities: roman a clef.) This elucidation confounds the ancient suspicion that fictions are lies. They are, in fact, scrupulously truthful at the next higher level of analysis: they are intended and taken as fictions by tellers and

38. Stewart, Nonsense (Baltimore and London: Johns Hopkins University Press, 1978), p. 62.

hearers. A solution to the generic puzzles in this story might be arrived at by locating legends, as Stewart does, "in a peculiar place between the fictive and the real".[39] However, once the Taleworld is distinguished from the Storyrealm, it is clear that legends are framed as true at the level of the Storyrealm though extraordinary at the level of the Taleworld. (Figure 27 schematizes the relations among fictions and realities; truth and lies.)

39. Stewart, "The Epistemology of the Horror Story", p. 35.

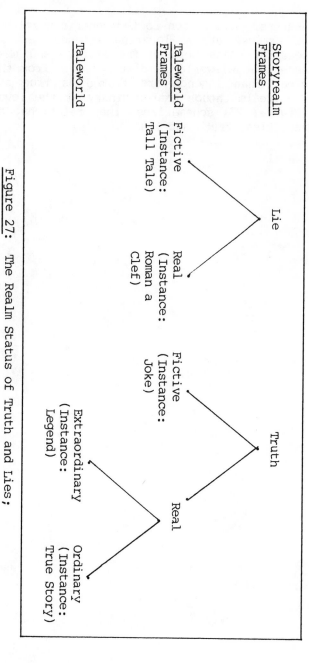

Figure 27: The Realm Status of Truth and Lies;

Fictions and Realities.

Disbelief calls into question either reality or truth, creating the suspicion, on the one hand, that the Taleworld does not exist and, on the other, that the storyteller is lying. Suspicions about reality can be disarmed by providing in the legend itself, ground for skepticism about the supernatural status of the events it unfolds. In this story, the orientation suggests an alternative interpretation ˌof Algy's experience as hallucinatory rather than supernatural. Suspicion about truth can be disarmed by reframing what first appeared to be reality as fiction. The imputation of lying is removed because no one is invited to believe in fictions. The reframe of this story asks hearers only to credit an illusion, not a supernatural manifestation. Kirshenblatt-Gimblett suggests that realm-shift can become characteristic of legends on account of the problem of belief.[40]

Solutions to the problem have produced a genre of demystification which Linda Dégh and Andrew Vazsonyi call "anti-legends."[41] The existence of anti-legends as a separate genre is attested to by José Limón's recounting of a Mexican-American version of Algy May's story which includes the demystification (translated from the Spanish by Limón):[42]

> Well, once this soldier was hitchiking on the highway from San Antonio to Laredo. It was at night, and it was very dark on the highway. He was right outside Pearsall and he was real tired, because he had been walking all day. He was walking up a small rise in the

40. Kirshenblatt-Gimblett, Personal Communication (1983). See also Linda Degh and Andrew Vazsonyi, "Legend and Belief" in Folklore Genres, Dan Ben-Amos, ed. (Austin: University of Texas Press, 1976), pp. 93-123, p. 49: Legend "takes a stand and calls for the expression of opinion on the question of truth or belief ... it is not necessarily the belief of the narrator or the belief of the receiver-transmitter that we have to consider; rather we must consider, abstractly, so to speak, the belief itself that makes its presence felt in any kind of legend. The legend tells explicitly or implicitely, almost without exception that its message was believed sometime, by someone, somewhere."
41. Dégh and Vazsonyi, "Legend and Belief", Genre 4 (1971), pp. 281-304, p. 297.
42. José E. Limón, "Legendry, Metafolklore, and Peformance: A Mexican-American Example", Western Folklore 42 (1983), pp. 191-208, p. 198.

road (informant imitates the tired walking motion of
the soldier). Then he saw a car coming very slowly and
coming to a stop as it came closer to him. Finally it
comes to a full stop as it gets to him and so he
figured, "Well, I'm going to get a ride!" and so he
opened the door, got in and said, "Good evening." But
nobody answered and as the car started speeding up, he
noticed that there was no <u>driver</u>! All he could see was
this old wrinkled hand on the steering wheel! And the
car moving faster and faster. And he said, "Oh shit!
What am I going to do!" And he was real scared
especially when he heard sounds like "Uh, Uh, Uh."
(Informant's voice pitch gradually rising.) Finally
the car slowed up as it got into Pearsall and at the
first stop light, the guy quickly jumped out and ran
like hell! And he made his way into a bar to get a
drink to calm down. And he sat there terrified and
shaking (informant imitates soldier). After a while
this little old man came in and sat next to him, and
the soldier said, "Oh sir, I have to talk to somebody,
I have to tell you about the awful thing that happened
to me!" And, he told the old man everything that
happened, about the car, and the hand. When he
finished, the old man glared at him and said, (loud
voice) "So you're the son of a bitch that got in while
I was pushing my car!"

Limón suggests that such a genre can be seen as what Alan
Dundes calls "metafolklore."[43] Jokes, humorous legends,
parodies of legends and anti-legends play on and thereby draw
out the conventions of the legend genre. As a storyteller,
Algy May manipulates the generic anomaly of that story. In
this light, multiplying or blurring genres must be regarded as
a strategy in the telling of legends.

Performative and Conversational Genres

Stories can be seen as the pivot between occasions and
events. They have two aspects: stories can be looked-at as
events in themselves or they can be looked-through to events
that are not themselves, to adopt Kirshenblatt-Gimblett's

43. Limón, p. 199; Alan Dundes, "Metafolklore and Oral
    Literary Criticism", The Monist 50 (1966), pp. 505-516.

suggestive phrases.[44] They have both presentational and representational properties. Attention to the presentations of stories to occasions is often termed aesthetic; attention to the representation by stories of events is often termed referential.[45] Both possibilities are present in every story so that stories make Taleworlds and Storyrealms available to occasions.

Each of these realms has its own affinities with the storytelling occasion. As the Taleworld moves away from the realm of the ordinary toward the realms of the past or the future, the realm of the supernatural, the realm of the dead, the realms of gods, demons, or fairies, the realms of dreams or madness, of mysticism or rationalism, of science, art, play, or thought, the gulf between the Taleworld and the realm of conversation widens.[46] However, as the Taleworld moves toward the ordinary, the boundaries between these two realms attenuate. Conversation is itself an aspect of the ordinary. Emphasizing its presentational aspect distinguishes the Storyrealm from surrounding conversation. Emphasizing its representational aspect renders story and conversation continuous: stories become an aspect of conversation. The storytelling occasion varies from the conversational to the performative. Performance is an enclave separated off from the ordinary, whereas conversation is continuous with it. Shifts toward the conversational draw the realm of conversation toward Taleworlds and Storyrealms. When all three coalesce in ordinary anecdotes about ordinary events on ordinary occasions, the genre is the true story.[47]

44. Kirshenblatt-Gimblett, Unpublished Lectures (University of Pennsylvania, 1978).
45. By Richard Bauman, for instance, in "Verbal Art as Performance", American Anthropologis 77 (1975), pp. 290-311.
46. See Alfred Schutz, "Transcendencies and Multiple Realities", in his On Phenomenology and Social Relations, Helmut Berger, ed. (Chicago and London: University of Chicago Press, 1973), pp. 245-262.
47. This analysis can be considered an application of Natasha Würzbach's contention that genre should be seen as "principles which govern the roles of participants in literary communication. Genre conventions, therefore, are related both to text and the socio-cultural context." "An Approach to a Context-centered Genre Theory in application to the History of the Ballad: Tradition ballad - street ballad - literary ballad", Poetics 12 (1983), pp. 35-70, p. 35.

Truth and reality align teller and hearers. A truth frame of the Storyrealm makes it transparent to the Taleworld. Hearers look through the story to the events it is about. The reality of the Taleworld, in turn, makes it transparent to the realm of ordinary events. Taleworlds dissolve into real ones. And the ordinariness of the events makes them transparent to conversation, an aspect of the ordinary. The boundaries among realms are attenuated. Thus, true stories draw together realms of experience and at the same time draw together the persons experiencing those realms. (See Figure 28 on the transparency of the ordinary in narrative genres.)

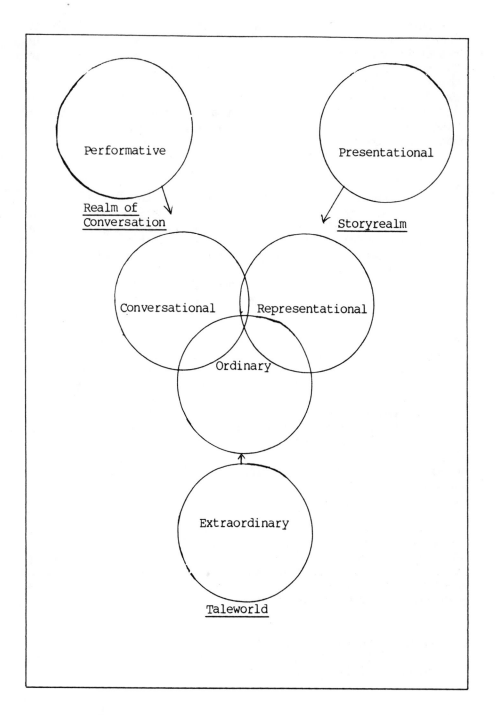

Figure 28: The Transparency of the Ordinary
in Narrative Genres.

Genre composes expectations. The movement of Taleworlds toward the extraordinary and Storyrealms toward the presentational moves the occasion toward the performative. By contrast, the movement of Taleworlds toward the ordinary and Storyrealms toward the representational moves the occasion toward the conversational. So a broad contrast might be drawn between conversational and performative genres, true stories being among the first, legends, jokes, and tall tales being among the second. Roger Abrahams, who arrived independently at the same distinction writes:[48]

> the continuum of situated stories from the conversational to the performative may loosely carry other co-variables, including shifts in pronoun system, and the relationship of speaker to hearer (or audience). Certainly we can point to the story correlation between personal narratives and conversational contexts, and a similar relationship between impersonal and conventional tales, legends and other widely extended forms with performance-like situations.

Of course the contrast between the conversational and the performative does not precisely overlap the contrast between the representational and the presentational, or the extraordinary and the ordinary. There is no one contrastive axis along which to distribute narrative genres. Still, each of these realms can be an aspect of the ordinary. So it is possible to suggest a distribution of genres in terms of laminations away from the ordinary, not necessarily along the same axis. On this view, personal narratives, ordinary anecdotes, true stories might be regarded as the core experience of narrative. In them, realms once perceived as discrete in the phenomenology of narrative are seen to blend into one another. The Taleworld, the Storyrealm, the realm of conversation, each turns out to be an aspect of the ordinary. Moves away from the transparency of the ordinary toward the performative, the presentational, or the extraordinary engender other genres of narrative. Hence, this inquiry has been concerned with interfolding as well as distinguishing the ontological presentations of stories.

48. Roger Abrahams, "The Play of Worlds in Story and Storytelling", Unpublished Manuscript (University of Texas Austin: 1977), p. 43.

APPENDIX

TRANSCRIPTION DEVICES

Speaking has two organizational patterns which could be called structure and rhythm. Structure includes not only conventional grammar but also repetitions, reruns, corrections and the like—all the structural possibilities of speech that can be written down in words. Rhythm consists of pitch, loudness, and duration, including pauses—the structural possibilities of speech that are not written in words. These two patterns can work together or against each other. When they work together, as for instance when the end of a sentence is marked by the typical pause (therefore called by linguists the obligatory end-pause), their redundancy makes a clear closure. However, since grammatical closure is clear enough by itself, it is possible to skip the end-pause for other strategic reasons and yet retain intelligibility. When the two patterns work against each other the structural, linguistic, or cognitive pattern usually overrides the rhythmic, audible, or mechanical pattern so that, for instance, even quite a long pause inserted mid-sentence will not be taken as closure. Rhythmic patterns that lie along the contours of the structural pattern clarify, intensify, or punctuate their import. Rhythmic patterns that cut across the grain of the grammar modify, gloss, or undercut it. Structural units are called sentences; rhythmic units are called utterances. Their coincidence creates redundancy or high-information. Lack of coincidence creates ambiguity or multiple understandings. The interplay between these sytems informs spoken language. Because our customary attention in written English is to grammatical sentences, an effort is made in the transcription used here to represent the intelligibility of rhythmic units in the form of phrases set off by breath pauses: written lines end whenever pauses occur in speech. In writing, commas do some of the work of pauses.

No one had ever seen them come shopping
and all they could find in the house
this is absolutely true
was a tin bath
full of snails.
And that's what they lived on.
And they took the old lady away
and buried her.
And the other one
remained.

Without any
visible means of support except this tin bath of snails.

(Algy May Tapes,
29 March 1975.)

The other three rhythmic possibilities, loudness, pitch, and duration, are not represented in this transcription since I felt that the complexities of intonation were difficult to represent intelligibly, and peripheral to the analysis developed here. The use of end-lines to mark rhythmic patterns was beautifully introduced by Dennis Tedlock in his transcriptions of Zuni chants.[1] It remains possible to read through the phrase pattern to the sentences. The layout of lines indicates how to phrase a passage of conversation in speaking it:

There were
three
teenage
Frenchs
sleeping in one bed over here
in the cottage- in the old house.
Thunderstorm
Father French comes down
finds the center one
struck
by lightening.
Three boys in one bed center one killed
Tchew.

(Algy May Tapes,
29 March 1975.)

Any one conversation has its own rhythmicity, a tempo articulated by a pattern of pauses, the rhythm being interactionally and culturally characteristic.[2] One

1. Dennis Tedlock, tr., Finding the Center: Narrative Poetry of the Zuni Indians (Lincoln and London: University of Nebraska Press, 1978).
2. See Edward T. Hall, Handbook for Proxemics Research (Washington D.C.: Special Publication of the Society for the Anthropology of Visual Communication, 1974) pp. 71-72 on interaction synchrony. Also see Birdwhistell, Kinesics and Context (Philadelphia: University of Pennsylvania Press, 1970) p. 215 on rhythm in communication of which synchrony is one aspect.

transcription convention is to note the duration of pauses by inserting in parentheses the number of seconds elapsed. However, the significance of pauses is not inherent in their span but in the understandings attached to that span. This transcription therefore attends to the appropriateness of what might be called felt pauses, judgement of appropriateness being made by a trained observer.

Pauses indicated are of three sorts. The first two aré, one, optional pauses in the middle of a sentence and, two, obligatory pauses at the end of a sentence, both indicated by line ends. Mid-sentence pauses phrase utterances without relinquishing a speaker's current turn at talk. End-pauses signal the closing of one utterance and/or the opening of another. The absence of an obligatory end-pause is marked by an equal sign:

M: And he- he'd sort of rushed out of Princetown Church
          and
      took off his surplice and put it on the roof of his car
      and forgot it was there.=
A: Forgot it.=
M: Forgot about it so it blew off on the way.

                    (Algy May, 29 March 1975.)

The equal sign indicates that a first speaker overran the next speaker's opening, or the next speaker cut into the first speaker's ending, or both. Skipping an obligatory end-pause is a way for next speakers to assure their turn at talk. And since pauses can signal sentence ends and completed sentences usually signal completed utterance turns, next speakers can sometimes treat mid-sentence pauses as if they were end-pauses and initiate utterances at this juncture. These two sorts of pauses are thought of as breath-length pauses. The third sort is a slightly longer pause felt as equivalent to an utterance-turn. That is, conversationalists will feel that someone might, could, or should have spoken up during such a pause. Utterance length pauses are marked by a slant line:

And they lived on snails.
/
Snails they gathered too.
Not escargots as such

                    (Algy May, 29 March 75, I 6)

Longer pauses are marked by series of slant lines. These transcription devices along with those that follow were adapted for me by Malcah Yeager from the transcription conventions in Semiotica.[3]

An utterance is the minimal complete turn at talk, ranging from a grunt to a story.[4] It may or may not be a complete or completed sentence. Usually speakers have the right to finish a sentence before relinquishing their turn at talk. But some turns are not sentences and some sentences are not completed in a turn. Utterance turns are set off by capital letters to indicate the start of an utterance, by periods to indicate down intonations at the end of an utterance, and by question marks to indicate up intonations at the end of utterances:

A: But in more recent times Miles will remember Foxy.
MF: Yeah.
A: Do you?
MF: Yeah.
A: Well he you know took seventeen tries to get a
   to be a parson.
MF: Did he?
A: Yeah and he
   got in the the eighteenth try.

(Algy May, 29 March 75.)

Since these are intonational markings, grammatical questions are not necessarily accompanied by question marks and grammatical statements sometimes have them.

Utterances are further clarified in the transcription as follows. Dashes indicate correction phenomena, that is, corrections made by speakers of their own or other utterances. What follows the dash corrects what precedes it. Parentheses

---

3. Malcah Yeager, Personal Communication (Philadelphia: 1976). Similar devices are conventional in James Schenkein's 'Towards an Analysis of Natural Converation, Semiotica V 4 (1972) pp. 344-377.
4. See Erving Goffman, Frame Analysis (New York: Harpor Colophon, 1974), p. 509.

enclose doubtful hearings or indecipherable recordings: ( ).
Parentheses enclosing aspirants indicate laughter; (hehe).
Double parentheses indicate editorial comments, including
specifications of laughter or other noises: ((laughter)).
Initials followed by a colon before utterances are used in the
script to abbreviate who is speaking. These are keyed at the
beginning of a transcription of any one occasion. Conventional
English spelling is used for British speakers, including
capital letters for proper names. No dialect spellings are
used to differentiate regional speech from received
pronunciation on the ground that neither accent is phonetically
represented in the orthography, with the exception of the
particle 'un,' meaning him, her, or them, which is not
represented in conventional orthography. Consistent spelling
captures the mutual intelligibility of speech but loses its
idiolectical, dialectical, or cultural variation:

    J: He was a lovely horse wasn't he.
    A: Great big fat horse hm.
    K: I'll bet ((chuckles)).
    MF: ((Chuckles))
    K: Hm
    M: Yeah but Michael- Michael also
    A: (Hoho)
    M: When he was out on the co-
         on the- on the common- on the (Denster) moor
         he managed to get into
         the local- the next door farm.
                                    (Algy May, 29 March 75.)

     Goffman points out that "transcription practices favor a
first actor's finishing before a second actor begins. That
finishing is what printed or spoken narration needs. But real
interaction does not need that waiting in the same degree.
While a first actor is still making his move, a second actor
begins his reply."[5] This transcription is designed to
reflect such overlapping moves. Double left-hand brackets
across two or more utterances indicate simultaneous speech: [[.
Single brackets around their utterances indicate the extent of
simultaneity: [   ].

    5.   Goffman, p. 212.

```
   [[ A:   [Fantastic story wasn't it.]
      M:   [He was always a bit-
   [[      [He was always a bit  ]funny actually wasn't he
      K:   [It was extraordinary.
      A:   Course he was funny.
           Damn funny.
```

(Algy May, 29 March 75.)

These events may or may not be interruptions.

Talk is organized into utterances. Utterances are in turn organized into larger units or speech events within conversation, the unit of interest here being stories. (Other speech events might be explanations, reports, descriptions, lists, recitations, tirades.) Interruptions, then, occur at two levels of analysis: technical interruptions cut into utterances, and thematic interruptions cut into turns. Turns constitute speakers' right to hold the floor and can consist of speech events as long as stories. Turns are at the next higher level of analysis after utterances. It is possible to cut into a person's utterance without taking away his turn. Consequently, technical interruptions can be discounted if they are not also thematic, and thematic interruptions can be counted even when they are not technical, but thematic interruptions cannot be discounted on the grounds of not also being technical: interruptions at the higher level control the determination. That determination depends on what Barbara Kirshenblatt-Gimblett calls the culture of interruptability.[6]

Conversation presents itself as already segmented into utterance turns. That segmentation offers a solution to the sociolinguistic problem of where to cut into discourse. Speech is the implication of language in situations. Its units are utterances not sentences, presented interactionally in the form of turntaking. Turntaking has its own limits as an organizing principle since "whether studied from the point of view of performance of a single actor or from the equally atomistic position of those who conceive of the world as made up of people who alternately speak and listen or move and watch, focus upon the actor and the reactor serves only to obscure the systematic properties of the scene,"[7] according to

6. Barbara Kirshenblatt-Gimblett, Personal Communication (Philadelphia, 1978).
7. Birdwhistell, Kinesics and Context (ibid.) p. 98.

Birdwhistell. Systematic properties are further obscured by
the linear sequential linguistic paradigm. As Hall writes,
"When discussing any system, it is helpful to be able to
conceptualize the entire system as a functioning whole. We are
inhibited in doing so because written English forces upon the
writer a linear progression of ideas that is poorly adapted to
describing most systems (that is, one thing at a time, coupled
with the unstated assumption that what happened in the past
will continue in the future). The system I have in mind is one
that relates _information_ in a _context_ to produce something man
calls _meaning_."[8] Hence, simultaneous speech wrestles in the
transcription with the linear sequential organization of
written English. Events never quite settle into their
formalizations. Transcriptions are one among several
descriptions intended to move stories into the contexts that
convey us our understandings of them.

Stories can be considered in light of the sequential
organization of talk. They are themselves sequentially
organized and they may also re-present the sequential
organization of the events they recount, so that form could be
said to reflect content.[9] However, stories are structurally
as well as sequentially organized and events consequential as
well as consecutive. More than recountings are at issue. As
Goffman writes: "For what a speaker does usually is to present
for his listeners a version of what happened to him. In an
important sense, even if his purpose is to present the cold
facts as he sees them, the means he employs may be
intrinsically theatrical, not because he necessarily
exaggerates or follows a script, but because he may have to
engage in something that is a dramatization—the use of such
arts as he possesses to reproduce a scence, to _replay_ it."[10]
For such theatricality, scripting may be an apt formalization,
one that catches some of its characteristics. But replays,
representations, recountings, stories in short, are tricky and
complex. Other descriptions capture other aspects.
Descriptions turn out to be a way of assembling realities.

8. Hall, _Handbook for Proxemic Research_ (Washington: SAVICOM
    Publication, 1974) p. 18.
9. See Labov, _Languge in the Inner City_ (Philadelphia:
    University of Pennsylvania Press, 1972) Chapter 9, "The
    Transformation of Experience in Narrative Syntax," pp.
    354-396.
10. Goffman, pp. 503-4.

Line-ends	≡	Pauses

From Dennis Tedlock, <u>Finding the Center</u>: Narrative Poetry of
the Zuni Indians (Lincoln and London: University of Nebraska
Press, 1978).

=	≡	Absence of obligatory end-pause
/	≡	One turn pause
Capital Letters	≡	Start of utterance
.	≡	Down intonation at end of utterance
?	≡	Up intonation at end of utterance
‒	≡	Correction phenomena
	‒	
( )	=	Doubtful hearings
(hehe)	≡	Laughter
(( ))	≡	Editorial comments
[[	≡	Simultaneous speech
[ ]	≡	Extent of simultaneity

Adapted by Malcah Yeager from James Shenkein, ed.,
<u>Studies in the Organization of Conversational Interaction</u>
(New York: Academic Press, 1978).

....	≡	Elisions
Initials plus :	≡	Abbreviation of speaker
English spelling	≡	English speaking, including captials for proper names

<u>Figure 29</u>: Transcription Devices

INDEX

aesthetics, 103, 245
alternation sets, 131
anecdote, ix, x, 34, 77, 103, 110, 133, 144-145, 154, 161,
    186, 198, 203, 248
"background expectancies",vi, 6, 7,9,48
beginnings, vi, 11, 28-31, 33-34, 36, 39, 41, 46, 53, 65,
    68, 208
belief, 238-244
bi-directionality, ix, 23, 45
boundaries, 11, 19, 22-23, 31, 36, 41, 45, 62, 77-78, 190,
    205, 226, 235, 246,
characters, vi-vii, 10, 15-17, 39, 57, 102, 104-107, 123,
    125, 127-131, 134-135, 138-156, 200-201, 226, 228,
    230-235, 239
closings, vi, 11, 31-36, 41, 46, 68
codas, 35-46, 50, 64, 66, 68, 107-108, 111-116, 123, 171,
    173-174, 236
codification, x, 20, 219-222, 235
"collaborative narration", viii, 182
consecutive, 28, 31, 170, 207, 215-218, 225, 255
consequentiality, 28-29, 31, 72, 170, 206-210, 214-218, 221,
    224-227,255
content, 21, 34, 64, 72, 87, 96, 99
context, vii, ix, 2, 4, 11, 14, 26, 48, 69-79, 85-86, 98-99,
    109, 131, 163, 191, 194, 196, 209, 221, 255
    multiple contexting, 69-70, 73, 78, 98-99
co-occurence, 131
description, vii, viii, ix, 20
discourse, vi, 7, 14, 19-20, 24, 28, 34, 72, 100, 103-104,
    157-158, 163, 178-185, 188, 191-196, 205-206, 211, 216
enclaves, vii, 9, 11, 12-16, 24, 31, 36, 45, 100, 156, 164,
    169, 211, 225-230, 236
ends, 11, 28-36, 41-42, 46, 53, 65, 68, 208
ethical puzzle, 200, 202
ethnomethodology, 1
evaluation, 20-21, 33-34, 53-61, 64-66, 68, 103, 132-133,
    169-170, 202, 224
event, x, 2, 11-12, 14, 19-24, 28, 31, 34-35, 39, 45, 53,
    58, 69, 71-72, 74-75, 102-103, 186, 188, 191-196,
    198-200, 202-209, 211, 214-215, 221-222, 244
    eventfulness, x, 202-209
extraordinary, 56, 58, 224-226, 228, 232-233, 235, 238-244,
    247-248
fictions, x, 8-12, 21, 55-56, 73, 186-198, 204, 208, 240-243
folktale, 21, 147

form, 72-73, 99, 101
    formal analysis, 70, 74-75, 99
frame, vi, viii, ix, 1, 8, 11, Ch. I, 69-70, 77, 103, 107,
    138, 156, 163, 197-198, 205, 211, 218-229, 234-236,
    240-242
frame analysis, 68
    -for, ix, 23, 31, 45, 51, 68
    -of, ix, 23, 31, 45, 51, 61, 68
function, 87-88, 98
genre, x, 21, 34, 144-145, 153-155, 187, 197, 212, 236-248
hearer, 16-18, 20, 35, 40, 50-51, 57, 59, 62, 72, 74-75, 77
    122, 162-163, 173, 176-178, 185, 197-199, 204, 209
    231-233, 240, 245
implication, 2, 5, 13-14, 29, 69, 185, 215-216
indexing, 222-227
interaction, vii, 72, 157-158, 161-178, 184-185
interruptions, 38, 163-169, 179-180, 184, 254
joint storytelling, 157, 175-178, 182, 185
lamination, vii, 24-25, 34, 40, 62-68, 104-107, 139, 142,
    156, 188, 201-202, 211, 221-222, 226-228, 231-232, 248
legend, 21, 55, 187, 216, 228, 235-244, 248
legitimation routine, 102, 104
level of analysis, ix, 22, 184-185, 219, 221-222
lies, x, 240-243
metacommunication, 20-21, 42, 165, 169, 205, 235
metanarrative, 20, 103
"metaphysical constants", 5, 6, 9-10, 15-16, 48
mutual construction, ix, 14, 100, 157, 162-163, 169,
    175-176, 182, 185
mystery, 214, 223-227, 237
narrative, ix, x, 1, 10, 12-13, 19-25, 31, 53, 103, 157,
    185-186, 205-206, 209, 211, 222, 248
narrator, 20, 59, 161, 185
nesting structure, 79-80, 92, 94-95
ontology, viii, 11, 14-15, 18-22, 45, 50, 62, 68, 101, 103,
    164, 185, 187-196, 198, 207, 211, 224, 227-228, 234,
    240, 248
    ontological presentations, viii, 19, 227
openings, vi, 11, 31-36, 41-42, 46, 66, 68
order of event, 21, 24, 31, 53, 169, 222
ordinary, vii, ix, 8-10, 12-13, 19, 21, 56, 110, 118, 156,
    188-190, 202-203, 222, 224-226, 228, 232-233, 235,
    238-248
orientations, vi, 1, 12, 14, 47-53, 56, 64, 107-124, 132,
    135-141, 146-149, 151-152, 174-175, 218
paradigm, 220,
performance, 14, 21, 62, 70, 75, 77, 103, 157-159, 162, 177
    184, 230, 245, 247-248
perspective, vi-vii, ix-x, 2, 5-6, 16-18, 50, 53, 68, 71-72,
    144, 162, 174, 200-202, 212, 219, 221, 229-236, 240
phenomenology, ix, Introduction, 19, 209, 231, 248

prefaces, 36-46, 65-66, 68, 171-172, 179
presentation, vii, ix, 15, 18, 21, 29, 69, 77, 102, 211-212
    245, 247-248
    -of self, vii, ix, 2, Ch. III, 199-200
reality, viii, ix, x, 5-11, 13, 15, 17, 21, 24, 55, 68, 73
    110, 186-199, 204-206, 238-243, 245, 255
    "multiple realities", vii, ix, 7-8, 188, 190
realm, vi-ix, 7-18, 19, 21-25, 31, 34-36, 43, 45, 47
    Ch. I, 73, 104-106, 110, 164, 184-185, 188-196, 199
    210, 211, 222, 224, 228, 236, 245-247
    -shift, 7-8, 11, 18, 66, 188-190, 224
    -status, 11, 14, 20-22, 24, 34, 62, 100, 103, 194, 198,
    222
recursion, ix, 229
referential, x, 11, 28, 73-74, 186, 196, 199-200, 205-206
    210, 245, 247-248, 255
representational, vii, 10, 23, 31, 191, 193-194, 245
"second storying", ix, 80-99, 101, 131
sequence, x, 28-29, 38, 48, 53, 57, 170, 176, 178, 200, 203
    205-210, 214-223, 226-228, 237, 255
serial stories, ix, 80-99, 101, 178
sociolinguistics, Ch. II, Ch. IV
space, vi-vii, 6, 10, 16, 19, 48-49, 55, 77, 99, 109-125,
    131-132, 134-144, 146, 148-149, 152, 154-156, 189
story, vii-ix, 12-18, 19-27, 31, 34, 39, 43, 53, 58, 69,
    72-75 78, 100-103, 107, 110, 131, 139, 142, 157-158,
    164, 186 196, 199-200, 203, 206, 209, 211, 215, 221,
    227
    -in-context, 74, 78-79
    storyability, tellability, x, 53-55, 103, 186, 202-209,
Storyrealm, vi-x, 14-18, Ch. I, 96, 98, 102-104, 156, 157,
    185, 186, 191-198, 205, 207, 210, 211, 214-215, 240
strategy, vii, 16, 59, 68, 99, 202, 217, 244
structure, x, 2, 10, 28, 48, 87-91, 93-96, 207-209, 219-220
    222-223, 236, 249, 255
surround, 70-71, 73
suspense, 203, 216-217, 223-227
syntagm, 220
Taleworld, vi-x, 12, 15-18, Chapter I, 73, 96, 102-104,
    107, 110, 116, 119-122, 131, 133, 144, 148, 156,
    186-188, 195-200, 205, 207, 210-211, 214, 236, 240
teller, storyteller, vi-x, 14-18, 20, 39, 54-57, 62, 72,
    74-75, 77, 101, 103-104, 107, 158, 162-163, 176,178,
    197-198, 204, 209, 229, 231-233, 240
telling, 19, 21, 40, 60, 72, 74, 103, 138, 158, 177, 199,
    227
time, vi-vii, 6, 10, 16-17, 19, 28-29, 43-44, 55-56, 77,
    99, 109-111, 114, 116, 122, 124-126, 131-135, 138-144,
    146, 149, 154-156, 187, 203, 206-210, 221

topical continuity (thematic relationships), 14, 64, 81-98
     101
transcription, viii, 249-256
transfix, 23, 48, 58, 157, 163, 169, 176, 184-185, 222
transparency, viii, 156, 246, 248
trickster cycle, 146-155,
true story, 186-187, 197-198, 236, 239-246
truth, x, 55, 188, 198, 238, 240-245, 248
turntaking, 14, 38-40, 77, 157-158, 163, 169, 185, 230, 252
     254
typification, 4, 5, 202-203

BIBLIOGRAPHY

Abrahams, Roger
  1975 "Negotiating Respect". Journal of American Folklore 88.
  1977 "The Play of Worlds in Story and Storytelling". Chapter of
        unpublished work-in-progress tentatively titled Goings On:
        Between Acts and Enactments. Universtiy of Texas, Austin.

Austin, John
  1965 How to do Things with Words. New York: Oxford University
        Press.

Barthes, Roland
  1974-75 "An Introduction to the Structural Analysis of
        Narrative". New Literary History ̚: 237-272.

Bateson, Gregory
  1968 Communication: The Social Matrix of Psychaitry. New
        York: W.W. Norton.
  1972 Steps to an Ecology of Mind. New York: Ballantine Books.
  1979 Mind and Nature. New York: E.P. Dutton.

Bauman, Richard and Joel Sherzer, eds.
  1974 Explorations in the Ethnography of Speaking,
        New York: Cambridge University Press.
Bauman, Richard.
  1975 "Verbal Art as Performance". American Anthropologist 77:
        290-311.
  1978 "Context in Contemporary Folklore". Unpublished lecture.
        University of Pennsylvania, Philadelphia.

Bell, Michael
  1976 "Tending Bar at Brown's". Western Folklore 35.

Ben-Amos, Dan
  1976 "Analytical Categories and Ethnic Genres". Folklore Genres
        ed. Dan Ben-Amos. Austin and London: University of Texas
        Press.
  1979 "The Ceremony of Innocence". Western Folklore 38,
        pp. 47-52.

Berger, Peter and Thomas Luckmann
  1967 The Social Construction of Reality. Garden City, New York:
        Anchor Books, Doubleday and Company.

Bernstein, Basil
   1973 "Social Class, Language and Socialization". <u>Language and Social Context</u> ed. Pier Paolo Giglioli, pp. 157-178. Middlesex, England: Penguin.

Birdwhistell, Ray
   1970 <u>Kinesics and Context</u>. Philadelphia: University of Pennsylvania Press, 1970.
   1971 Unpublished lectures. University of Pennsylvania, Philadelphia.
       "Some Discussion of Ethnography, Theory, and Method". <u>About Bateson</u>, ed. John Brackman. New York: Dutton.

Bremond, Claude
   1970 "Morphology of the French Folktale". <u>Semiotica</u> 11, pp 247-276.

Culler, Jonathan
   1980 "Fabula and Sjuzhet in the Analysis of Narrative". <u>Poetics Today</u> 1, pp. 27-37.

Degh, Linda and Andrew Vazsonyi
   1976 "Legend and Belief". <u>Folklore Genres</u>, ed. Dan Ben-Amos, pp. 93-123. Austin: University of Texas Press.

Douglas
   1970 <u>Purity and Danger</u>. Middlesex, England: Pelican.
   1977 Introduction. <u>Rules and Meanings</u>, ed. Mary Douglas, pp. 9-13. Middlesex England: Penguin.

Dundes
   1962 "From Etic to Emic Units in the Structural Study of Folktales". <u>Journal of American Folklore</u> 75, pp. 95-105.
   1964 "Texture, Text and Context". <u>Southern Folklore Quarterly</u> 28, pp. 251-265.
   1966 "Metafolklore and Oral Literary Criticism," <u>The Monist</u> 50, pp. 505-516

Edwards, Jane Spencer
   1979 "Orientation to the Contexts of Oral Narrative". Presented at the American Folklore Society Meetings. Los Angeles.

Ervin-Tripp, Susan
   1972 "On Alternation and Co-occurrence". <u>Directions in Sociolinguistics</u>, ed. John Gumperz and Bell Hymes, pp. 213-250. New York: Holt, Rinehart, and Winston.

Evans, David
    1976 "Riddling and the Structure of Context". Journal of
    American Folklore 89, pp. 166-188.

Gabriel, Gottfried
    1982 "Fiction and Truth, Reconsidered." Poetics 11, pp. 541-551.

Garfinkel, Harold
    1977 "Background Expectancies". Rules and Meanings, ed. Mary
    Douglas, pp. 21-23.

Geertz, Clifford
    1980 "Blurred Genres: The Refiguration of Social Thought".
    The American Scholar, pp. 165-179.

Georges, Robert
    1969 "Toward an Understanding of Storytelling Events". Journal
    of American Folklore 82, pp. 313-328.

Glassie, Henry
    1973 "Structure and Function: Folklore and the Artifact".
    Semiotica 7, pp. 313-351.
    1979 Folk Housing in Middle Virginia. Knoxville: University of
    Tenessee Press.

Goffman, Erving
    1959 The Presentation of Self in Everyday Life. New York:
    Anchor.
    1974 Frame Analysis. New York, Evanston, San Francisco,
    London: Harper Colophon Books.
    1981 Forms of Talk. Philadelphia: University of Pennsylvania
    Press.

Goldstein, Kenneth
    1964 A Guide for Field Workers in Folklore. Hatboro,
    Pennsylvania: Folklore Associates.

Goodman, Nelson
    1978 Ways of Worldmaking. Indianapolis: University of Indiana
    Press.

Goodwin, Charles
    1975 "The Interactive Construction of the Sentence Within the
    Turn at Talk in Natural Conversation". Given at the American
    Anthropological Association Meetings. San Francisco.

Hall, Edward T.
    1974 Handbook for Proxemics Research. Washington D.C.: Special
    Publication of the Society for the Anthropology of Visual
    Communication.
    1977 Beyond Culture. Garden City, New York: Anchor.

Hymes, Dell
    1974 Foundations in Sociolinguistics. Philadelphia: University
    of Pennsylvania Press.

Hymes, Dell and Courtney Cazden
    1978 "Narrative Thinking and Storytelling Rights: A
    Folklorist's Clue to a Critique of Education".
    Keystone Folklore 22, #1 and 2, pp. 21-36.

Husserl, Edmund
    1932 Ideas: General Introduction to Pure Phenomenology. tr.
    W.R. Boyce Gibson. New York: MacMillan; London: George
    Allen and Unwin.

Jason, Heda
    1972 "Jewish-Near Eastern Numskull Tales: An Attempt at
    Interpretation". Asian Folklore Studies 31 #1.
    1975 Studies in Jewish Ethnopoetry. Taipei: The Orient
    Cultural Service.

Jones, Steven
    1979 "Slouching Towards Ethnography: The Text/Context
    Controversy Reconsidered". Western Folklore 38, pp. 42-47.
    1979 "Dogmatism in the Contextual Revolution". Western Folklore
    38, #1, pp. 52-55.

Kaplan, Abraham
    1964 The Conduct of Inquiry. San Francisco: Chandler
    Publishing Company.

Kirshenblatt-Gimblett, Barbara
    1974 "The Concept and Varieties of Narrative Performance in East
    European Jewish Culture". Explorations in the Ethnography of
    Speaking, ed. Richard Bauman and Joel Sherzer. New York:
    Cambridge University Press.
    1975" Personal Experience Narrative as a Primary Form". Given
    at the American Folklore Society Meetings. New Orleans.

Labov, William and Joshua Waletzky
    1967 "Narrative Analysis: Oral Versions of Personal
    Experience". Essays on the Verbal and Visual Arts, ed. June
    Helm. Seattle and London: University of Washington Press, pp.
    12-44.

Labov, William
1972 "The Transformation of Experience in Narrative Syntax".
Language in the Inner city. Philadelphia: University of
Pennsylvania Press.

Labov, William and David Fanshel
1977 Therapeutic Discourse. New York, San Francisco, London:
Academic Press.

Lee, Dorothy
1959 Freedom and Culture. Prentice-Hall.

Limon, Jose E.
1983 "Legendry, Metafolklore, and Performance: A
Mexican-American Example." Western Folklore 42, pp. 191-208.

Marcel, Gabriel
1960 The Mystery of Being. Chicago: Gateway Edition, Henry
Regenery Company.

McDowell, John
1979 Children's Riddling. Bloomingdale and London: Indiana
University Press.

Merleau-Ponty, Maurice
1964 The Primacy of Perception, ed. James M. Edie. Chicago:
Northwestern University Press.
1964 Signs, tr. John McCleary. Chicago: Northwestern
University Press.

Natanson, Maurice
1962 Literature, Philosophy and the Social Sciences. The Hague:
Mouton.
1970 The Journeying Self: a Study in Philosophy and Social
Role. Massachusetts, California, London, Ontario: Addison
Wesley.

Prince, Gerald
1982 "Narrative Guides". Chapter in manuscript of forthcoming
book, Narratology. The Hague: Mouton.

Propp, Vladimir
1968 Morphology of the Folktale. Austin and London;
University of Texas Press.

Radin, Paul
1972 The Trickster. New York: Schocken books.

Ricoeur, Paul
    1980 "Narrative Time". Critical Inquiry 7:1, pp. 169-190.

Ryan, Marie-Laure
    1980 "Fiction, Non-factuals and the Principle of Minimal
      Departure." Poetics 9: 403-422
    1881 "The Pragmatics of Personal and Impersonal Fiction."
    Poetics 10: 517-531

Sacks, Harvey
    1966, 1967, 1968, 1970, 1971 Unpublished Lecture Notes.
    University of California, Irvine.
    1972 "On the Analyzability of Stories by Children." Directions
    in Sociolinguistics: The Ethnography of Communications, eds.
    John Gumperz and Dell Hymes. New York: Holt, Rinehart, and
    Winston, pp. 325-345.
    1977 "An Analysis of the Course of a Joke's Telling in
    Conversation." Explorations in the Ethnography of Speaking,
    eds. Richard Bauman and Joel Sherzer. London and New York:
    Cambridge University Press, pp. 337-353.

Schegloff, Emmanual and Harvey Sacks
    1974 "Opening up Closings". Ethnomethodology, ed. Roy Turner.
    Middlesex, England: Penguin.

Schenkein, James
    1972 Foundations in Sociolinguistics. Philadelphia: University
    of Pennsylvania Press.

Schenkein, James, ed.
    1978 Studies in the Organization of Conversational Interaction.
    New York: Academic Press.

Schultz, Alfred
    1967 The Phenomenology of the Social World, tr. George Walsh and
    Frederick Lehnert. Evanston, Illinois: Northwestern
    University Press.
    1973 On Phenomenology and Social Relations, ed. Helmut Wagner.
    Chicago and London: University of Chicago Press.

Searle, John
    1975 "The Logical Status of Fiction," New Literary History 6:
    319-332.

Seitel, Peter
    1969 "Proverbs: A Social Use of Metaphor". Genre 2:2.

Smith, Barbara Herrnstein
    1978 On the Margins of Discourse. Chicago and London:
    University of Chicago Press.

Shuman, Amy
    1981 Retellings: Storytelling and Writing among Urban
    Adolescents. Ph.D. Thesis. University of Pennsylvania,
    Philadelphia.

Stewart, Susan
    1978 Nonsense. Baltimore and London: Johns Hopkins
    University Press.
    1982 "The Epistemology of the Horror Story". Journal
    of American Folklore 95, pp. 35-50.

St. Leger-Gordon, Ruth
    1972 The Witchcraft and Folklore of Dartmoor. Wakefield,
    England: E. P. Publishing.

Sutton-Smith, Brian and David M. Abrams
    1977 "The Development of the Trickster in Children's
    Narratives". Journal of American Folklore 90.

Tedlock, Dennis
    1978 Finding the Center: Narrative Poetry of the Zuni
    Indians. Lincoln and London: University of Nebraska Press.

Turner, Victor
    1980 "Social Dramas and Stories about them". Critical
    Inquiry 7. pp. 141-168.

Uspensky, Boris
    1973 A Poetics of Composition, tr. Valentina Zavarin and
    Susan Wittig. Berkeley, Los Angeles, London: University
    of California Press.

Van Gennep, Arnold
    1960 The Rites of Passage. Chicago: University of Chicago
    Press.

White, Hayden
    1980 "The Value of Narrativity in the Representation of
    Reality". Critical Inquiry 7:1.

Whorf, Benjamin Lee
    1969 Language, Thought and Reality. Cambridge: M.I.T. Press.

Williams, Raymond
    1977 Marxism and Literature. Oxford: Oxford University Press.

Wittgenstein, Ludwig
   1933 *Tractatus Logico-Philosophicus.* London: Routledge
      and Paul.
   1952 *Philosophical Investigations*, tr. G.E.M. Anscombe.
      New York: Macmillan.

Wollheim, Richard
   1968 *Art and Its Objects.* New York, Evanston, London:
      Harper and Row.

Woods, John
   1982 "Animadversions and Open Questions, Reference, Inference,
      Truth in Fiction." *Poetics* 11, pp. 552-562.

Würzbach, Natasha
   1983 "An Approach to a Context-centered Genre Theory in
      Application to the History of the Ballad: Traditional Ballad -
      Street Ballad - Literary Ballad." *Poetics* 12, pp. 35-70.